RED DUST AND CICADA SONGS

Caitlin Press Inc.
3375 Ponderosa Way
Qualicum Beach, BC V9K 2J8
www.caitlin-press.com

Cover design by Rhonda Ganz
Cover painting: Mary Bomford
Cover illustration of baobab: Wayne Thom
Drawing on page 178: Josephine Fletcher
Photos on pages 172 and 173: Erik Bach
All other photos: Mary and Larry Bomford
All other illustrations used under licence from Shutterstock.com

Printed in Canada

Caitlin Press Inc. acknowledges financial support from the Government of Canada and the Canada Council for the Arts, and the Province of British Columbia through the British Columbia Arts Council and the Book Publisher's Tax Credit. Library and Archives Canada Cataloguing in Publication

Red dust and cicada songs / Mary Bomford.
Names: Bomford, Mary (Author of Red dust & cicada songs), author.
Identifiers: Canadiana 20220232083 | ISBN 9781773860916 (softcover)
Subjects: LCSH: Bomford, Mary (Author of Red dust & cicada songs) | LCSH: High school teachers—
   Zambia—Lundazi (Town)—Biography. | LCSH: Lundazi (Zambia : Town)—Bi-ography. | LCGFT:
   Autobiographies.
Classification: LCC LA2388.Z2 A3 2022 | DDC 370.92—dc23

A MEMOIR

RED DUST and
Cicada Songs

Mary Bomford

"Africa…gave her the privilege
of a second childhood…a time of awe."

—Judith Thurman in the
introduction to *Isak Dinesen's Africa*

CAITLIN PRESS 2022

For my husband, Larry,
and my sons, Michael and Mark,
my fellow travellers.

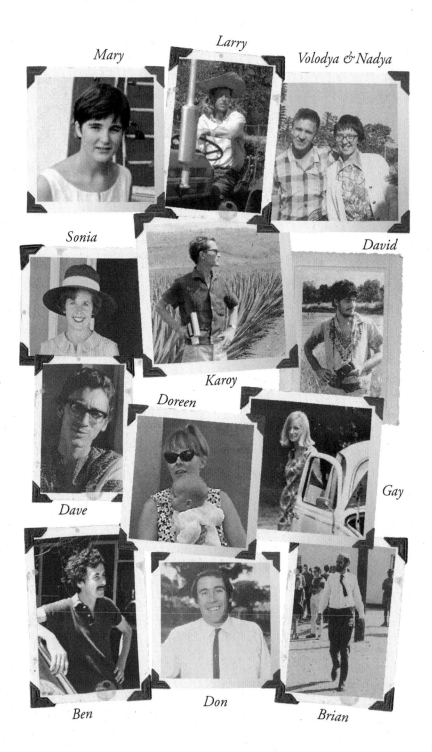

Mary

Larry

Volodya & Nadya

Sonia

David

Karoy

Doreen

Dave

Gay

Ben

Don

Brian

This story is a love letter to the hopeful time when Zambia was newly independent; to the people; to the landscape; and to those of us who came wanting to help and went away with more than we could ever give.

The events are supported by letters of the time, and the revisiting and retelling of memories over fifty years. Many individuals retain their names, others are changed for clarity, or altered to protect their experience when it conflicted with mine. Some details are condensed but hold the heart of the events as I recall them.

CONTENTS

PREFACE

"Why was I born in Zambia? What were you doing there? Could you write something down for the kids?"

My son asked those questions when he became a new father. When he was a child, we had shared stories of elephants and snakes but not our early adult life in a new country. His questions sent me on an exploration in memory, back to 1969, when my husband Larry and I landed in Lusaka, the capital of newly independent Zambia. We were idealistic CUSO volunteers, in our early twenties. We were about to begin an adventure in Africa, and we were excited to teach in a Zambian secondary school.

Fifty years later, does my story of a young Canadian woman teaching English to Zambian teenagers relate to the challenges raised by issues of race in Canada today? I believe the roots of my response to today's issues began in the mid-1960s and continue to evolve.

The young Canadians who made up our group of CUSO volunteers became aware of the world's imbalances as we moved from our late teens into adulthood. In the world of the 1960s, words like poverty and prejudice and injustice were the words we used to hold this knowledge. We looked for a way to respond. We were keen to share what we saw as the strengths of our culture and optimistic that the "developing world" could also enjoy our standard of living. We joked that we wanted to save the world. We were confident that education and technology were the keys to solving the imbalance. CUSO offered us an opportunity. Founded in 1961, CUSO (Canadian University Services Overseas, now Cuso International) recruited newly graduated Canadian teachers, nurses and agriculturalists to share their skills in developing countries until their new universities could graduate their own citizens.

But I had never met an African, the people I thought I could help. Nor were they represented as real people in books, television, movies, or songs. Driven by the human desire to explore differences, arriving in Zambia became the first step in my education that we all live lives of mutual connection.

CUSO issued Frantz Fanon's *The Wretched of the Earth* and Chinua Achebe's *Things Fall Apart* as required reading for our group of Canadians preparing to live and work in Zambia, the former British protectorate of Northern Rhodesia. Fanon, a Black psychiatrist and philosopher, drew on his experience as a Black man in the French Colony of Martinique and on his psychiatric practice in Algeria to explore the damaging effects of colonial rule on the imaginations and souls of colonized persons. Achebe describes the disintegration of a tribal leader in Nigeria as he comes up against the new values imposed by colonialism and Christian missionaries.

Personally, it was a challenge to relate to Fanon's or Achebe's ideas. I saw myself as a citizen of an independent country, free from Britain and our colonial history for over one hundred years.

I didn't consider that I was taught British history with heroic references to WWII, Churchill, and Dunkirk and thought Canadian history was pedestrian. My parents still played 78 RPM records of "Bluebirds over the White Cliffs of Dover" and I was proud to be part of the pink bits on the map of the Commonwealth. My high school literature syllabus was predominantly British. Canadian writers' voices, Atwood, McLennan and Cohen, were popular but not part of the syllabus. Instead I was taught the poetry of Duncan Campbell Scott describing the demise of Indigenous culture. As teens we looked to the USA and Britain for our music. Gordon Lightfoot was pleasant but the Rolling Stones and the Beatles drove the energy of the coming cultural shift.

Within my childhood home, colony was a benign word with unquestioned hints of the White Man's Burden. But my parents made it clear that the racism of the USA was wrong and Martin Luther King was a hero. At church I learned that Africa was the destination for missionaries and we were encouraged to share our pennies to help children there who had no shoes. We were taught that prejudice against another human being was wrong, even a sin.

The only time Africa was mentioned in my school life was in Grade 6 when Sister Myra taught us about the growing independence movements. She said, "They will rise up in anger against us.

We have so much to account for."

"Account for what?" I wondered.

I had not yet learned to ask questions about Canada's Indigenous history; the links between Africa, slavery and the Civil Rights movement in the US. It didn't occur to me that Canada had a colonial history of its own but questions were planted by my high school friend, who was a member of the Stó:lo First Nation. I wondered why he had joined the Red Power movement. During the summer of Expo 67 in Montreal, I realized that the Quebecois were pushing back against the tenacious grip of English speaking influence in Quebec's business world.

I arrived in Zambia with minimal knowledge of Canada's history and even less of Zambia's. I carried a teaching diploma, good will, optimism and curiosity.

I tucked away the ideas of Fanon and Achebe but they slowly challenged my thoughts as I began the pragmatic job of teaching English to teenagers in a Zambian secondary school. This memoir, begun at the request of my son, explores the events and people that changed my responses and attitudes. Over time, I abandoned the concept that I needed to change the lives of those I met. I realized that I was learning more than I could ever teach. Eventually, I developed a deeper awareness of my own country's imperfect history.

We were privileged to work and live with Zambians and with dozens of nationalities, as we filled the acute teacher shortage in the early years of the country's independence. My life in Zambia continues to inform every aspect of my life and thought since I returned to Canada. What remains with me is the deeply rooted knowledge that, through the reciprocity of everyday relationships, through misunderstandings and the struggle to resolve them, and through connections that overcame culture and colour and history, I learned to recognize and rejoice in our common humanity. I began to grasp that we are all interwoven. Now, as our world tumbles into social and environmental turmoil, we need to come face to face, work together, rediscover we are the same under the skin, both flawed and beautiful, and reignite the belief that together we can save this world.

The Elephant and the Baobab

The elephant stood in a sunset-tinted pink puddle under an acacia tree. In the spring of 1998, my fiftieth birthday approaching, I cut him out and flipped through the magazine until I found a baobab tree. The baobab was the invasive tree Saint-Exupéry's Little Prince had to weed out of his small planet every morning. But the baobab was my favourite tree in East Africa, the one that looks like its roots are sprouting from the top of its fat, cylindrical trunk. I pinned both pictures, elephant and tree, onto a small corkboard and set it on a shelf in my studio.

More than twenty years after we left, I yearned to return to Africa. I wanted to see our friends from Lundazi, wherever they might be.

My New-Age friend admired the corkboard collage and said, "This is your letter to the Universe. Without it, how can you expect your wishes to come true?" A totally rational, non–New-Age friend gave me an elephant-shaped, leather piggy bank for my birthday. It had small ears, like an Asian elephant, not the large, wing-like ears of the African elephant, but it would do. She suggested I put a few quarters into it for good karma and see what happened. As I thought about turning fifty, I pictured myself approaching the rise of a smoothly rounded hill, then arriving at the summit and looking down into a wide valley filled with the glow of fading light. Two hackneyed phrases, "over the hill" and "sunset years" nattered in my head and simple math told me that even if I lived to one hundred, I was halfway through my life. Our sons, Michael and Mark, had left home and it didn't look like they would boomerang. Larry was talking about retirement planning. At school, I had just committed to two years of retraining that would give me new techniques to revitalize the frustrating familiarity of teaching wriggling, often snotty-nosed, dyslexic primary children.

A few weeks later, on a sunny morning in June, a group of marimba players who played Zimbabwean music visited my school. They set up their instruments at the end of the soccer pitch. The pale, Caucasian musicians were trained by Zimbabweans and they adopted vibrant Zimbabwe-style clothing. They created a dissonance in me because I couldn't make their music, with its truly African sound, fit with their pale white bodies. But when their mallets met the marimba's wide wooden keys, the vibrations conjured up the rhythm of tropical rain storms. The wooden hammers drove the bass notes down into the ground and up into our bodies. Six-year-old Cherry, my dreamy student, with hair like a dandelion puff, a child for whom printed words were an insoluble mystery, stood nearby and I watched as she began to move. Around us, three hundred children danced on the grass with the angularity of North Americans, feet pounding straight down and arms flailing. Cherry's body picked up the counter rhythms; her hips shifted, one up, one down and her feet connected firmly with the earth. Her elbows tucked into her body, then shot out from her torso in sync with the marimba beat. She danced like the Zambian children I had worked with, moving with the body-memory from millennia before, when some of us walked out of the Olduvai Gorge and began the exodus out of Africa. I watched her, unbelieving. My eyes teared up and I began to tremble, so I turned, slipped inside the school and hid in the staff washroom where I hunched over and cried uncontrollably but quietly, from deep in my belly.

Bonnie, my petite vice-principal, cracked open the door, "Are you OK?"

"Yes. Yes. It's OK. I need to go back."

"Don't worry," she said. "Take your time."

The crying settled and I returned to the schoolyard. The leather elephant piggy bank and the photos of the baobab tree and the elephant in the puddle gathered dust on the top of a shelf for five more years.

Several times since returning to our Canadian life in 1975, a photograph, a snatch of music, meeting African exchange students on the university campus in Victoria, or the overheard sound of an East African accent, would trigger embarrassing, irrational and barely controllable tears. I could not understand the power of the memories that bloomed within me.

Zambia

THE GREAT EAST ROAD

Heads together, three men leaned over, under the raised hood of the one-ton flatbed truck. One man reached down into the guts of the motor, yanked out the snapped fan belt, lifted it over his head and let out one of the crudest of British curses.

Except for the curses they reminded me of my grandad, who ran a machine shop on the other side of the world in Canada. He was a genius at diagnosing ailing vehicles and, as a child, I had listened to him talk through a problem in words like crankshaft, gear box, fuel pump and rotor. I didn't understand them, but they had a comforting familiarity. The men under the hood of the broken-down truck used the same tone of voice and similar gestures as Grandpa, but I couldn't understand a word they said except for the emphatic cursing.

The truck was en route to Lundazi Secondary School, but was stalled on Zambia's Great East Road, in August of 1969. We were four hundred and thirty miles from Lusaka, the capital city, and seventy miles from the school, our destination and new home. Larry, my husband of eight weeks, and I climbed down from the truck cab and waited. The driver, in his white shirt and tattered tie, and the other men, one in a red shirt and the other in a blue shirt, slide-stepped down the road embankment and walked into the bush, each in a different direction. As they walked, they paused to run their fingers over the bark of several trees until the man in the blue shirt stopped at one tree and called the others over. The driver touched the tree with his fingertips, nodded, took a knife from his pocket, sliced open the grey bark and stripped out strands of orange, fibrous cambium.

Within minutes, the men had stretched and twisted the inner bark, woven it into a rope, measured it against the broken fan belt, connected the ends into a loop and attached the makeshift belt to the engine. Then, just like in a good movie, our hero, the driver, slammed down the hood, jumped back into the cab and turned the key.

The engine roared. The two men I called red shirt and blue shirt leapt over the sides of the truck into the back; we climbed back into the cab and were off.

One week before this fan belt repair, Larry and I had been in Lac Charlebois, Quebec, completing our CUSO orientation. We were part of a group of fifty idealistic Canadians in their early twenties, ready for adventure and full of confidence that we could contribute our skills to what was called, in 1969, the Third World. With input from Canadian experts, Western- trained African academics, and urban Zambians, we devoted hours to intense discussions about imperialism, colonialism, racism, African independence movements, cultural differences and culture shock. Together we ate, drank, talked and danced through all our waking hours. After Lac Charlebois, we moved like an ever-changing, soaring, multicoloured flock of birds, first to London, then on to Dar es Salaam. Some of the flock dispersed from Dar to postings in Tanzania, while others, including us, landed finally in Lusaka, where we were welcomed by Kenneth Kaunda, Zambia's president. He shared with us his vision of Zambian Humanism, based on the values of interdependence rather than on Western individualism. We shared his belief about the importance of community and earnestly hoped to experience that in Zambia.

From Lusaka, Larry and I flew in a refurbished WWII DC-3 to Chipata, the capital of Eastern Province. The unpressurized former troop carrier flew low over the savannah. For one long, magical moment we looked down on the broad backs of dusty brown elephants, black shadows stretching from their feet as they moved through dry honey-coloured grass lit by shimmering afternoon light. That was the moment I believed we had truly arrived in Africa.

The school's headmaster had arranged for us to be picked up in Chipata, along with a load of supplies. When the one-ton flatbed truck pulled out of Chipata, we shared the cab with the driver. The load in the back was covered with roped-down tarps. Our two canvas duffle bags (WWII surplus from the Capital Iron store in Victoria) packed with everything we thought we would need over two years, were jammed into a space between the tarp and the sides of the flat deck. The driver gently eased my guitar and its flimsy pressed cardboard case into the back and promised it would travel safely.

Chipata Airport

When everything was ready, half a dozen men jumped into the back and balanced on the load or hunkered down along the edge.

Ten miles after the first fan belt repair with woven cambium, the engine began stuttering and stopped again. The men hopped out, found the cousin of the last tree, repeated all the steps and the journey began once more. The trip went stop-start through three more fibre fan belts.

I felt like Alice falling down the rabbit hole, with characters running in and out of the foreign landscape in response to rules I didn't understand. It didn't help that we had minimal information about our destination. We had to trust it was somewhere along this road. We had found Lundazi on a basic map but had seen no photographs of the town. The one letter we'd received from the Canadian CUSO couple teaching there was full of warnings about the colonial attitudes of the British, the inept administration and the unruly students.

The fourth time the fan belt broke, Larry and I climbed down from the cab. Larry said, "Let's walk a bit. My legs are getting cramped."

"I figure we've covered fifty miles," I said. "We've got another seventy to go. Do you think we'll make it before dark? What if they can't fix it? Where will we sleep?"

Christopher and Mary

We walked along for a few hundred yards, in the direction of Lundazi. The road ahead lay flat and straight, diminishing until it hit the horizon, like an introductory exercise in perspective. Behind us, the same. The earth to the left and right, and the road itself, was rusty red, completely unlike the chocolate brown soil we knew from home. The trees were short with open branches, nothing like a cedar or a fir. Their leaves were rust and maroon with a few splashes of acidic lime green. Soon we'd learn these were the colours of August and the dry season.

We looked back to the truck, where most of the men leaned against its sides, smoking. The driver was still searching the bush for the right kind of tree bark. A mile or more down the road we saw a moving plume of golden-red dust. It grew into an expanding cloud drawn forward by a black box that got bigger and bigger until it became a Land Rover that stopped next to the broken-down truck. Then it started up again and headed for us.

The Land Rover pulled up beside us, and out stepped a Zambian police officer. His black, polished boots held their shine in defiance of the dust. His uniform was crisply pressed and he wore long tan socks rolled over just below his knees, held in place by a black tab garter.

"How can I help you? Sir? Madam?"

St. Christopher, I thought, Patron Saint of Travellers. The nuns who taught at my elementary school had promised there was a saint to call on for all occasions. St. Christopher always appealed to me. I thought he was second only to St. Bernard and his dog, but St. Bernard was the saint to call on when you were lost in the Alps and here there was no snow in sight. St. Christopher was the perfect saint for this moment.

"We are happy to meet you. I am Larry and this is my wife, Mary. We are going to Lundazi. My wife and I will be teaching there. The headmaster is expecting us this afternoon, but as you can see, the lorry keeps breaking down."

"So, Mr. Larry (pronounced more like *rally*) I am happy to assist you. My name is Christopher Manda and I am travelling to the Boma in Lundazi."

I wondered if I had heard correctly and even checked for a halo.

He offered to carry us to Lundazi and to alert the school that the truck needed a new fan belt. Of course we accepted. I looked back towards our duffle bags. They had travelled ten thousand miles so far, but I resigned myself to never seeing them again.

I had romantic notions about Land Rovers, connected to movie images of safaris, lions and big game hunters. Christopher directed me to the front passenger seat, while Larry sat in the back seat of the sturdy and practical metal box on wheels, designed by the British to go anywhere. The space was tight and the minimally upholstered seats were not sprung. Metal bolts grazed my shins at every jolt over the corrugated road. Larry's shins jammed into a petrol can at every lurch.

There is an art to driving a washboard road. One theory says there is a perfect speed, not too fast, not too slow, that will take you over the peaks of the corrugations with a minimum of juddering. Christopher drove on the go-as-fast-as-you-can theory. The Land Rover was built to handle the thumping, but our bones rattled and jarred. Over the racket he told us about Lundazi.

"You will see we have a very nice Boma."

"What's a Boma?" I asked.

"It is the place of our government office. It is a very old word.

From the old times, it means a safe place for keeping the cattle."
Christopher continued, "We are having three primary schools and
one secondary school. And two churches, the R.C.s—you know,
the Catholics—and the Presbyterians. There is a mosque. We have
some shopkeepers, Asian. Mulla, he has the biggest store and the
two petrol pumps. There is an airport, very big, just near the secondary school. The airport is necessary because of Lenshina, the crazy
woman."

We wanted to know more about this story, but Christopher did
not want to elaborate. He said there was an uprising, maybe five
years ago, but all was calm now. Lenshina was dead and we should
not worry. He changed the topic to emphasize that there was a good,
clean hospital with two doctors, and a post office where you could
send a telegram anywhere in the world.

"I am very sorry, but we are not having a bank. Two times
a month, Barclay's Bank are coming with their special Land Rover
which is carrying money. At that time, we police are providing guards."

Near the end of our journey together he said, "There is one thing
in Lundazi, v-e-r-y famous. I will be showing you."

After seventy miles of mostly straight road and open forest on
both sides, we could see the shapes of low buildings. We knew we
had arrived when we saw two petrol pumps on the right hand side of
the road. Christopher turned to the left as we entered the town and
drove for about half a mile. He stopped in front of a scaled-down
Norman castle built of sun-dried brick, the same colour as the soil
around it. We stepped out of the Land Rover to have a look. The
castle had two circular turrets two storeys high, capped with conical
roofs. The doorways were arched like praying hands. Later we would
discover the matched pair of elephant tusks that framed a doorway
inside the castle.

"But what is this?" Larry asked. "Why is it here?"

"The D.C., the British district commissioner. He built the
castle, starting in 1948. Now it is a hotel. It is also having a restaurant. If you come this way, I will show you the dam. The
commissioner ordered the construction. Now the Lundazi River makes Lundazi Lake. From here we are getting our water for
the town."

We followed him to the edge of a murky, weedy lake created by a

Lundazi Boma

hand-built earthen dam. In time we would learn the lake was home to a family of energetic hippos who had an impact on water quality in the dry season. We would drink, cook, clean and bathe in this water while Lundazi was our home.

Before we could grasp the incongruity of the Castle Hotel, Christopher got us back into the Land Rover and drove us through town. We went past two beer halls, with local beer brewing in recycled diesel drums propped over low fires. The centre of town was full of houses that must have been designed by the imaginative district commissioner. The red brick buildings, possibly intended for British colonial staff, were raised about six feet off the ground and supported by brick arches, two or three to a building. The houses looked like they were on stilts or reaching up on tippy toe, but for what reason? Whatever the original purpose of the arches, the current residents stored wood and bicycles under them.

Our tour was complete. Christopher delivered us to the school office and left us with the headmaster. We never saw our rescuer again.

The incidents along the Great East Road are so clear I can shut my eyes and watch them replay a full colour video of that day. From the moment of our arrival and through the first two days, the memories are rough snatches of impressions. I remember the warmth of the headmaster's handshake. He was a Zambian who played no part in our history. He finished his contract soon after our arrival and Brian, British, stepped into the position. That was the first hint that staff changes would be a constant. I remember long one-storey buildings laid out on the open campus. Red dirt pathways connected the buildings. Whitewashed bricks embedded in the soil at 45 degree angles created zigzag borders along the paths. There were trees, many leafless, waiting out the dry season, and the grass was baked to a brown stubble.

The other Canadians, Barb and Len, tall and slender prairie people, welcomed us in for the first two nights. They introduced us to Lundazi's main street and helped us navigate its small shops. On the second day, the truck—that we had learned to call a lorry— arrived, fitted with its new fan belt, along with our precious luggage, nothing stolen, nothing damaged. I dug into my duffle bag, anxious to put on clean clothes, and chose an ankle length caftan I had sewn before we left Canada. Then Larry and I went off to explore the school site. We met Ben and Doreen, soon to become our new neighbours; and Dave and Joyce, who invited us to tea. Early in the introductions I exclaimed, "We've been married for just one month, three weeks and four days!" The precision of my announcement, while wearing what looked like a sturdy nightgown, provoked friendly teasing for the first few weeks.

Movie Night

In spite of the warm welcomes from everyone over our first three days, by the end of that week I feared we had landed among a group of lunatics. We arrived on a Tuesday and Friday was Movie Night. David, one of the single Brits, invited us to come along. Everyone was welcome to meet in the school's thinly stocked library next to the small audiovisual room.

My mind was a blur of new names and new faces. We had met the headmaster, the deputy headmaster, most of the thirty-eight staff (a few were still on holiday) and some of the support staff. The eight hundred students would arrive the following week. I was glad of a chance to have a look at everyone in one place and see how many names I could remember. I needed a cue card like those at the beginning of Russian novels.

We had become acquainted with eight African teachers: two South Africans of mixed heritage, and six Zambians ranging in age from their early twenties to late forties. There were three East Indians who taught math. But at Movie Night everyone in the room was European. We had quickly figured out that all the Caucasians, who made up more than three-quarters of the staff, were referred to as Europeans whether they were British, Canadian, Australian, Irish or Danish. That evening, I had no intimation that the ones who gathered on this Friday would play parts in our life story for years to come.

Brian was the deputy headmaster, soon to be headmaster. He was tallest of all the men, with wavy, almost blonde hair, and a booming voice easily heard across the schoolyard. Sonia, his wife, was quieter and impeccably groomed. We learned later that Brian sewed all her clothes. Sonia was head of the English department.

Ben and Doreen, Brits, were our across-the-school-path neighbours. Ben was six feet tall, thin and wiry, with curly hair. This description fit most of the British men at the school, the majority of whom were born in 1944 or 1945 and grew up on a diet of post-WWII food rations that seemed to have fuelled them with a frenetic energy for life. Ben was a master of puns and verbal repartee. Doreen was blonde and shorter than me, maybe five feet tall. She had an encyclopedic knowledge of anything relating to jewellery, gems or fabric. We both taught English.

At first sight, Dave and Joyce, also British, seemed similar to Ben and Doreen, and it would take me a while to learn their different characters. Dave was a bit taller than Ben and never stopped moving—physically or mentally. Joyce taught domestic science and had already initiated me into how to find groceries in Lundazi's shops.

Grant, a single Brit, came from a military background and taught geography. Duncan, also single and British, had an Irish girlfriend who lived in town and worked as a midwife at the local hospital. He was soccer-mad, organizing games at any opportunity.

Whippet-slim Gay was British, and the only single woman on staff. She taught English.

Don, an affable Australian, taught agriculture and economics. Don was single and had been assigned his own house, but he lived with Gay most of the time. Zambia stipulated couples must be married before they came to live and work in the country, but the two had met soon after their arrival. Don maintained his house and provided a courteous façade that acknowledged the official rule and seemed to satisfy everyone in authority.

Erik, Danish, our across-the-fence neighbour, was quiet and soft spoken. He had left a girlfriend in Denmark and was pining. I had noticed he was a photographer.

Hans and Lisbet, also Danish, were both tall, with fine blonde hair. Lisbet was also a midwife at the local hospital.

Father Roy was a Canadian White Father working at Lumezi Mission, twenty miles south of the school. He was French Canadian, and a fluent speaker of Chitumbuka, the local language. He explained that the White Fathers were called White not because of the colour of their skin but because of their white habit. Their outfit, chosen in 1868, was modelled on the Arab gandoura as a symbol of solidarity between Christians and Muslims in North Africa.

Barb and Len, the other CUSO couple, were near the end of their contract and we would replace them as the Canadians on staff. And there was David. He ran the projector. David taught technical drawing and industrial arts, but we learned that he had a Classics degree and could read Latin and Greek. He could fix anything. He recycled and recreated found metal into car parts, generator parts, or whatever a good machine shop would provide. His mind was filled with enough projects for two lifetimes. Without him, we would not have found our own car.

David set up the two spindle arms on a cranky film projector. Three military-green, round metal cases held the spools of film that had travelled five hundred miles by bus from the British Council office in Lusaka. David attached the first feed reel to the top spindle and looped the film leader through the projector and onto the take up reel at the bottom. When the sound of celluloid clicking its way evenly onto the sprockets was established, he turned off the overhead lights and switched on the hot, white projector lamp. Jerky, grainy, black and white cowboys and their horses leapt off the screen. The silent film, starring Tom Mix, was ludicrous and plotless, with men and horses rushing off in all directions. Twenty minutes later, as Tom's horse carried him down a cliff face, the first spool ended, and the tail of the film flapped and snapped around the take up reel. David turned on the room lights and quickly set up the second reel. The horse slid to a stop with Tom still in the saddle and off we went for another twenty minutes. David put on the final reel, but someone had forgotten to rewind it before they shipped it to our school. We watched it backwards. Cowboys slid off their horses, the horses galloped backwards, bullets were sucked back into gun barrels, the dead were raised and the heroine was unkissed.

Everyone was laughing and outdoing each other with snappy quips pointing out the quirkiness of the reversed story. My sense of humour eluded me. I didn't know where to look. I wished I was back in the plush red seats of the movie theatre in Quebec where we had watched *Les Parapluies de Cherbourg* just four weeks earlier. I could tell that these people had been too long away from "civilized" life. "Gone bush" I thought, like the old trappers who spent too long in their log cabins in the Canadian north and couldn't adjust to town life ever again.

I would, over the next few months, learn to let go of my superior seriousness and find a sense of humour. In fact, I'd realize, it was the best antidote to "going bush."

Our House

"Let's see what you've got in here." Dave, the British teacher we met on our first exploration of the school, used a school master key to open the door of our new home.

Thursday morning, after we had stayed two nights with the Canadians, Barb and Len, the headmaster assigned us a house. The back door looked out to the girls' dormitories. A path ran from the school past the front door and on to town. Our house faced Ben and Doreen's identical house across the path.

Sheets of asbestos roofed the house. The metal framed windows and doors were designed to frustrate termites. Our front door opened into the large living/dining room. The sunlight picked out dust motes and shone on the coral pink walls and the worn, burgundy coloured, termite-proof concrete floors.

A settee, two armchairs and a table with four chairs filled the room. All the furniture was made of wood, but the settee and armchairs were fitted with firm cushions for comfort. Each of the three bedrooms had a large built-in closet and a metal framed single bed with a foam mattress covered in reasonably clean pink brocade. The kitchen had cupboards up and down, a counter, a stainless steel sink and a drainboard. A cast-iron woodburning stove stood in a recessed alcove.

"A wood stove? Won't that warm the house up?" I asked.

"You'll be surprised how much heat stays in that alcove. The school generator only runs from sunset till ten to power the lights. How else would you cook anything?"

Dave pointed out the pipes that ran up into the ceiling behind the stove.

"Your water tank is up there, in the attic. The stove heats your water. The tank is big. It'll give you enough hot water for washing up, bathing, even laundry."

A toilet stood in a small room off the kitchen. A hand basin and

Firewood delivery by oxcart

bathtub were in a separate room.

"The dry season is coming up. The lake behind the dam will start to shrink. Then the hippos really stir up the mud."

"Hippos?" I asked.

Larry answered, "Remember? When the policeman brought us to the Castle Hotel, he showed us the hippos in the dam."

"That's them," Dave said. "Less water, same hippos. The water gets cloudy at first. As the dry season goes on you won't be able to see your feet when you stand in the tub. Sheets won't come white when they are washed. But it all clears up when the rains come, usually November. You'll get used to it."

"You mean we drink that too?"

"You boil it, then filter it. You want to get a proper two-part filter with porous ceramic filters. That'll give you nice, clear drinking water. Let's see about getting you a better settee. We'll check in down the road."

We followed him to an empty staff house where he used the master key again to let us in. Dave decided the standard issue settee in this house was in better shape than the one in ours.

"I'll bring the car and switch this one for you."

By the end of our first term we were used to this Robin Hood method of redistributing furniture. It happened whenever a teacher left. You could also bargain in advance with a departing teacher and trade up on your furnishings the day before they departed. Garden plants were part of this reshuffling system too, but it seemed that digging up plants happened mostly after dark.

After the settee was traded and we were alone, we opened our duffle bags and pulled out sheets, towels, the orange daisy patterned Melmac dinner plates we'd brought, cutlery and a few plastic mixing bowls. It looked like we were camping, but we were in our first home almost two months to the day from our wedding.

Dave told us that Dennis, from South Africa, had been the previous tenant in our house. Dennis had broken his contract at the end of the previous term and left town, carrying his farewell gift. I found a quote from Jean Paul Sartre, printed in splotchy ball point pen on a scrap of white paper and glued to the back of the closet door in the main bedroom.

"Man…must count on no one but himself;…he is alone, abandoned on earth in the midst of his infinite responsibilities, without help."

It made my heart sink to read these words and wonder how they could be his guiding quote. The posters that had decorated my walls in my university dorm had sayings like "Today is the first day of the rest of your life" superimposed over soft focus photos of sunny fields of daisies.

Dennis was Cape Coloured, a South African label used to name people of mixed black and white ancestry. Days after we had settled into his old house, he reappeared, claimed his old job and moved into another, identical, house across the road from us. It was rumoured that he was a spy, possibly for one of the anti-apartheid freedom-fighter movements. There was also speculation that he should return his farewell gift because he didn't actually leave.

The house was ours to make our own. All Dennis had left behind was the quote in the closet.

WHY?

We never asked each other, "Why?" "Why did you leave England? Or Canada? Or Australia? Or Ireland?"

Could any of us have explained why we had left the familiarity of home? We, the expatriates in Lundazi, had slipped into Zambia through a small window in time, when the new country needed teachers. A degree would do, even without teaching experience. Most of us were in our twenties, part of the population boom that followed the troops returning home after WWII. "Never trust anyone over thirty" was our mantra. We had entered our teens in the social revolution of the 1960s, when the Beatles let their hair grow from brush cut, to mop top, to androgynous shoulder length. The time when bell bottoms appeared as a crisp, naval style, then morphed into wider flowing fabric with swirling neon patterns. Tie-dyed T-shirts appeared, sunburst symbols of freedom and do-it-yourself art. The birth control pill was invented, LSD unleashed.

Larry and I emerged from strong farm and church roots. We were conservative in our adoption of the new culture, but we embraced the desire for freedom from the constrained 1950s. We were intrigued by new versions of living, especially the idea of communal farms. We were sure the world needed changing and we wanted to be part of that change. We were driven by a sense of duty, an unacknowledged reflection of our parents' values. Larry's degree in economics pointed to a suit, a tie and an office, but for him, that path was abhorrent. My teaching diploma gave me limitless job opportunities. Canadian school boards were desperate to staff their classrooms. I had six job offers in hand, no interview required. That seemed too easy. I'd rather step into Zambia's teacher shortage than stay at home. Our understanding of our motives was limited to an urge to break free of clearly defined, easy-to-fill roles and set off on an adventure that would "change the world."

In 2010, thirty-five years after the close of that adventure, Michael, our eldest son, phoned and asked us the question, "Why?"

Our first grandchild, four-year-old Liam, Michael's eldest child, had asked his father, "Daddy, tell me stories about what you did when you were four."

We had learned not to tell our Zambia stories. The passion and energy generated by those experiences flared forth and overwhelmed the person who had asked a polite question, "Oh, so you lived in Africa. What was it like?" We would launch into our tales with the enthusiasm of evangelists, not realizing the person only wanted a quick, sunny summary. Eventually, we settled on a brief answer that would satisfy the questioner. We slipped into amnesia, wrapped in undefined yearning, and struggled to become Canadians again.

When Michael said, "I don't really know why I was born in Zambia. Why were you there? What were you doing? We left when I was four, didn't we?" we were amazed that he wasn't familiar with the defining heart of our young adult lives.

As I thought about his questions, a kaleidoscope of memories from my own childhood flashed and turned in my mind: Sunday dimes. Jam sandwiches. Newspapers. Sister Myra. Martyrs. Grandpa Charlie.

The first memory was about dimes. Dad gave each of us a weekly allowance of ten cents for the church collection. My dime would bounce quietly against the green felt lining of the deep, circular collection plate attached to a long wooden handle held by a church usher. The usher would lean over and stretch his arms out all the way to the centre of the pew, like a dancer handling a pool cue. I could either drop my dimes into the collection plate or I could save them up for twelve weeks and slip them into the half-moon-shaped pockets inside a folding card with a sweet painting of the child Jesus on the front. He was depicted as about five years old, with blue eyes, chubby cheeks and softly waved blonde hair, even though he was actually Jewish and would have had olive skin and dark hair. He wore a white robe with a finely stitched blue and gold collar. Behind him was a globe turned toward Africa. I knew that my twelve dimes would go to Africa to help Black babies with curly hair.

Next, I recalled that across the road, on what we called the Indian Reserve, there were many children with straight black hair, runny noses, and thin sweaters inadequate for a winter's day. My brothers Tom and Mike and I were sure the kids were hungry. We knew about the Beatitudes from catechism class at St. Mary's School—"Blessed are the hungry"—so we raided our cupboards and made jam sandwiches to feed the children out behind the snowberry bushes that grew along the gravel road separating our yard from the Reserve. A week later, a social worker from Indian Affairs came to our house and asked our mother to stop us. It became clear to me that it was good to send money to feed children in Africa but it was not right to share food with the kids across the road.

My third memory was about my mother trying to toilet train her three boys, who often missed the mark and stained the wall beside the toilet. Mom followed a tip from *Cheaper by the Dozen,* which tells the story of how Lillian Gilbreth used the principles of time and motion study to manage her large family. Mom taped a sheet of newspaper on the wall beside the toilet to catch the boys' errant pee stains. When a fresh sheet was needed, she tore off the old one and replaced it. She made the paper do double duty by selecting articles about poverty and hunger in Africa to reinforce her dinner time mantra when we complained about our food. "Eat up, children in Africa are starving." As a girl, both addicted to reading and needing to sit down on the toilet, I paid more attention to the stories on the wall than the boys did.

Next I thought of my Grade 6 teacher, Sister Myra. She was slender, six feet tall, sizzling with Irish passion and intensity and insisted we read *Time* magazine for our current events class. She taught us about the independence movements in Africa years before most of the world had noticed. My historical and political awareness of Africa began in her classroom in 1960.

The fifth memory was about the stories we heard at St. Mary's, tales of the martyrs who helped the poor and who refused to be coerced into denying their beliefs. As the hymn "Faith of Our Fathers" said, they held firm "in spite of dungeon, fire and sword." The early Canadian Jesuits had their hearts cut out and eaten. St. Lawrence was roasted on a gridiron. St. Catherine was stretched on a wheel. The stories always ended with the demand that we too should aim to be selfless, brave and unbending. I agonized over my limits, until one warm summer Sunday evening, just before the seven o'clock Benediction service. I was alone under the arch of the free-standing bell tower next to St. Mary's, our parish church. My mind was encamped with martyrs flayed, pierced and beheaded. They writhed together, cried out and urged my commitment to heroic deeds. I stood under the four pillars of the bell tower and looked up at the fat, looped rope dangling above my head. My sandalled feet and bare legs soaked up the pleasure of the low-angled sun. I squinted into the golden light and decided I would never be a first class hero and I was unfit for martyrdom. My twelve-year-old self resolved I would try to be a good person, but I would run from anything that threatened my life or safety. Then I walked into the church, knelt, breathed in the spicy incense and sang "Faith of our Fathers" one more time.

The final piece of my kaleidoscope of memories was Grandpa Charlie, my mom's father. He wasn't too keen on church and plaster saints, but he did put good teachers on a pedestal and talked about their power to inspire children. He watched me play school with my dolls and with my brothers and sisters. He encouraged me to become a "real" teacher. He'd had to leave school early to find work as a mechanic—or what he called a "grease monkey." I think he equated education with clean hands. For him, education had a capital E.

I didn't recall any of these memories when I filled out the application to teach overseas with CUSO.

Recently I asked Larry, fifty years after we'd made our decision together, "Why did you want to go to Africa?"

"For an adventure. I wanted to travel. So many of my English relatives travelled all over the world. I wanted to do something I thought was useful. Besides, you wanted to go too."

So, in the spring of 1969, we found ourselves seated under fluorescent lights at a fake wood grain, Formica-topped conference table watching our reflections in the uncurtained, nighttime windows of a university seminar room.

Our CUSO interview felt like we were at a large dinner party with only glasses of water for nourishment. The panel of fifteen expounded on colonialism, independence and apartheid, and only sometimes addressed questions to us. I said emphatically that I could not work in a humid climate (a summer working in Montreal during Expo 67 had wilted my mind and sapped my energy). That plea removed us from potential jobs in hot and humid West Africa and narrowed our choices to the dry heat of two of the former British colonies of East Africa—Zambia or Tanzania.

If I had asked our new Lundazi acquaintances, our fellow teachers, "Why did you leave? What brought you here?" I am sure that no one's story would match mine in any way. I wonder how much my church-tinged images of Africa influenced my decision to leave home, or if the stronger pull was the tide of our particular moment in history. Whatever its origin, that moment brought us to Lundazi, along with dozens of others from around the world, ready to begin an inadvertent experiment in communal living on a school compound inside a newly independent country.

I wanted to answer Michael's question, "Why was I born in Zambia?" So, I assembled old photos from that time, wrote up the stories I thought would appeal to our grandchildren and created a picture book that answered part of his question. By the time that book was printed, I was pulled deeper into emerging memories. I wanted to understand the power of those years for me and for Larry, but also to share them with our sons. In the stories, I hoped they might recognize how those experiences have reverberated and influenced all our lives.

You Need a House Boy

"The first thing you need to do is hire a house boy," said Dave as he offered Larry a brown bottle of warm Castle beer. Joyce, Dave's wife, served me black Chombe tea in a rose patterned teacup that chimed in its saucer.

After Dave helped us move into our new house, we accepted his and Joyce's invitation to tea. I imagined that British teachers were more accustomed to the idea of hired help, given their history of grand country houses, butlers and below-the-stairs staff; but this was 1969 and we were Canadians. We were the offspring of working class families, fresh from student protests, at one with the ongoing civil rights marches in the US. The thought of me, a twenty-one-year-old woman, hiring a house servant seemed pompous and just plain silly.

"I don't think we need a servant," I said.

Dave answered, "We said that too, but think about it. The generator only runs from sunset until ten, then it's lights-out in the dorms and in all our houses. You need a steady supply of wood for the kitchen stove. It heats your water and cooks your food. You'll need your bread baked for you because the stuff in the market is full of grit. It ruins your teeth. Besides, it's usually burnt because they cook it on an open fire. Your drinking water needs boiling and filtering. You don't have a washing machine and there isn't a laundromat in the whole country. Everything, absolutely everything, right down to your knickers, needs to be ironed to kill off the putzi fly larvae that burrow into your skin. You're both teaching full time. How are you going to keep on top of all that? You'll need a boy."

Boy. The ghost of Martin Luther King trembled.

"Doesn't anyone just look after themselves?" Larry asked.

Dave's reply was patient but clear, "Last year, the Irish bachelor tried it, but he didn't stick it. Left at Christmas break. Look at it this way. You are expected to provide a job. It's a good one. You don't want to deny someone a job, do you? The school has hous-ing for house boys and their families, down behind the soccer field. Whether you like it or not, as soon as word gets out new teachers have arrived, there will be a lineup at your door."

A job. OK. We can give someone a job.

"So if we change our minds and actually decide to hire someone, how do we go about it?"

"Don't worry. I'll tell my boy. He'll put the word out for some-one good. Then you just interview the blokes who come and make up your mind who you want. More tea? Beer?"

We said, "Thanks, but we really want to unpack and settle into our house."

We had rarely been alone since leaving Canada two months be-fore. For the first time, we could cook our dinner in our own home. The huge gaps in my cooking skills were about to become obvi-ous. Larry, an experienced Boy Scout, was accustomed to campfire cooking, so between us we made a basic meal on our one ring, pres-sure-pumped, kerosene-fuelled Primus stove. The day before, I had walked the dirt path into downtown Lundazi with Barb and explored the single row of shops to find out what we could heat up from tins: slender Danish sausages, South African sardines in tomato sauce, and Fray Bentos steak and kidney pie would get us through the first few days. We couldn't use the wood stove because we didn't have any wood and we didn't know how to get it.

On Saturday, two days later and the morning after Movie Night, a lineup began at our door. There were thin teenage boys anxious for a job because they had missed the cut getting into secondary school. There were old men, arthritic, barefoot, with tight twists of white in matted, tight-curled black hair. Every applicant had ironed his threadbare shirt and trousers to a sheen.

Bedford Silungwe stood out. He was taller than the others, solidly built, a young man, not a teenager. He arrived at our door wearing spit-and-polish shiny black shoes, white knee socks, sharply pressed shorts and a white shirt. He had a lively, deep, slightly hesitant voice and spoke reasonable English. I thought he had kindly eyes behind his black rimmed glasses. Most important, he said he could bake bread.

By the end of Bedford's first day there was an oxcart at our back door with a load of firewood, and the woodburning stove in the kitchen was heating up. We decided to reserve the Primus stove for boiling water because its fast kerosene-fuelled heat was more efficient than wood for heating up a kettle for tea.

At first, I thought it made no sense at all to have a wood stove in an African kitchen since it was more than warm enough without burning a fire in the house. In my experience, heat and light happened magically with the flip of a switch. I had failed to make the connection between power and the availability of natural resources—water, oil reserves, coal mines, and hydro dams—connected to power lines. In our isolated corner of Zambia, we depended on expensive, imported diesel for electricity and on the local forests to provide wood for cooking.

Larry and I began a stumbling relationship with Bedford, trying to balance out who would do what in the house. I would cook our meals, but he would bake our daily bread. As a university student, I tried to bake my own bread to save money. My first yeasty brick splashed and sank into the lagoon at Stanley Park when I offered it to the ducks.

On his second day in our kitchen, Bedford baked bread while we were at school. When I got home at four he had finished and gone home. Our tiny kitchen was spotless and smelled of a slow wood fire, yeast and bread crust, but I couldn't find the loaves. I checked all the cupboards then tried the drawers under the counter. In the bottom drawer, wrapped in a page from the *Times of Zambia*, I found a tidy beige brick that looked exactly like my first student loaf. I hurried to the market before it closed, to buy another dozen charcoal-crusted, gritty buns.

The next morning, Bedford was apologetic. "Today, Madam, I am baking good bread."

That afternoon a second brick joined the first. Larry and I ate up the last of yesterday's market buns. I noticed that Bedford's glasses were simply frames with no lenses and that his bright white knee socks, seen close up, were threadbare and enhanced with white shoe polish. I began to wonder who we had hired and how we might quickly unhire him. Reluctantly, I asked Gay, who taught English with me, what I could do.

"No problem. Send him over to Joseph."

Don and Gay's cook, Joseph, had the reputation of being the

best cook in the compound. He was older than anyone on the entire teaching staff. His hair was salt and peppered and he moved with the quiet, grounded authority of someone who has found his place in the world and is content. In the kitchen he wore a soft white chef's hat. Out of the kitchen he was a skilled poacher and he supplied impala and duiker meat to those who were on his list. Gay, as his employer, was the gatekeeper of the list and, in addition to offering us Joseph's skills as a baker, she invited us to join Joseph's queue. After that, small packages of rich game meat showed up randomly. It was manna from heaven after fish and sausages from tins.

After a day spent with Joseph, Bedford made high rising, golden-crusted loaves, occasionally decorated with spiralled or s-shaped twists of leftover dough.

Much later, I asked him, "So, tell me, what are these designs?"

"Ah. Madam, they are snakes."

At first I was startled, then my fingers tingled with the memory of how, as a child, I loved the sensation of rolling out rainbow coloured snakes and worms from leftover bits of plasticine.

Once bread was solved, we just took it for granted that Bedford always arrived on time, even though, in this new country, most people lived without clocks or watches. He washed our clothes in the bathtub, stepping on them the way I imagined Italians stamped grapes in a vat. He used the dining room table as an ironing board and heated the metal base of the heavy iron on the wood stove. He polished our concrete termite-proof floors with a glossy sepia wax that stained our bare feet. In our sleep, our waxed feet brushed the bedsheets with hazy, rust-coloured abstractions. The wax, imported from South Africa, was called Sunshine Stoep Polish, and was labelled with a cartoon of a bright yellow rising sun, complete with wide-open eyes and a generous grin. Bedford managed the wood stove so there was always ample hot water and the stove was hot enough for us to cook supper when we came home from school. He used stove blacking to buff the heavy cast-iron body from ashy grey to clean, matte black. Bedford told us the things he needed to keep the house clean to his standards, and we bought them.

He introduced us to his wife and new baby. We still have a photo of them taken in front of our house. His wife wears a striped dress and large white towel as a skirt wrap. She stands behind Bedford who is seated on our lawn chair. He holds his child on his lap and looks directly at the camera, new-father proud. A few weeks after I took the photo, he introduced another wife, his first, who had come down from Chitipa, his home area north of Lundazi. Bedford said, "There are many things she does not like to eat. I am looking, looking very hard, trying to find the foods she likes."

Eventually, I worked out that Bedford and I were the same age. At twenty-one he had two wives and two children. This man who wore empty glass frames could read and was keen to learn. He began experimenting with recipes. Near the end of our first term, Phyllis, Larry's mom, sent us a Penguin cookbook from the southern USA filled with recipes from the Deep South based on cornmeal similar to Zambia's gritty cornmeal. In our kitchen, both Bedford and I learned how to cook polenta, shoofly pie, spoonbread and cornbread. The dishes looked anemic to me because Zambian cooking corn was white, not like the egg-yolk-yellow sweet corn I was used to from Chilliwack, my hometown, famous for its fresh corn.

The cookbook's pages became dotted with margarine and the margins filled with Bedford's printed notes about alternate ingredients. Although our supplies were limited, he became an expert at making substitutions. Peanuts stood in for pecans, walnuts and almonds. Instead of butter, he used Danish margarine in tins. We mixed lumpy milk from Nestlé powder. A chocolate chip cookie recipe evolved, after substitutions, into a plain white sugar cookie with home roasted peanuts and no chips.

Bedford taught me how to rescue a burned saucepan using fine sand and baking soda. I asked him how he knew these things. "My mother taught me this. She is so strong she is like a man." I tried to imagine his mother. I would have liked to meet her, this woman who raised a son who could read in a time when there were few schools, a man who dressed creatively for his profession. His knee-high socks, in addition to being enhanced with white polish, had no soles. There was just enough fabric in the foot to go under the arch and hold the leg portion in place.

When I got to know him better I asked about his name. He told me, "It is like a very strong lorry." Then I remembered the chrome, box-capital letters on the hood of British Bedford trucks used by many businesses and government offices to transport everything from

Bedford and family

people, to goats, to sacks of grain. Bedford told me it was good to choose an English name. Larry and I were often amused by the English names chosen by our students; names like Cigarette and Typewriter. The most creative was Tiny Killer McTavish. Years later, a colleague from Malawi, Teddy Phiri, told us that he and his wife had chosen traditional African names for their children. However, when they started school, they adopted English names and abandoned their African ones. They didn't care about "colonial influences." They wanted something "cool." For himself, Bedford had chosen a name associated with strength. Over time, he came to feel like a distant cousin to us. As we became more comfortable with each other, we would have endless arguments about family obligations. As a man with a salaried job he was the target of never-ending requests from cousins, uncles, brothers and aunts begging for loans or bags of mealie-meal: the hundred-pound sacks of ground corn that fed a small family for a month. I insisted, "They are taking advantage of you." He argued, "No. This is our way. It is my duty. When I am needing help, they will also be helping me."

I tried to imagine my brothers and sisters asking for a portion of my salary each month. Irritation and resentment were the only emotions that rose in me. When President Kaunda had spoken to our volunteer group in Lusaka he said, "Zambians do not follow the Western path of Individualism. They practise Zambian Humanism, the path of mutual aid and loyalty to their community." That sounded lovely at the time, but in practice it didn't appeal to me, despite my fantasies about living in a peaceful commune. One month, the family demands on his wages were more than his salary, and he asked us for a loan. We hesitated, but finally agreed. He repaid that loan and others in small installments and never defaulted.

Bedford became the dependable constant in the background of our ever-changing lives throughout our time in Zambia.

THE SCHOOL

The school was built at the peak of optimism and hope just after Zambia's independence from Britain in 1964. Inspired by Canada's Prime Minister Lester Pearson, many Western countries provided foreign aid to help Zambia develop its school system.

When we arrived in 1969 there were six Zambian teachers and one Zambian administrator. These were the rare ones who had managed to get a secondary education when Zambia was the British colony called Northern Rhodesia. Among the Caucasian staff, I was the youngest at twenty-one—most were in their mid-twenties. Brian, the deputy headmaster at the time we arrived, was the oldest at thirty-three.

The in-country teacher training, experienced by many of the Brits on staff, was one of the many schemes the new government used to attract teachers to the fledgling state-run secondary schools. Zambia advertised at teacher training colleges abroad and appealed to the volunteer organizations springing up in North America and Europe, such as CUSO in Canada and VSO in Britain. As a result, the Lundazi teaching staff was a melange of international volunteers and contract teachers from Britain, India, Canada, Australia, Denmark, Northern Ireland and South Africa. Later, teachers arrived from Norway, France, Guyana, the USSR, and the USA, as well as a steady stream from Britain.

The school was laid out with classrooms, dormitories and cooking facilities. Twenty-eight staff houses were spaced along two roads that radiated out from the campus. The now headmaster, Brian, and the deputy headmaster, Manyinda (I never knew his first name) lived in larger homes tucked right against the border of the school grounds. At the farthest edge of the school property, on the far side of the sports field and running track, thirty-six one-room homes housed the school maintenance workers and "house boys," men who worked in the teachers' houses as cooks and cleaners. I didn't notice these tiny homes until weeks after our arrival.

Our school was almost as well-equipped as a Canadian rural school in the 1960s. Like the staff houses, the classroom blocks had asbestos roofing and termite-proof, steel-framed doors and windows based on a British design but manufactured in Zambia. Five years later, when we lived in England, a friend invited me to visit the primary school where she taught. The windows, latches, doors, and door handles were identical to the ones in Lundazi and were so familiar I found myself reaching out to twist a window latch. It swivelled and creaked in the same way as the latches in my Zambian homeroom. Even the muscles in my hand carried Lundazi memories—I found myself back in my African classroom, before the first class of the day, opening the windows to let the breeze flow through.

The one-storey classroom blocks were laid out like a capital H: two parallel lines of four classrooms and a covered walkway across the centre to connect each side. There were classrooms assigned for the pen and paper subjects: English, history, geography, maths, and religious knowledge (RK). Separate buildings housed the science labs, domestic science rooms, and classrooms for technical drawing and agriculture. There was space dedicated for a library, and an audiovisual supplies room.

The students were ranked from First Form to Fifth Form. At first, I found "Form" a confusing concept. First Form was the Canadian equivalent of Grade 8. Fifth Form was the equivalent of Grade 12. In 1964, less than three percent of the secondary school–age population was in school and there were no Zambians ready to graduate from either technical school or university. Most of our students were aged from twelve to seventeen, but several older ones were "flying under the radar." The pent-up thirst for education was so intense that men with grey in their hair sat at the back of some of my classes. At registration they claimed, "I do not recall the year I was born." At best, I was four years older than the seventeen-year-old Fifth Form students and could be the daughter of some of the adult students.

The boys and girls came from all over the country. Once they gained a secondary place, they were sent where there was room. They represented multiple tribes: the warrior Ngonis from the east, the urban Bemba from the Copperbelt, Chewa from the Chipata area,

First form girls

and the local Tumbuka. Each tribe carried history and stories to prove they were superior to the others, but as a teacher I was not aware of tribal differences playing out in the classroom, which might have been a reflection of my naivety or the students' capacity to find common ground. David, with a linguist's ear, noted that the students spoke a mixture of the dominant languages Chichewa and Chitumbuka.

Our students lived in dormitories, eights units for the girls and eight for the boys, at opposite ends of the school campus. Each unit held about fifty students, who slept in two long rows of bunk beds pushed up against the windows. There were two washing blocks for the girls, with sinks, toilets and showers, and two blocks for the boys. Each dormitory had an older student assigned as prefect, with supervisory responsibilities in exchange for the luxury of a cubicle with walls, shelves, and a single bed.

The dormitory windows were hung with cotton curtains—solid colours of red, yellow or orange. Some of the curtains had odd shapes. I eventually made a connection between the misshapen curtains and the bell-bottom trousers worn by some of the boys. A boy would entice a girl to cut two triangles from the edges of her dorm curtains. Then he would beg her to sew the triangles into the lower inseam of his black school uniform trousers to create bell-bottoms. The

School kitchen

transformed trousers reminded me of the flash of mating plumage on a Canadian red-winged blackbird. Only the boys wore bell-bottoms, as girls were not allowed to wear trousers. The same "no trousers rule" applied to the women teachers also.

The students ate in the huge dining hall built with concrete cinder block walls, under an asbestos roof supported by metal rafters. Our eight hundred students were served nshima—their traditional staple food made from hard, white milled corn cooked with water—for breakfast, lunch and dinner. Southern US cooking uses yellow milled corn boiled in water to make polenta. Recently, I was astonished to see prepared polenta—wrapped in a plastic sleeve and looking like a fat, yellow sausage—at our health food store for three dollars a pound. At that rate, it would have cost over a thousand dollars per meal to feed our student body rather than the ten dollars a day for two hundred and twenty pounds of ground corn that provided three meals for everyone.

The porridge was cooked outside the dining hall under a ramshackle metal roof, in large round-bottomed kettles. Wood fires were set into low fireplaces beneath the kettles. The cooks lit the fires, poured water into the kettles, heated it to boiling, then added cornmeal and stirred it slowly with long, wooden paddles until it was the

Students

consistency of stiff oatmeal. They scooped the cooked nshima into rimmed metal plates and topped it with relish, a stewed concoction of tomatoes, peanuts, onions and various seasonal greens spiced with locally grown cayenne called piri-piri. Meals were served at long tables in the dining hall.

About twice a week, the students ate meat mixed with their relish. Local farmers sold chickens, pigs and cows to the school boarding master. The cooks cut up the carcasses to give each child two ounces of meat in their meal. Occasionally, the local game department sold wild meat to the school at bargain rates after the game guards culled hippos and elephants that ravaged the farmers' fields.

One evening, when I crossed through the empty hall just after dinner en route to the staff room, I saw local children, about seven and eight years old, carrying spoons and empty two-quart tins previously used for floor polish. They scuttled across the floor and scraped up anything that had dropped under the tables. Then they slipped out into the darkness. These images play back to me as a black and white silent film, with small bodies lit by the cool flicker of fluorescent light as they crab-walked over the floor. My mother's voice still speaks over this moving picture to my eight-year-old self, "Children in Africa are starving. Eat your dinner." I still clean my plate.

The student dining hall also served as an assembly space and gymnasium. After the evening meal, the tables and chairs were folded

Brian and staff on the way to assembly

and stacked. At seven every Tuesday and Thursday morning, before the heat ramped up, the whole school gathered for assembly. Len played a hymn on the school piano and eight hundred voices rang out in a multiplicity of harmonies that could not be confined within the labels of soprano, alto, tenor or bass.

Each school assembly closed with the Zambian national anthem sung to the tune of the Pan-African anthem. Apartheid was still in full force in South Africa and there seemed no reasonable possibility of it ever ending, however, the anthem was sung with hope. My musical ear was pedestrian, but I could feel the power of the students' singing even though I didn't fully understand its complexity. I wish I could go back in time to listen again.

Because we were close to the equator, sunset was at six, varying only by fifteen minutes throughout the year's imperceptible shift from equinox to solstice. When the sun disappeared, the school's diesel generator growled awake and provided light for students and staff. The students ate in the dining hall, then returned to their classrooms for homework. At ten, the generator sighed and gasped to a halt. The students settled into their dormitories, while the teachers lit candles and kerosene lamps in their homes. Once our ears adjusted to the silencing of the generator, new noises began to lay down the sound tracks that would haunt our memories forever: high-pitched cicadas, the irregular gulping voices of frogs and the liquid calls of owls.

Shopping in Lundazi

When I was a teenager my mom would say, "Watch the stew, stir it and don't let it burn."

"OK. Yeah. Yes."

My intentions were excellent, but a good book always led me astray until the smell of charred beef yanked me away from time travelling with the Princes in the Tower or the Medici poisoners. Mom gave up and reassigned me to keeping The Kids (my five younger siblings) distracted while she prepared dinner.

When I left Mom's home cooking, I moved on to dining hall meals at university, then to TV dinners every night throughout my first year as a primary school teacher. When I arrived in Lundazi I could boil water and open a box of Kraft Dinner. I accepted that we needed Bedford to manage the wood stove, keep our water supply boiled and filtered and bake our daily bread, but I reasoned I was a married woman now and it was time to learn how to cook. I did not want to drift into the potential expectation that Bedford would prepare our meals. That felt too "lady of the manor" for my taste. But, first, I needed to learn how to shop.

Lundazi's main street was bracketed by the butcher on one end and, at the other end, Mulla's hardware store, which also sold petrol from two hand-cranked pumps. In the middle was a series of small, cinder-block shops that carried the same items, with minor variations from one store to another.

Two wide concrete steps led to a veranda in front of each shop door. Every shop had barred windows, one on each side of the entrance. Depending on the day of the week, two or three tailors set up their treadle sewing machines along the veranda. The tailors, always men, could size a person up without measuring and sew a man's short sleeve shirt or a woman's shift dress overnight. One of the tailors drew my eye, but I tried not to stare. The left side of his face from his cheekbone to his lower jaw was a folded mass of glistening pink and red. Leprosy had disintegrated the skin that should hide his cheek muscles and sinuses. His dark, intense eyes looked directly at me when I walked up the steps to the veranda, while he kept on pumping the treadle and running a straight seam down the side of a shirt.

The first time I stepped into a Lundazi shop on my own, the smells of dust, dried fish, and wood smoke filled my throat and stifled my breathing. Four women, with their babies snuggled into bright cotton back-wraps, and two men, barefoot but wearing dusty fedoras, filled the space to capacity. We waited our turns in front of a concrete counter that divided the customers from the shopkeeper, whose products were displayed on rickety wooden shelves behind the counter. I watched as a woman pointed to what she wanted and the shopkeeper brought it down and placed it on the counter. When it was my turn, I copied her gesture and asked for three bars of soap, a tin of fish and a bag of rice. I felt victorious at the success of my transaction.

After a few more trips to town, I wrote home,

> Shopping means we need to find our shopping bags and baskets. You must bring your own containers. No one has heard of brown paper SuperValu bags around here. The first stop is usually the largest shop on the street. Imagine going into a yellow cement warehouse about fifty feet long and twenty feet wide. All the stock is behind counters. You have to fight your way through twenty people and catch the attention of the storekeeper. Then you begin calling out your list and waving frantically in the direction of the stuff you want. You don't ask for cookies and ketchup, it's biscuits and tomato sauce because that is what the British call them. The stock is very strange, no vegetables or tinned soups. Lots of tinned meats…better than what we'd get in tins in Canada, thank heaven, because we live on it most of the time. The weirdest one is Fray Bentos beef pie with puff pastry in a pie-shaped tin. There is always beer and Cinzano vermouth and Mazoe squash—a coloured concentrated cordial that comes in lemon and orange. Fanta and

Coke crates are stacked near the door. There's plenty of washing soap and lots of cigarettes. No shampoo. Lots of toothpaste, lots of baby powder. Since there are plenty of babies around here, every store has lots of baby cleaning supplies, but no tinned baby food, much to the dismay of the English mothers on staff. One of the English women at the school got fed up last week. She packed up her kids, marched them to the school, stood outside her husband's classroom and demanded that he take her back home to England. She has calmed down a bit now and they will stay on.

After I decided to teach myself how to cook, I often took my questions over to Ben and Doreen's house. Doreen willingly offered suggestions, loaned me cookie sheets, measuring spoons and recipes, then put the kettle on. Over tea, I moaned about the tedium of eating tinned meat day after day.

Doreen said, "Come with me. I'll show you how to get the best cut of fresh beef. The butcher comes into town about once a week and opens shop in that peculiar boxy building, the first one in the row of shops."

The next Wednesday, Doreen and I walked to town. When a cow had been gutted, skinned, hung, and was ready for sale, the butcher used a metal rod to strike on a three-foot section of railway tie that hung out front of his shop. The furious clanging rang all over the town site and carried as far as the school. Doreen seemed to have a second sense as to when the clanging would happen. The day of my shopping lesson, the clatter began just as we arrived at the butcher's shop.

We entered the high-ceilinged cube and waited at the blood-smeared concrete block that served as a counter. I looked up and saw that the shop was tall enough to hang skinned cow carcasses, full-length, on meat hooks drilled into the ceiling. The cows' black, hairy tails were still attached and arced out at painful angles. The ceiling was black: every inch of it covered by ecstatic flies that shifted and shimmered from black to purple, accented with flashes of green. I thought of how my mom diligently controlled germs by keeping a bottle of Lysol near the kitchen sink and separate towels for dishes, counters, floors, and hands. I thought, "Momma really wouldn't like

Lundazi shopping street

this," which fuelled my triumphant determination not to give in to the queasy feeling in my guts.

Doreen pointed to the smaller of the two upside-down carcasses, "You see that spot, below the haunch and above the ribs. That's the fillet. That's what you want."

She said to the butcher, "I would like five libs of fillet." He took a machete with a two-foot blade, wiped it across his stained apron, then deftly sliced out the piece. Later, I learned this was beef tenderloin, the least used muscle in the cow's body and the most tender cut of meat. The butcher flopped the fillet over the rusty pan of a chipped enamelled weigh scale. He moved the sliding weights back and forth and said, "Five and a half libs, Madam."

Doreen indicated the beef was for me, so he wrapped it in newsprint from last month's *Times of Zambia* and charged me "thirty-five ngwee a lib" (equivalent to fifty-four cents a pound). It was then I realized that *lb.*, the abbreviation for *pound,* had become a word in its own right, *lib.*

Following Doreen's instructions, I took the slab home, washed off the printer's ink and set it on a plate at the back of our small kerosene-fuelled fridge. She told me to wait at least a week, until the meat developed a blue-green sheen that indicated it had aged enough. The next step was to scrub off the slippery green coating, cut the meat into cubes and simmer it with onions for at least three hours. The result was very chewy but intensely flavoured beef stew.

"And if you burn it," Doreen said, "you disguise the nasty charred flavour by sloshing in half a cup of sherry. It works every time."

But I rarely burned it. I had too much invested.

OUR GARDEN

Years after we left Zambia, during a frigid Fort St. John winter, when our kitchen garden was frozen under snow, I discovered Isak Dinesen's memoir, *Out of Africa*. She began, "I had a farm in Africa." In our own way, we had a farm in Africa from the time we arrived until we said goodbye.

Once Bedford learned how to bake bread and settled into managing our house, the next expectation was that we should also have a gardener. With reluctance, we hired Francis. Francis, the antithesis of Bedford, was a barefoot, roll-your-own chain-smoker who leaned on the rake and stared off in the direction of the girls' dormitories a stone's throw from our back door. He worked on his own timetable and the vegetables did not thrive.

Francis taught us two things: how to make raised beds and how to plant sweet potatoes. He heaped up soil into a grave-sized mound, then raked it flat into the shape of a single bed raised six inches off the ground. He cut up chunks of sweet potato, buried them in the raised bed, and within weeks, leaves and trailing stems emerged. They looked familiar, but it took a while before I realized the connection between the lush, lime-green tangle of vines that covered our soil and my mother's do-it-yourself houseplants.

When I was a child, Mom sometimes set aside half a sweet potato from the six tubers meant for dinner. She stabbed two toothpicks into its sides like skinny arms, then balanced the toothpicks over a jam jar filled with water. After a few weeks, the eyes of the sweet potato sprouted and began to send out coiled triangular leaves, unfurling along vines that she looped up and over the kitchen cupboards.

Our Zambian vines produced more than greenery. In the middle of our second term, Francis dug up enough sweet potato tubers to fill two baskets. One potato weighed five pounds. By this time, our patience with Francis and his random work ethic was exhausted.

Our garden

We let him go and decided to manage the garden ourselves, with a little help from Bedford.

The garden soil of my childhood was chocolate brown but our new soil was rust red. Into it we planted carrots, squash, beans, onions, sugar cane and spinachy greens with unfamiliar Chitumbuka names. Don, the agriculture teacher, gave us seeds for a delicious sweet, white, thin-skinned South African squash with firm orange flesh. However, onion seeds from South Africa did not thrive because onions are sensitive to how long the days are. Even though we lived under what seemed like never-ending sunshine, we were close to the equator and had only twelve hours of light. Those seeds knew what they wanted, and what they wanted was the full thirteen and a half hours of sunlight that shone on South Africa.

When the rains came in November, the garden flooded and water sluiced away the soil. But the raised beds held together and our crops stood firm. Years later, when we returned to Canada, we heard about the new fad for French intensive gardening in raised beds, but we knew that Zambia had them first. We still rake our soil into beds every spring.

On a blue aerogramme, stuck with Zambian stamps postmarked December 1969, Larry wrote home,

I'm cooking dinner. Making hamburgers using our own garden onions, tomatoes, lettuce, our homemade bread, and eggs from the school farm.

Michael, our eldest son, who was four when we left Zambia, became a university lecturer in organic and sustainable agriculture. Forty years later, he wrote an article on energy use and climate change. He began the article by describing how, throughout his childhood, dinner always began with grace, followed by a litany, "and the potatoes, the onions and the beans are from the garden" or "and the tomatoes and the peas" depending on what we had cooked that evening. Neither Larry nor I were aware of this pattern until Michael pointed out the ritual.

Outside the back door of our new Zambian home, I pushed stubs of frangipani branches into the ground. A few months passed and five-petalled, creamy, whorled blooms opened. We planted cuttings of spiny crown of thorns that spread along our driveway and made a low, needled barrier that stopped students from criss-crossing our yard. Larry put up a bamboo trellis on two sides of the veranda. I dug in slips of morning glory at the trellis base and ten weeks later the vines reached the roof, offering up dozens of daily purple blooms with pink throats. Small lizards came to live in the vines and watched us with swivelling eyes. I sliced open a green skinned papaya and admired the sweet orange flesh that surrounded a cavity filled with a generous handful of black seeds. The seeds went into the ground and days later double-winged leaves sprouted from the soil. The trunk shot up in small sections, like a telescope opening out, and within seven months there was a six-foot-high tree with fruit to harvest and seeds to begin the cycle again. Deep green mango trees grew everywhere and provided welcome shade for people and cattle, but the fruit tasted like turpentine.

I came to know and anticipate the extravagant red blooms of the flame tree and the delicate violet flowers of jacaranda. Each of those trees grew to the size of large oaks. Their fiery red and light purple array of blossoms came before the leaves, then, at the end of the season, eighteen-inch-long pods filled with slender rattling seeds hung from the flame tree, and seed pods like frilled castanets decorated the jacaranda. It was impossible to take a colour photograph of the jacaranda flowers because the Kodachrome slide film of the time did not pick up the delicate shade of violet. The transparent developed slide, in its square cardboard frame, showed a large, grey-trunked tree covered with a grey blur instead of soft purple flowers.

There were so many trees and shrubs I did not notice—the common, quieter trees of the miombo forest that provided shade, fibre, poles for building, wood for fire, and medicines. The European nurses at the local hospital saw evidence of patients treated by herbalists using powerful blood coagulants and wound-healing poultices derived from local plants, but I didn't connect these rumours with actual trees. In the heart of the dry season some of the trees opened lime green leaves in defiance of the rest of the dusty, tan coloured landscape as they waited for rain.

A tree cured Larry, despite his scepticism. One morning he woke with a painful spasm in his neck. He couldn't turn his head and it was impossible to disguise his discomfort. He struggled through his agricultural science class until his best student, Simon, raised his hand, "Please sir. You have been witched. That farmer, the one whose cattle came into our school farm and smashed our peanut field, he has witched you. You tied his best cow to a tree. The calf was crying for his mother. Now you are witched. To stop the witching you must find a mubanga tree."

Larry pushed off the suggestion, but three days later, his head still immobile, he found Simon after class and asked for help. Simon agreed.

"Sir, you will be finding this tree very near your house."

As Larry followed Simon, other boys from the class took notice and joined the parade. Simon directed Larry to the tree and explained, "Now Sir, you must be standing very near to the tree. Now you must be resting your head upon its bark. You must be standing very quiet. Then you will be cured."

As his students watched and chuckled, Larry followed Simon's directions. A minute passed. He lifted his head. The pain was gone.

A NEW WAY OF SEEING:
WHAT IS A DIET?

As we settled into the routines of the school year, my life had moments of uncertainty, some pleasant, some disturbing. Moments when things were not what they appeared, and assumptions were upended. Moments when I sensed the world was more various, beautiful or strange than I had imagined. It was as if I had opened a door and found new rooms in my home, spacious and airy, filled with hints of divergent futures, incomprehensible puzzles, and new ways of seeing.

Our students craved sweets. They got a few teaspoons of sugar in the morning to sweeten their breakfast nshima but depended on the small shops in town to provide technicolour hard candies—fuchsia, lime and yellow—in exchange for their pocket money. My students' English essays were full of the raptures of sugar and honey, with expressions like "Too, too sweet," and "So sweet." In their stories, love was always sweet.

In the first year, when we still depended on British-based texts, I taught standard comprehension lessons. The students read an essay, followed by the five Ws: "Who, What, When, Where, and Why?" One story was about a man in London who went to his doctor with knee pains and was told to go on a diet to relieve the pressure in his joints. Waysi put up his hand, pushed back his metal-legged chair, then stood by his desk and asked respectfully, "Please Madam, what is a diet?"

"When you are on a diet you must not eat too much food, especially sugar." I almost said, "No doughnuts or ice cream," but I quickly stopped myself. I had not seen doughnuts or ice cream since we arrived in Lundazi.

Waysi looked at me with incomprehension and sat down, unsatisfied. Other hands went up. Davison shouted out, disbelieving,

"Please, Madam, how could anyone have too much food? It is not possible." My words began to sound nonsensical and my mouth went dry. I could not begin to explain the abundance of food in Canada, the plates of half-eaten French fries left on A&W trays, nor the heaped plates of spaghetti and meatballs unfinished. Every student in front of me was wiry and slender. They would look scrawny standing beside a Canadian teenager. I couldn't think of a single overweight kid among the eight hundred students. The only round person was the boarding master, Joel, who shovelled sugar to the point of saturation into his recess coffee.

They looked at me sideways and broke into incredulous comments among themselves. I ended the lesson early and dismissed them. I had no idea what to say.

LETTERS AND PARCELS

Once or twice a week, on a school night or a weekend afternoon, we wrote letters to our friends, our parents and our brothers and sisters. The letters were written on eight by eleven inch onion-skin, a thin, nearly transparent white paper, or on blue aerogrammes. Aerogrammes were six by twelve, with two lines on the front to show where to fold the paper into thirds. The paper was tabbed on three sides. When our letter was complete we folded the sheet twice to make a six by four inch packet, licked the tabs, and folded them over to create a light, all-in-one letter and envelope. We wrote the destination on the front and our address on the back. Then we selected the best stamps the Lundazi post office had to offer: butterflies, elephants, African shields, or the Zambian flag, and glued them to the upper right hand corner.

Larry and I were familiar with aerogrammes because soldiers had used them in WWII. In both our childhood homes there were packets of aerogrammes, keepsakes from fathers, uncles and boyfriends who fought overseas. Messages were still legible.

"I miss you darling."

"I got the socks."

"We are moving out tomorrow."

My mother, Yvonne, saved the letters we wrote and stored them in her filing cabinet. Thirty years after our return, she put them into a crinkled pink paper bag and gave them back to us. After Larry's mother, Phyllis, died, we found two shoeboxes filled with our Zambia letters, bundled in chronological order and held together with disintegrating elastic bands. I have reread our aerogrammes and the sheets of onionskin looking for clues—thoughtful comment or carefully observed details about our life in Zambia, something that would explain why those years set the template for the rest of our lives. Instead, I find diatribes on the evils of capitalism and colonialism,complaints about staff and students, and endless wish lists. As I read, I think, "God preserve me from my twenty-something self on paper." I am amazed at our demands. Larry's mom and dad, Phyllis and Norm, still had three children at home and four others, newly launched, beginning their adult lives. My parents, Lou and Yvonne, had my five siblings at home and a business to run.

The letters are filled with cajoling, teasing requests that assumed our parents would supply anything we needed to pursue our adventure in Africa. We asked them to arrange magazine subscriptions for *Maclean's, Chatelaine, New Republic,* and *Commonweal* (a left-wing Catholic magazine from the US which landed me on the FBI "persons of interest" list for subscribing to it). I asked for more cookbooks.

Another request,

Please send me Fleischmann's yeast packets.

Every shop in Lundazi sold imported British yeast in tins. It seemed I was incapable of measuring loose yeast by using a tablespoon. Amidst so much newness, I wanted the security and precision of pre-measured Canadian yeast in its square yellow envelope.

The home ec department needs dress patterns. Could you send pattern discards from the shop?

Our family business sold sewing machines and dress fabric. I knew that at the end of each season my mom directed her staff to toss hundreds of patterns from Butterick, McCall's and Simplicity. She mailed some to the school.

We need music. The evenings are long.

My brother recorded Beatles music and Joan Baez onto seven inch reel-to-reel tapes, packaged them up and mailed them. When they arrived, we sent enthusiastic thanks and asked for more.

Larry's request: *Could you send some balsa wood airplane kits. It would be fun to start a model airplane club at the school.*

We needed car parts and someone to track down papers for our Canadian income taxes.

Our mothers took on the part-time job we created for them. They shopped, scrounged, wrapped up parcels in heavy brown paper or reusable burlap, then took the trip to the post office and paid generous sums for overseas parcel mail.

Phyllis found used books and Larry's godmother sent a *Reader's Digest* subscription for my Third Form English classes. I wrote,

> The books arrived this week. Dave grabbed all the stamps. Because of these books I was able to create a library for all my Third Form English classes. Now we have ninety books for a hundred kids. I hope not everyone decides to borrow at the same time.

Parcels could take three months to arrive but, despite the time and distance, it was rare to lose anything in transit. Along with all the Europeans on staff, we lived in cycles of orders placed or items begged for from family, followed by months of anticipation, culminating in a parcel wrapped in paper, tape, string, customs labels and postage stamps. News of a parcel's arrival and its longed-for contents was the social coin of staff room chat, sometimes with a hint of bragging about whose mother showed the most ingenuity and generosity. A parcel was the highlight of the day, a tangible link to home, family and the abundance we had left behind but were confident we could demand at any time.

Luangwa Valley Game Park

Nine weeks after Larry and I arrived in Lundazi, we were in the Luangwa Valley, trapped under a mosquito net, naked and yearning for sleep. The combined temperature of the air and our skin was so irritating that we did not touch except for our feet, his left and my right, tilted together to connect lightly at the edge of our soles.

When I remember the Luangwa Valley, I remember heat.

According to the shared wisdom of the teaching staff, the dry season, when the red line on the thermometer climbed to its peak just prior to the coming of the rains, was the best time to visit the game park. In October and November, the roads were intact, the grass was dry and sparse, and that made for good viewing of impala, kudu, rhino, elephant and lion.

Lundazi was relatively cool most of the year, but October's heat conquered me. I was slow, edgy and resentful and I wanted someone to blame. In late October, Barb and Len, the other Canadians, invited us to join them for a weekend at the game reserve in the Valley. We didn't have our own car yet, so it was a generous offer and we accepted. We left on Friday afternoon as soon as school was out, with Larry and I in the back seat of their Austin station wagon.

Our destination was a twisting, ninety-mile descent to the floor of the valley. No one had explained that lower elevation meant rising heat. As the four of us switchbacked down this escarpment at the southern end of the Great Rift Valley, cut by the Luangwa River, the air got hotter, the road got rockier, the landscape drier and the plants spinier. I was not a gracious fellow traveller. The skin of my legs stuck to the car seat, my mouth dried out and my internal monologue disintegrated into, "Why would anyone want to come here? Why did they ask us? Why did I say yes? Is this a test or a miserable trick?" I wanted to moan like a six-year-old, but was distracted by someone waving at us on the side of the road.

Two uniformed men flagged us down at a tsetse fly checkpoint. Len and Barb told us we needed to get out and stand away from the car while the men used hand pumps to spray the wheel wells and the undercarriage of the car with clouds of DDT, the insecticide that Rachel Carson had warned the world about in 1962. Tsetse flies carry sleeping sickness, which affects people, and trypanosomiasis, which debilitates cattle. The flies and their diseases are linked to poor health and poverty. The spray stations aimed to control the transmission of disease between the valley, where the flies were endemic, and the populated areas. When the clouds of insecticide had settled, we could return to the car and continue our trip into the tsetse zone.

After two hours of driving, the sun moved towards the horizon and the light shifted to amber. As we swung around another turn in the road my resentment evaporated. In front of us a river—chocolate brown, shallow and broad—flowed in ribboning channels that broke apart, slipped around bands of islands, rejoined, and widened again. An uncountable number of elephants moved in unison across the river, their flowing bodies bronzed by the setting sun. Until that moment, "to move like an elephant" had meant clumsy and awkward. But what I saw in front of me was grace and grounded weight. The elephants reminded me of the heavy velvet draperies that swooped over the screen of the Paramount, my hometown movie theatre, at the end of the Saturday matinees. The river reflected the brassy sun and stretched in a wide horizontal band intertwined with the dark, flowing wave of elephants. The two lines, river and elephants, braided into one.

Our destination was Nsefu Camp, with its half-dozen cylindrical grass thatched rondavels (sleeping huts) on the bank of the Luangwa River. We had made our camping reservations by mail because there was no telephone in Lundazi or at the game camp. In October, the rondavels sat a good distance from the river that had dried up, dropped down and pulled away from the riverbank. In the rainy season, when the river swelled, it rose to within yards of the rondavels. The landing for each flight of steps was three feet from the ground to provide protection when the river escaped its banks. The design worked. The rondavels built in 1951 under the colonial government of Northern Rhodesia still house tourists today.

Luangwa rondavel

Each rondavel was just big enough for two metal-framed single beds with mosquito nets, and a small table. A common washing block served the six units with toilets, sinks and a tub that filled slowly from a large galvanized water tank. A large table and eight chairs set under a grass thatch roof defined the dining room area. The table, chairs and poles were made of mubanga, a hardwood so resinous that termites would not eat it.

In 1965, four years before our first trip to Nsefu, a British couple visited there and shot an 8mm black and white film of their family sitting outside around the dining table that was draped with a white linen tablecloth. Their film has been immortalized in a YouTube clip that advertises Nsefu Camp as the longest established safari camp in the Luangwa Valley. The historical clip doesn't show the kitchen that stood away from the sleeping huts. A simple grass roof shaded the rough table that served as a prep counter for the cooks who lived and worked at the camp in the tourist season. Next to the table, a blackened metal grill balanced over a campfire. The cooks used the grill to cook meals for the guests. Like all the other guests, we brought our own food and kept it locked in the car for safekeeping from animals. The first night, we gave the cooks the sack of potatoes meant to last us for our three day visit. They spoke rudi-

Camp cooks

mentary English and our Chitumbuka consisted of "Hello," "Thank you," and "Good morning, did you sleep well last night?" We asked them to prepare a dinner of potatoes, tinned fish and tinned peas. The cooks must have been amazed at our appetites, but that didn't curb their creative skill at producing a meal with minimal equipment. They cooked all our potatoes and served us mashed potatoes, fried potatoes, baked potatoes, potato chips and croquettes (mashed potatoes rolled into small cylinders, dredged in flour then fried gently to a crispy golden brown.) I can't recall if we ate the whole array or not.

By the time we finished our meal, the sun had set and the temperature eased towards lukewarm. After the cooks cleaned up, they settled beside the remains of the kitchen fire and smoked hand-rolled cigarettes. The four of us sat on well-worn slung-canvas chairs around our own campfire, piled on sticks to make a blaze, tipped our heads back to search for the Southern Cross and told stories. In spite of the heat, we enjoyed the fire because the smoke befuddled the mosquitoes and the flicker of flames kept animals at bay. When the fire died to embers, we said our goodnights, took our flashlights and walked to our rondavels. The shape of the hut was a circle, so there was just one wall that curved around the space, without right angles or corners. The rectangular beds stood free in the room with space to walk around them on all sides. I felt like I was standing inside a round Quaker Oats box.

I was uneasy in the curvilinear room. I wanted to straighten out the edges, to make the furniture and our suitcases fit up against the walls in a way that implied the control of an invisible underlying grid. The desk was pushed to the wall, but it touched at just two of its corners. I felt unsettled knowing that my pencil and pen might roll into the curved gap and onto the floor. For a moment I was gripped with longing for the familiarity of my childhood bedroom, its single bed, the desk, and the low metal cupboard that I had pushed against the walls in the places I had chosen. I wanted to push the rondavel furnishings flush with the wall and hear the satisfying *thunk* of two straight surfaces meeting.

I wondered what happened to a person's mind when they lived inside round spaces. I did not ask what had happened to my mind after a lifetime inside square and rectangular rooms. Larry and I pushed the beds together in the centre of the hut. The darkness was absolute beneath the circular thatch and the heat so unrelenting that it baked the sweat from our skins. We tossed pajamas and night shirt because they intensified the discomfort. Sleepless for a long time, I gave up, crawled from under the mosquito net and wrapped myself in a towel. I opened the door, stood on the top step and looked up to the moonless sky with its spangle of stars drilling silver holes in the matte black darkness. Erratic, hot red sparks from the embers of the camp's cooking fire shot upwards to meet the stars.

Finally, we slept, circled by the round wall that protected us from the curved and twisted landscape; the fractalled trees and sandbars; and the sinuous muscle of snake and leopard.

The next morning I felt disoriented again when, just after dawn, we followed the camp's game guard into the bush, along trails that veered east, south, and west around contours and clumps of bushes. I wanted a straight path and a clear view of my destination, without surprises.

As we walked in the filtered shade of the dry-season trees, the air touched our skin with the remnant of pre-dawn's coolness. We took photos of each other. In his picture, Larry wears black trousers, suede desert boots and a short-sleeved shirt I had sewn for him. He is

Larry and the game guard

following the game guard, who is dressed in a sharply pressed, olive coloured uniform of short sleeved shirt and shorts. The guard also wears a brown fedora with its wide brim turned smartly up on the left, a leather belt over his shirt, a large black watch on his wrist, and a rifle slung over his right shoulder. In my photo, I'm wearing open-toed sandals and a sleeveless, miniskirted dress that rises to six inches above my knees. I am not wearing a hat or sunglasses. I had never heard of sunscreen.

We were tracking a lion. I was sure we would see one. It would be beside a particular tree, maybe a thorn tree, where it sat every morning and waited for the tourists to walk by, just like in a zoo. Because my mind was on lion, I did not notice the birds singing to the sunrise nor did I take in the significance of the rifle on the game guard's shoulder. I gave his weapon about as much importance as his hat. I didn't grasp that this was not a controlled and scripted landscape. We were in one of the last truly wild places on earth, a place that would become inaccessible when the rains came and the river flooded and moved through the landscape to enrich the soil, uproot trees, and wash away the roads and the temporary buildings. For the moment, the ground was hard packed, covered with tawny, dry grass. The sun, at first low and gold, became smaller, whiter and hotter as it rose.

I didn't understand what I was seeing or hearing. I didn't know how this environment worked. I had no context to frame all this newness.

The game guard was there to protect us, to be our eyes and ears, and to remind us to walk softly, in silence. He was not an affable naturalist ready to translate this world for us. His knowledge of the valley was so intuitive that he wasn't aware of what he knew. He couldn't explain it to us in the vocabulary of English, his fourth language. We were disappointed we did not see a lion sitting by its particular tree, but it saw us. The guard tensed, slipped his rifle off his shoulder and pointed into the grass. He saw the lion that was invisible to us and firmly directed us back to camp.

The expatriate teaching staff made regular trips to the Valley and filled us with advice about how to respond to the dangers of the Luangwa. "If elephants block the roadway, don't drive forward or stop to look. Put the car in reverse. Fast!"

We loved to tell stories of high-centreing the car on fibrous, hassock-sized lumps of elephant dung. The shared wisdom was, if you were walking in the bush and met an elephant, the safest thing to do was to climb a termite mound—the rough conical rust-red chimneys that grew up at least ten to fifteen feet out of the ground, like wonky Dr. Seuss illustrations. Larry and I believed that advice until one day we walked around a group of trees and saw an elephant balanced on top of a termite mound, trunk stretched upward reaching for seeds pods over its head, as if it was playing Dumbo in a circus act.

Everyone who visited the valley had a story—the game drive where a rhino charged the Land Rover while Brian shot the attack on his 8mm movie camera; how Len stepped in lion tracks on the path to the communal shower block; the time elephants boxed in David's car on the road to the camp.

My Luangwa story happened one night in our second year, when Larry and I spent a weekend in the Valley on our own. I was lost in a deep sleep, and in a dream that placed me back in my first Canadian classroom, a repurposed WWII army hut with tall, wood-framed windows. I was sorting loose sheets of paper covered with the hieroglyphics of stories written by my eight-year-old students. Stories of African animals: giraffes and lions and elephants. I leaned over to pick up empty brown-paper lunch bags off the floor, but there were so many that I couldn't help but step on them. They crackled and crunched and multiplied around my feet. I couldn't gather all of them up in my sleep, so I woke up to solve the problem in another reality. Moonlight brightened the white curtains on the window. I could still hear the paper bags rustling and crackling. I got up, walked cautiously across the room and pulled the curtains back just enough to look outside.

Impalas, the tightly sprung ballerinas of the antelope world, capable of leaping ten feet in the air to soar over obstacles, were gathered outside the window so close I could lean out and touch them. At least twenty of them, their tiny sharp hooves en pointe, stepped daintily around the tree next to the cabin. They nuzzled through the dry leaves on the ground searching for something delicious. Each hoof punched through leaves that rustled, crackled and crunched like the uncontrollable paper bags in my dream. The impalas' daytime coats of café-au-lait on their backs and white cream on their underbellies had translated to soft charcoal and grey in the darkness. The males' lyre-shaped, spiraled horns picked up the moonlight, and I could see the perfect jet-black spheres of the females' Nefertiti eyes when they raised their heads to check for danger. Above them hung the dried, salami-shaped seed pods of the sausage tree, grey in the day but glowing white under the moon. So much beauty. I felt my heart contract in awe then open like a sigh. I went back to our bed, leaned over and shook Larry's shoulder. "Come. Look."

Larry loved the Luangwa Valley and its evocation of *Boys' Own* adventure stories: the possibility of a lion lying sun-lazy in the shoulder-high grass or an elephant charging, ears flapping wide, and stamping down on its flat leathery feet, pounding up dust. He saw a landscape that was magnificent, monumental and without boundaries. For me, the valley was too large, too incomprehensible, too full of uncertainty and potential dangers. I was overwhelmed by crocodiles, snakes, malaria-bearing mosquitoes, relentless heat and winding paths with no clear view. Years later I was emptied out, in the same way, by the size and scope of the Rocky Mountains when we drove between Jasper and Banff. On another trip, the Grand Canyon left me fumbling for words and burdened by its expanse. Faced with the Luangwa Valley, I couldn't grasp its unlimited edges. My feeling of awe and disorientation overflowed the cup of my imagination. I was fearful of all the uncontrollable unknowns of the valley, but I am grateful for that experience of wildness; the memory that sits in me today in a separate place. The memory taunts me in crowded supermarkets and malls, in pretentious restaurants and in pristine city parks. I recall the experience of no edges, of a river flowing from a source unknown to an ocean I had never seen; the experience of land stretching out into places inhospitable to humans and their needs; the experience of walking among untamed animals; the experience of not knowing how to travel in safety without the help of a guide. Now I wonder, as the human world moves into the lines and squares of cities, how will my grandchildren know wildness?

BRAVE

Back in Canada, if I shared a piece of our Zambia life, someone would say:

"Weren't you scared?"

"I think you were so brave."

"I couldn't do that."

But I never felt brave.

My mother always assured us "Everything will turn out all right," followed by, "Maybe we can try this."

I was heartbroken at the start of Grade 4. There wasn't enough money for crayons. Notebooks and pencils came first. Mom's solution: she gave me a small box and showed me how to collage it with leftover gift wrap. Then she told me to search the whole house and find all the stubs of broken crayons. She bet me I would fill the box. I went to school with my beautiful box, the only one of its kind. No one had to know that every crayon inside was already middle-aged.

Grade 6. Again, no money. This time I needed white shoes for choir. Mom had just bought me sensible brown lace-up oxfords to last the whole year. When I burst into tears because I knew we couldn't afford another pair, she said, "Just wait, something will turn up."

I think my grandmother dug deep. I got the shoes, white, with an angled pleat across the toe. The next year I needed the next size up. Mom sliced the toe box across the angled leather pleat line.

"There," she said, "now you have open-toed sandals."

She told me stories of how her mother cut up second-hand party dresses and made dazzling costumes for my mom and her sister to wear at their tap dance recitals. The outfits were topped off by huge sateen hair bows passed down from an aunt.

When I left home, I knew how to fix, patch and repair most clothes: holey socks, snapped underwear elastic, or snagged hems. I knew how to do without and how to improvise. Mom didn't realize she had given me the perfect skill set for life in Zambia.

Dad's training was tougher.

My dad wanted us to be brave. He told us the story of how he had fallen down his family's hand dug well, the one they used to water their horses during the drought of Saskatchewan's Dirty Thirties. He told us how he was not afraid, and convinced us that when he looked upwards from the bottom of the black cylinder, he could see the stars at midday (my dad was never one to let facts get in the way of a good story). His mother threw down a rope and rescued him. That night he was the champion, the hero of his large family. If we, his children, ever exuded even the scent of fear or hesitated over a difficulty, he said with frightening intensity, "Don't be silly. Get going!" and gave us a sharp push on the shoulder with his index finger.

One summer he gave my brother and me a lesson about diving into fear. Dad had taken all six of us camping in our Volkswagen van up to Seton Lake, near Lillooet. Mom was at home. The doctor told her she needed to rest. Lillooet regularly hits forty degrees Celsius in the summer. The heat baked our skin and dried our mouths. This was not a time when everyone carried a personal water bottle. Instead, the six of us pretended to be drought-stricken camels.

After we set up camp, we followed Dad down to the beach. He chivvied me to the top of the diving tower installed on a float near the edge of the lake.

"Up you go. Don't be afraid. You can jump in to cool off."

"You too," he told my ten-year-old brother.

Tom was four steps behind me. I could not back down. The steps, made of four-by-four planks, bit my feet, the tower trembled, the view of the water shimmered and flashed white sparks through the spindly architecture. I reached the top and stood on the square landing platform, no rails, nothing to grasp.

"Step out," called Dad. "Tom, don't back down."

I walked the plank, picked up a sliver in my right foot and froze. There was no way back. Tom's head appeared at the edge of the landing. His lips were blue, and his thin hands gripped the platform.

"Jump!" called Dad.

I did. Feet first.

I loved jumping off the dock near my cousin's cottage at Cultus Lake, a two-foot drop into welcoming water, but this rickety diving tower was at least twenty-five feet high. The drop was so long I had time to think, to breathe in terror, to feel my arms and legs flail out of control. I did not belly flop. My feet struck first and down I went into amber liquid that darkened to sepia. My feet hit muck, then I ricocheted upwards. I kicked, I grabbed for the ochre light that was too far above my head. My lungs were desperate.

I broke into the light and dog-paddled my way to the beach. I heard Tom's splash as I stepped out onto the sharp beach stones. I held myself perfectly still until I heard him break the surface and gasp for breath. Then I sucked in air and felt my knees tremble.

Dad called, "There. See? It wasn't that bad," in his hearty, don't-contradict-me voice.

I knew I couldn't cry. After all, I had survived.

From him I learned repeatedly I could push myself through fear, make no fuss, and pull through.

Maybe I was trying to live up to his demands when, at eleven, I decided I would not be a "silly girl." I would not despair over the ugly brown oxfords that supported my flat feet. I would just wear them and pretend I didn't care. I would not swoon at my girlfriend's autographed photos of handsome movie stars, not the surly rugged ones, nor the sweet blonde cheeky ones. I would not scream at spiders or snakes.

Years later, during a gut-stripping crisis involving one of my children, a friend offered me the image of a lotus flower. The lotus root anchors in mud and reaches up with a sturdy, snake-like shoot that rises through tea-brown water towards blurred yellow sunlight to open in white petalled symmetry. The lotus image promises something might be harvested from an anxious, tedious, blundering struggle.

I remembered my dive into the lake and the pudding texture of the muck mixed with bits of sticks and gritty stones as I kicked up from the bottom of the lake and reached for light and air.

I had no awareness that Dad's rough challenges and Mom's it-will-turn-out-all-right-in-the-end reassurances were buried deep in me, unacknowledged resources, as I dove into my Lundazi life.

THE RAINS

The heat intensified after our trip to the Luangwa. It could be intolerable by seven in the morning and there would be no hope of reprieve until sunset. Our students were preparing to write the end-of-year government exams. The pressure for fifth formers was more acute because their exams, prepared in England then shipped to Zambia, would determine whether they could join the growing cohort of young Zambians who had graduated since their country achieved independence in 1964.

Together with the rest of the teachers, we became testy with each other and sharp with our students. We heard rumours of food riots at secondary schools in the cities of Ndola and Kabwe, where heat and exam anxiety had fused and exploded.

We ached for the relief of rain. Every afternoon we watched the thunderheads roil and billow above us. They soared like grey-bottomed ships with bleach-bright sails as they moved across the hot blue sky. Then, late one November afternoon, after weeks of taunting promises, the rain began to spit, then drum, then hammer. Water poured off the roof and overflowed the gutters in sheets. We could not speak and be heard inside the staff room. Together, a dozen of us walked outside. The rain smashed down the dry thirsty soil and kicked it up into the air, releasing petrichor, the blood of the gods, the scent of rain on parched earth. I tipped my face to the rumbling clouds, accepted their stinging, cool relief and breathed in the exhilarating spicy smell of raindrops on dust.

I had not felt rain for five months. The last time was a gentle July shower during our orientation at Lac Charlebois. Growing up in British Columbia, I had never waited for rain. It came and it went, sometimes drizzling for grey days on end, sometimes brief and sweet, with slanted sun shining it into rainbows. Now I knew another rain. Rain that held itself aloof for most of the year, then arrived in power and majesty, evoking the sound of kettle drums and demanding gratitude and complete attention. Now I understood why the rainy season was called The Rains.

Two years later, I would recall my introduction to The Rains and the exquisite release of tension that accompanied their arrival. In that future November, no amount of rain could wash away the fear that would grip our school.

But in this, our first November, civility returned with the rain. The students wrote their exams and our first term was complete.

A New Way of Seeing:
Caterpillars

With the rains came the promise of the return of green. Life crawled out of the soil: flying ants, crawling beetles and pulsing grubs.

I had an early morning English lesson with my all girls class. The air was still cool from yesterday's downpour. The girls were happy. They were feeling beautiful. Each one wore a large barrette, emerald green with ruby red, amethyst and gold spots, attached to her tight curls. I assumed a new shipment of bright plastic adornments from India had just arrived at Mulla's store.

Prisca's barrette dropped off her hair and onto her desk. She squealed, "Oh!" When she picked up the green barrette, it twitched into a C shape as she nudged it to fit behind her ear. She looked at me and her eyes flashed.

The other girls watched for my reaction as I realized the barrettes were alive: caterpillars thick as my thumb, as long as my middle finger, nourished by the riot of green leaves that come with the rains.

I smiled and pretended I was calm, interested and curious. I picked up the chalk and found the lost thread of my lesson.

After class I rushed home to collect a forgotten pile of assignments. Bedford was in the kitchen baking something. He startled when I entered. He held a full cookie sheet, but there were no cookies. The tray was covered with dark, roasted, three-inch caterpillars lined up in tidy rows.

"Excuse me," he said. "These are too, too delicious. They are coming with the rains."

He slid the tray back in the oven and closed the door.

So, the barrettes were edible, an annual delicacy.

I realized two things: the girls wanted to startle me and test me, but Bedford wanted to protect me. I began to have an inkling that the people we lived among kept many things hidden from us out of concern for our sensibilities, or from their conviction that we simply couldn't understand.

DRUM

Nigel was on the search for a drum and we were ready to help. In mid-December, at the end of our first term, Peggy and Nigel, new friends from our CUSO orientation, now stationed in Lusaka five hundred miles to the south, drove up to join us for an adventure across the border into Malawi. They were both musicians, and Nigel wanted to visit villages along the shore of Lake Malawi in the hope of finding a good traditional drum. The four of us loaded our luggage onto their roof rack and crammed ourselves into Peggy and Nigel's tiny white Renault 4, with its stick shift that looked like a fat umbrella handle.

We headed east and took the border crossing ten miles from the school. A pole, trimmed from the trunk of a slender tree, blocked the road and indicated the border line. A mud brick guard house about six feet square sat next to the barrier. The guards and their families lived in three small, metal-roofed homes. It took three men to maintain round-the-clock shifts on what appeared to be the sleepiest border crossing in the world.

Sometimes the border guard asked for our passports. Sometimes he asked us to sign the official register embossed with the Zambian government seal and filled with cream-coloured pages lined in light green ink. Sometimes he simply wrote down our licence number and waved us through. On this day, the guard came out to greet us, "Good afternoon. Where are you going?"

Larry said, "Tonight we will stay at the rest house in Mzimba. Tomorrow we will sleep at Nkhata Bay."

Mzimba was a small market town forty miles from Lundazi. Like many towns in Malawi and Zambia, it had a rest house built in colonial times to house civil servants travelling on government business. Zambian government officials continued to use the rest houses and ordinary travellers could also rent rooms. The houses were inexpensive, basic and clean, and were often the only accommodation in town. Built of brick and brightly whitewashed, they usually had a shaded veranda, but each had a unique floor plan.

Restaurants were rare, so travellers brought their own food, gave it to the caretaker, and asked him (always him) to prepare their meals. The Mzimba rest house had a shared dining area and lounge with locally made tables, chairs and armchairs that resembled the simple style of William Morris Arts and Crafts furniture. I am not sure if there was a connection to Morris via the British colonists or if the designs evolved from what a local carpenter could make with basic tools and wood from the nearby forests. The results would be compatible with Morris's idea of designing functional but beautiful furniture for ordinary working people.

December 16, 1969, blue aerogramme,

Hi Mom and Dad,

We're at a rest house in Mzimba along with Peggy and Nigel. We've discovered gorgeous scenery just over the border, not more than forty miles from the school.

When we stopped at the rest house the proprietor told us he wouldn't allow unmarried couples to stay. Once we convinced him we were married Canadians and not loose-living Americans he let us in. For 90 cents each (if we used our own blankets on the beds) we had the whole place to ourselves—two large bedrooms with single beds and mosquito nets, rugs on the floor, a sitting room with easy chairs and a fireplace, dining table and a refrigerator full of lots of cold, filtered water. We gave our food to the caretaker and told him how we wanted it cooked. He set the table, served the meal, and cleaned up.

After we unpacked, Larry and Nigel went to explore the market. They returned holding aloft an eight-foot-long stalk of sugar cane.

Peggy said, "That's very impressive, but how are we supposed to eat it?"

The caretaker's six-year-old daughter was watching us like a miniature anthropologist. Peggy broke off a piece as long as her forearm, offered it to the girl and mimed that we wanted to know how to eat it. The child rested the cane along her cheek for leverage then bit off the tough outside layer, spit it out and chewed into the fibres. When I tried, it was like sucking golden syrup through slim silk straws.

Later, a Canadian dentist who worked in Malawi told us, "People in the villages eat lots of sugar cane. They have good teeth and healthy gums. If they move to town and switch from sugar cane to store-bought sweets, they quickly develop the same dental problems I used to treat in Canada."

After sugar cane and dinner that night, I filled the wide, deep, claw foot tub. The combination of steam and the yellow glow cast by the Tilley lamp on the cream-coloured walls created a cozy cave for a luxurious soak. When I got out to dry, something about four inches long crept out from under the bath mat. My breath stopped. I couldn't tell what it was. A huge insect? A toad? A mouse? Then I could see it was a bat, blind and creeping across the floor.

I wrote home and made much of the drama, ending with,

> I'm getting used to this sort of stuff. I did not scream.

The next morning, we drove farther north and stopped at the rambling open market in Mzuzu. We got out for groceries and I itemized them in my letter home.

> I bought a mushroom (one foot across, two cents), a pineapple (twenty-four cents), long tomatoes (eighteen cents), papaya (ten cents) and bananas (twenty cents), then stuffed everything in a basket.

The plastic bag hadn't been invented yet. I had learned to carry a basket to hold shopping items that might be wrapped in newspaper or, occasionally, placed in a flimsy paper bag. When I read my letters they sound like a catalogue or a sale flyer with endless details of what we bought and how much it cost. I think of Oscar Wilde's maxim: "Nowadays, people know the price of everything and the value of nothing."

Larry and I grew up after WWII when our parents had to count every penny, so both of us were energetic penny-pinchers. I suppose that is a better combination than one penny-pincher with a spendthrift partner, but it makes for irritating reading when I am searching the letters for some thoughtful comment about our everyday life only to find another excited paragraph full of exclamation marks about a great bargain I had discovered in toilet paper or tinned peas.

Supplied with fruit and one enormous mushroom from the market, we continued our journey to Nkhata Bay on the shore of Lake Malawi. The lake's size is a geography teacher's dream, a beautiful mnemonic. From north to south it is 365 miles long, as the days in a year, and at the widest point from east to west it is 52 miles, the same as the number of weeks in a year. From Lundazi to Nkhata Bay the journey is 250 kilometres on a gravel road. (I am reminded that, in conversation, we switched back and forth between miles and kilometres. Back then, odometers were still calibrated in miles, but kilometres were the official standard.) We often found ourselves behind yellow graders that stirred up thick, rusty clouds of dust as they scraped down the washboard, reset the road camber and smoothed the carved tracks of storm washouts. We kept our distance from the billowing grit and grumbled about the inconvenience, without appreciating the consistent quality of road maintenance.

As we left Mzuzu, a teenage boy flagged us down with his right hand while his left hand balanced five textbooks on his head. He was grinning and hard to resist.

Nigel pulled over and asked, "Where are you going?"

"I am travelling to my village just near Nkhata Bay."

Nigel turned around to check our space in the back seat, "What do you think guys?"

"I think we can squeeze." Larry answered.

When he had folded himself between us and placed his textbooks at his feet, the young man said,

"My name is Alec, Sir. I like to practise my English."

Nigel said, "Maybe you can help us. I want to buy a good drum. Do you know where we can find one?"

Alec answered, "I am knowing exactly. There is a village. It has made a new drum. They will sell their old one now. Do you stay at the rest house? The one at Nkhata Bay?"

"Yes, we will be there for a few nights."

At the edge of Nkhata Bay township, Alec gave us directions to our destination and asked us to drop him off.

"We will meet at the rest house in the morning. I am coming at eight o'clock. I will be taking you to the village to see the drum."

He rebalanced the books on his head, stepped into the bush, and disappeared down a narrow footpath.

The Nkhata Bay rest house was built on a rise and at first sight gave the impression of a grand mansion. A flight of six steps led to the wide veranda that wrapped three sides of the building. The floors were cool concrete, polished with the red floor wax that was now a comfortable constant in our lives. The ceilings were almost twelve feet high, so the heat of the day would rise and leave the living space cool. The dining room filled the centre of the building and each bedroom opened onto the veranda. Mosquito nets for the beds hung from chains connected to ceiling hooks far above the sleepers.

Throughout the first night, Larry and I heard gentle, high-pitched, trilling chirps and I wondered what kind of birds sang in the dark. In the morning I said to the head cook, "I thought I heard birds chirping inside the house last night."

"No, Madam, not birds, but those ones."

He pointed up to the corner of the dining room ceiling where a few ceiling panels sagged and formed a triangular opening. Clustered around the edges of the opening, waving their inquisitive antennae, were dozens of cockroaches as long and as wide as my hand. I put my palm to my throat to restrain a gag.

The dining room was so large and so sparsely furnished it had an aura of monastic simplicity along with the bright spaciousness of an art gallery. The four of us ate our breakfast at the heavy wooden table that could seat ten. We ate from our food supply: Weetabix with reconstituted powdered milk, and bread toasted British style, lovingly cooled in a toast rack. We spread our toast with tinned orange margarine and intensely sugary mango jam. The rest house offered a choice of strong black tea or orange squash to drink.

I was thankful there were no holes in our bedroom ceiling now that I knew what made the subtle skittering sounds overhead. On the nights following, I imagined thousands of cockroaches playing and singing in the rafters above us as we slept.

Alec surprised us because not only did he turn up, he was early. We had adjusted to living in a country where time was elastic. The five of us shoehorned into the Renault 4 again, drove out of town, and headed south. Alec directed us along a dirt road that rose and fell around the feet of gentle hills, past a tea plantation, through a tunnel of jungly growth with vines that scratched over our roof rack, then out again to a road fringed with grasses more than six feet high. The track curved back toward the lakeshore and led to a village set back from a beach of fine white sand that stretched south to the vanishing point.

We were impressed by the village's well-kept look. In addition to the traditional round mud and wattle rondavels, many houses were made of sun-dried brick laid out in a rectangular shape. A few had glass windows. The area around the houses was carefully swept by women using brooms made from bundles of fine twigs. Their sweeping, designed to clear potential hiding places for snakes and scorpions, resulted in the look of combed sand. Years later I saw the same patterns recreated in the Zen garden of the Ryōan-ji Temple in Kyoto. The same brooms generated safety in Malawi, sacred art in Japan.

Alec called, "Stop," in front of a small house with four chairs set out in front. We realized he must have sent word ahead, because the villagers were prepared for us. At the sound of our car, people came out to greet us, mostly women and girls. Peggy and I shook hands with everyone and said hello in our best tourist version of Chitumbuka. "Muli uli?" for "How are you?" and "Nili makola," for "I am fine."

When it seemed the greetings were complete, Alec stepped in, "Now we will walk to the beach. You must bargain slow. Lots of chat chat. You must discuss. It is not polite to go quick. The whole village is owning this drum, but the manager of the drum he is waiting for you for talking."

Boys, who looked to be ten or twelve, rushed up to look at us, then darted away shrieking and giggling. Four young men with trumpets made of dried gourds walked along with us. They played a few notes and encouraged us to try. The gourds were about twelve inches long, with bulbous bases and thin, curved necks. A sound hole, about two inches in diameter, was cut out of the base and covered with what looked like a thin, fibrous white fabric that vibrated when the musician blew into the mouthpiece cut into the neck of the gourd.

"What is this white stuff?" I asked.

Alec said, "It is coming from the nest of the spiders. We use mango juice for the glue. The juice makes it stick to the hole. Do you want to try to make some music?"

I accepted the gourd and managed to produce a muffled bleat. Larry took a turn and got more sound out of it because he had spent his childhood creating trumpets out of kelp that tossed up on the beach in front of his family's summer cottage on Cowichan Bay. The entourage of children clapped their hands, laughed, and leapt into exaggerated dance steps.

Alec directed us towards a group of men making fishing nets, but they paid us no attention.

"Now you will be meeting the headman. You must approach with respect. A man of his position, he will not run after you like children."

At this point, we noticed the small boys had drifted towards the bush and all the women and young girls had disappeared. Peggy and I were the only women on the beach. We followed Alec towards the men and he indicated where we should stop and wait.

Alec translated our greetings to the headman—the eldest in the group and the manager of the drum—who remained seated with the other net makers. Alec explained that Nigel was a musician who wanted to buy a good traditional drum. Early in the conversation the headman shifted from Chitumbuka to English and said, "And so, we are all equal, being created by God." I wondered if he was letting us know that he would treat us fairly or if he was warning us that we must not assume we could take advantage of him. He made it clear he could understand English but continued speaking in Chitumbuka. Maybe he was not talking about bargaining at all, rather, he was stating his ethics and welcoming us.

Through Alec, Nigel explained he was interested in many kinds of instruments. He asked about the wood and the animal skin used to make the drum. Larry, a fisherman since childhood, asked about the hand carved boats on the shore and the making of nets. Eventually Larry realized that the headman must have the last word, so he asked a final question. The headman replied, then sat a while in silence. He made a thoughtful "Hmmm…" and gestured to the man beside him, who lifted a small hessian-wrapped bundle and presented us with

Nigel and Larry with drum

a gift of six fish and three eggs. We accepted with our rough versions of the gestures of politeness that we had learned since we arrived in Zambia, hands together in a slight bow. I took photos and promised to send prints.

From behind a screen of trees about thirty feet away we heard the sound of our drum being prepared. The animal skin of the drumhead needed to be heated over a fire each time before it was played, in order to tune it and fatten the sound.

Alec said, "Now it is time to be sitting and wait—not so close to the headman—over here."

We sat down where Alec pointed and spent our time grinning at the little boys who had filtered back to the beach. Alec left us, returned to the headman, and continued to bargain. About ten minutes later he came to sit beside us on the sand.

"Now I am telling you, the top price will be twenty dollars. The lowest price will be fifteen. To get the best price you must show the headman you are talking and discussing and complaining that the price is too high. You must look serious."

When Alec explained that the headman would ask between fifteen and twenty US dollars, he also said that payment could be made with the equivalent amount in Malawi kwacha. The headman knew the correct exchange rate. (Twenty US dollars in 1969 would be worth about a hundred today.)

Then two drummers and twelve dancers came out from the screen of trees and began to demonstrate the voice of the drum. I felt like we were in a dream, the four of us sitting on white sand by the long blue lake, mango trees behind us and grass houses beyond them, as the two men beat out a fantastic rhythm on the drum. At the same time, we tried to look serious and intense while we speculated about the price of the drum.

Finally, Alec came back to us and said, "You can pay the lowest price, fifteen dollars, and then your business will be done. The headman has decided you can have the lowest price because you are strangers to this country."

Once the transaction was complete, our thank yous and farewells done, we said goodbye to Alec at the village. He had relatives there who had invited him to stay.

I have a photo of Larry and Nigel as they sandwich the drum

between our molded Samsonite suitcases, one red and one mustard coloured, on the Renault's roof rack. Both men have curly hair in need of a cut and a comb and they are grinning like schoolboys playing pirates, delighted with their loot.

We returned to Nkhata Bay along the winding road and through the lush forested spot we had admired in the morning. We stopped by a rickety wooden bridge that crossed a quick flowing stream. Under the bridge on a wide patch of mud at the stream's edge were hundreds of butterflies, bright yellow, orange with black spots, turquoise with long swallowtails, ink-blue, and green.

Our day had begun with singing cockroaches and ended with a drum and butterflies.

NKHATA BAY

Nkhata Bay pulled us back again and again. It was like an illustration from a children's book—a tiny town with the essentials for a good life, nothing else. At its centre was a market under a group of mango trees. The vendors sold fresh tomatoes piled in pyramids of ten, kapenta—an intense tasting dried fish about the length of my little finger—and newly harvested peanuts, unroasted, wrapped in a newsprint cone twisted out of yesterday's newspaper.

The best fresh vegetables came from the prison gardens up the hill. The prison was an open arrangement, without fences or retaining walls, where the prisoners even played weekend soccer games with the local police. During the week, the inmates tended a market garden lush with spinach, squash, cabbage and sweet potatoes.

A stone's throw from the in-town market was the fishermen's beach, where the men pulled up their dugout canoes and sold fresh fish from their boats. The canoes were about twenty feet long, carved in one piece from a single tree trunk, without hint of a keel. They were shaped like empty pea pods with a slit just wide enough for a fisherman's legs.

At dusk the fishermen spread their nets to dry over the spiky green grasses that grew along the shore where the sand met the water. The nets floated over the tips of the grass and created hundreds of miniature interconnected gauze tents, tinted pink by the setting sun.

Farther along the beach was the government wharf where the *Ilala II,* a fifty-year-old passenger ship, docked. It travelled the length of Lake Malawi once a week carrying passengers and goods. A terrific blast of the ship's horn brought hundreds of people to the dock to see, be seen, meet travellers or get on board.

About a mile from the centre of town was Chikale Beach. The road to the beach climbed over a hill with a lookout that gave a bird's-eye view of the market, the prison, the mosque, the shops and the rest house, all set among red-blossomed trees, aptly called flamboyants or flame trees. From the lookout, the road dropped down to the wide, sandy beach dedicated to swimming and camping.

If the Nkhata Bay rest house was full, we would bring our tent and camp under the giant baobab tree that anchored the beach. I thought the baobab was the most exotic piece of creation I'd ever seen—a tree that looked like an inflated, grey rubber glove standing upright in the earth. It was leafless for a good part of the year and its huge trunk stored water so the tree could withstand long droughts. A traditional story said that at creation, God gave each animal a tree. The hyena received a baobab. The hyena was sure that all the other animals had trees that were far more beautiful than his. He envied the fine leafed jacaranda with its soft violet flowers and the frangipani with its cupped whorls of creamy white petals. Even the tubular trunked palm with its pleated windmills of green leaves was better than the leathery obese baobab that looked like the hind leg of an elephant. In disgust, the hyena turned his tree upside down and planted it with its roots sticking up in the air.

The baobab was a favourite of birds and animals, and it housed all of them indiscriminately. I loved to fall asleep in our small blue tent under the baobab, listening to the lake lapping the shore, as I imagined the kindly, luminous eyes of night creatures looking down on us from the branches above.

Mornings, after our camp-style breakfast, we rolled out the reed mats we had bought in the market and found shade under the baobab. When the sun slid west in the afternoon, we moved a few yards over, closer to the reeds and brush that formed a protective thatch over the stream that fed the lake. Here, weaver birds made their nests from grasses and anchored them in the bushes. The brilliant yellow birds flew over our heads, in and out of the circular entrances of their woven teardrop nests, and fed their babies. I remember lying under the arch of a branch one afternoon, close to the stream's hidden flow, propped on one elbow, while I read one of the first detective novels, Wilkie Collins' *The Woman in White*. My attention drifted from the intricate plot to the flashes of yellow wings flickering over my head.

When I grew up in Chilliwack, I learned to brave the cold water in nearby Cultus Lake. I loved to swim, but getting into the water

Nkhata Bay prison

required many refined calculations. Was the pain of jumping straight in better than the protracted process of easing in inch by inch, past the backs of the knees, the chill to the groin and worst of all, the cold shock to the armpits? My father favoured the short, sharp, jump. I went for the slow agony method, pushing back against his insistence that a quick splash was better in the long run. At Chikale Beach, the closest place to paradise I have experienced, the water was generously accommodating and enveloped us in warmth. I slipped in and side-stroked my way to a partly submerged rock thirty yards offshore. I made a shallow dive and opened my eyes to see flashes of royal blue, lemon yellow, and black-and-white striped fish swimming around the rock and in and out of its crevices. The fish, three to four inches long, were just a sample of the hundreds of varieties of cichlids that live in the lake and supply the world's freshwater aquariums. I didn't know their names, but I swam through their colours.

We often had the beach to ourselves. Residents from town might walk by en route to somewhere else, but rarely stopped. Three or four local boys splashed around in the water, darting glances our way, and then moved on to something more interesting. One morning, Larry and I woke up inside our tent and looked out to see the rising sun through the netting of the tent door. A hairy, knobbly jointed, black spotted spider, larger than Larry's hand, clung to the outside of the net and blocked the view. It decided to leave when Larry prodded at it with his sandal. That was the most dangerous thing that ever happened at Chikale Beach.

Even when we stayed at the rest house, we returned to Chikale once or twice a day to swim.

My memory of the spacious rest house pulls up the sensation of fine beach sand still between my toes as I stand on the polished concrete floor of the high-ceilinged bedroom and peel off my damp bathing suit. Then, in my light cotton dress, I wander along the shaded veranda and into the cool, empty dining room with its white-washed walls and its long wooden table. On the sideboard, filtered water and drinking glasses are set out on a bamboo tray. Later in the evening, the wide arms of the veranda's easy chairs hold a sundowner of turpentine-flavoured Malawi gin mixed with sweet orange juice. Sometimes we are alone. Sometimes the soft voices of other travellers float in the space lit only by the moon.

My final memory of Nkhata Bay begins after sunset on the veranda. Larry and David are relaxing in comfortable wooden chairs and enjoying a rare, imported Carlsberg beer, a change from Castle or Lion, the local brews. I feel restless, so walk to the quiet end of the veranda, where I catch a sound on the night air, somewhere below the rest house, towards town.

There are no streetlights, but the moon is full in the night sky. Alone, I walk down the step towards the whisper of staccato. I hear a few soft sounds, the conversational rise and fall of voices from modest homes with candlelight sifting through the windows, the barking of a dog far away, and the scrape of my sandals on small stones. I stop near the closed-up market at the bottom of the hill and look up the rise of the main road that leads out of the sleeping town.

A dozen men in flowing white robes, belted at the waist, full-circled at the hem, swirl down the road, groaning in a slow, rumbling chant. Each carries a drum anchored by a strap over his left shoulder. Each has two drumsticks shaped like large question marks, with straight shafts and a C-shaped head. Each man strikes the drum sharp and clean with the tip of the C to free small detonations of sound. The moon lights their white robes and the skins of their moon-shaped drums, while percussion laces their chants.

In memory's eye I can still see the soft-focus white shapes swaying with their drums, appearing and disappearing in and out of the mottled grey moonshadows of the trees above them, before they evaporate behind the dark shape of a building. I imagine it was a procession for the month of Ramadan.

I protect this image and hold it, a memory from an innocent time. I want to be there again under the full moon.

In 2004, I returned to Nkhata Bay and Chikale Beach accompanied by Chimwemwe, a Malawian woman, part of our team implementing a CIDA project at the University of Malawi. As we drove from Mzuzu towards the lake, I replayed images from twenty-five years before, of afternoons when we stretched out in the shade of the baobab and listened to the music of weaver birds. My reverie was broken by the sight of eroded maize fields, crowded villages pushed to the edge of the road, and forests razed for cattle and crops. Midway, we stopped at a small shop to buy Fanta, and I used the washroom. Over the sink hung a mirror circled with words painted in red, "Who can catch HIV/AIDS?" "You!"

As we entered the town, it was obvious that Lonely Planet had discovered Nkhata Bay. Young travellers had read the description of the small paradise and come to embrace its beauty. In response, the town outgrew itself. Dozens of new shops, painted in hot pink, acidic lime and raw orange crowded up against each other and filled the once-treed market square. We drove through town and up to the rise of land above the beach. I looked down and saw cabanas, hostels and bars. The stream that had trickled under the bushes filled with weaver birds had dried up. The baobab had died and rotted away.

I could not go further. I turned back to the car where the driver waited for us and said, "I don't want to see any more."

As we retraced our route, I could not avoid seeing two clinics, the posters commanding, "Wear a condom." Along the roadside, carpenters' displays of wooden coffins were stacked two and three high. I had to acknowledge that travellers of all kinds had carried more than their backpacks in and out of town. Nkhata Bay had become the densely populated AIDS capital of Malawi.

Our First Christmas, 1969

By mid-November I was worried about Christmas. Christmas has its highs and lows, but my memory always dropped the lows and distilled the highs. Each year the ante rose as to what would make the day emotionally complete. In 1969 I had twenty-one Christmas memories behind me, but this would be my first without the loud chaos of my brothers and sisters. It would be a Christmas without my Uncle Lawrence playing a soulful "White Christmas" on his saxophone. We were half the world away, south of the equator with no hope of snow, and no hint of a fir tree.

For Larry and me, it was our first Christmas as a couple and the first without our families. For both of us, Christmas meant brothers, sisters, parents, all the grandparents and the remaining fragile great-grandparents gathered around a dining room table augmented by extra leaves and a card table pushed against the end. In Larry's family the spillover of siblings and cousins sat in the kitchen at the kids table. In my family the three eldest, the Big Kids, sat on chairs with the adults. The youngest of the three Little Kids got the highchair, and she was wrapped and held in place with a red Christmas apron. The toddler was propped on a cushion and the four-year-old sat on the telephone book.

At Larry's family table they flamed the Christmas pudding, then everyone snapped Christmas crackers, put on the red, orange, yellow or purple tissue paper hats they found inside, and read their fortunes aloud. In my house, after the mincemeat tarts, the music began. In my memory, Aunty Delphine was always there with her violin, Mom played the piano and Uncle Lawrence played his clarinet or his accordion. We sang "Silent Night," "Come All Ye Faithful" and "Good King Wenceslas." I always begged for a run at "O Holy Night" to see if I could hit the highest notes. Then the carols slid into big band tunes and "Autumn in New York."

Table set for christmas dinner

Larry had memories of occasionally attending Midnight Mass in the tiny wood-frame Anglican church near his family's farm. My family never missed Mass on Sundays, Christmas or the Holy Days of Obligation. My church Christmas had choirs, priests, altar boys (never altar girls), incense, bells, beeswax candles, and a crèche with angels, shepherds, and three kings waiting with Mary and Joseph around an empty manager. On Christmas Eve, a young child, accompanied by the choir singing "Away in a Manger," walked slowly down the length of the church carrying a small plaster Christ Child lovingly wrapped in a white cloth, and laid him in the manger.

Larry's family opened one gift on Christmas Eve. All of ours waited for Christmas morning because waiting was considered beneficial for the soul and for the development of our character. The six of us would lie on our bellies in front of the tree. We'd poke and prod and guess, then hold on until Christmas morning. One year I crept downstairs at about three a.m. and gently squeezed and shook every parcel with my name on it. I made good guesses. The next morning, I experienced the deflation that comes from being completely correct in my guesses and bereft of surprise.

As our first Zambian Christmas approached, we were still dependent on others for transport. Larry and David waited for parts and worked on the derelict Toyota David had discovered in the bush near Chipata. It was going to be our new car. David said it should be ready by the first week of January. Most of the teaching staff would travel to Tanzania, Malawi or the Seychelles over the four-week-long school break. We wouldn't be completely alone—Peggy and Nigel planned to spend Christmas with us—but I looked ahead to a Christmas without family or most of our new-found friends.

Larry said, "I think there will be ten adults and a few kids left at the school over the holiday. Why don't we invite them here?"

I thought for about two seconds and said, "Great. Let's."

I announced in the staff room that anyone on site at Christmas was welcome to join us for a turkey dinner.

Dave and Joyce planned to stay. In early December they gave me yet another lift to Mzimba, where I found candied fruit and tinned Brussels sprouts from England.

As a child, I loathed Brussels sprouts and choked at them every Christmas of my childhood, "Do I have to eat them?"

"Just three," said my mom.

In Mzimba I bought four tins of Brussels sprouts. I hated them, but they were essential for our feast. On the first of December, I wrote to Mom,

> I actually bought tinned Brussels sprouts. Can I be homesick for them? They'll probably be worse than fresh ones. I made a Christmas cake on Saturday. That's a major feat considering that Lundazi has no ingredients except for flour, sugar and tinned butter. I scrounged stuff from everywhere.

Peggy and Nigel returned home with us to help prepare our Christmas meal. Pulled by the thought of Christmas dinner with friends, more teachers than we expected drifted back early from their holiday travels with the question, "Do you still have room at the table?" When the headcount got to nineteen for our midday feast, I knew our living room would be full, so Peggy and I began planning an afternoon tea for the overflow.

We made up my Mom's Christmas chocolates recipe from icing sugar (or confectioner's sugar as the Brits called it), sweetened condensed milk (always available in Lundazi), and vanilla flavouring (borrowed with Joyce's help from the domestic science department.) Peggy and I mixed the ingredients then rolled the fondant into one-inch balls. At home, Mom would coat them by dipping the fondant mix into melted semi-sweet chocolate. To make the coating stick she added a cube of paraffin wax (the kind used to seal jam jars). I had bitter chocolate, chopped from a block in a Mzimba general store, but no sealing wax, so I cut an inch off one of our white paraffin candles and dropped it into the melting chocolate. Dave was horrified at the idea of a chunk of candle in the mix, but after a test taste he ate seven of the chocolate-coated sugar bombs. Peggy and I filled two large cookie sheets with the candies.

Father Roy, the White Father from the Catholic mission station at Lumezi told us, "There is this farmer, a good one. He raises turkeys, big fat ones. His place is just outside Chipata." On Christmas Eve, David drove the two hundred and forty mile round trip to pick up the fresh turkey. He packed it in ice for the drive back in one hundred degree heat.

The afternoon before Christmas we took a long walk through the schoolyard and the town.

Larry said, "Let's try to find a Christmas tree."

We walked under bushy mango trees and arching jacarandas just finishing their soft purple blooms.

"Lovely," I said, "but hopelessly huge."

We examined dozens of spindly bushes, but none of them looked like they wanted to be a Christmas tree.

"This one has great red flowers," Larry said.

We tentatively touched a low hedge made of spiky crown of thorns plants with brilliant red flowers. Those would never do, as they were named for the cruelty of the Crucifixion, thirty-three years after the night of Christmas angels and shepherds. We settled for a tall branch of bamboo. We picked armfuls of dusty pink, raw orange, lemon yellow and rusty red wild zinnias that grew taller than Larry in their December exuberance.

I removed the rattly bamboo fly screen from the front door, stretched it across the living room wall and attached the zinnia blossoms to create a wall of flowers next to our banquet table.

On December 26, I wrote home,

Mary and peggy inspecting bamboo

We started about 7:30 in the morning—stuffed two turkeys, eight pounds and twelve pounds. One was raised in Chipata, the other in Denmark and we cooked them in the school ovens. Cleaned up the house and made a Christmas tree out of an eight-foot piece of bamboo decorated with zinnias. I covered one wall with a fly screen covered with more zinnias. We had sit-down Christmas dinner for fourteen adults and five kids at one o'clock, with turkey, potatoes, salad, peas, carrots, Brussels sprouts, cranberry sauce (from Barb's mother in Alberta), Christmas pudding, and punch (Cinzano, gin, orange juice and chopped fruit). Then we had eighteen adults and seven kids for tea at 4:30. For tea we had my Christmas cake and your Christmas chocolates. Peggy and I made them in five flavours. Bedford had a few days off so we even cleaned everything up at the end of the day.

Father Roy brought Châteauneuf du Pape, a wine entwined with the history of the papacy, a fitting gift from a Catholic missionary. The three bottles had been stashed under his bed waiting for a grand occasion. During our first visit to the Lumezi mission station he showed us how he had constructed his bed out of empty wooden beer crates and planks, topped with a single foam rubber mattress. I was honoured that he considered this day a grand occasion.

My beliefs about Christmas hospitality were fuelled by my mother's passion for Charles Dickens' *A Christmas Carol* and the annual telling of the Nativity story. Mom always emphasized the part about the innkeeper who told Mary and Joseph there was no room in the inn. The message was that we should make room. On this, our first Christmas in Zambia, innocence and naivety won the day. I expected that everyone who would be alone on Christmas would want to come.

And everyone came: Christian, Brahmin; White, Black; brunette, blonde; adult, child. The sun shone all day, as it did most days. November's heavy heat was gone, broken by the rains of December. The land around us, spiky and tawny brown since our arrival, blushed lush green.

Mr. Manyinda, the newly appointed deputy headmaster, his wife Veronica, and five children had joined us for our midday feast. Later we learned that this was the first time, despite many invitations, that he and his family had come to a party at the home of a White teacher. On Boxing Day, he invited everyone back to his home for afternoon tea, another first. Over the next three years Manyinda would be an incomprehensible, constant provocation in our lives at the school. A man of raw pride, anger and deceit. But just for this day the lion lay down with the lambs and we could say with Tiny Tim, "God bless us, every one."

VALIUM

After the adventure of the drum, our discovery of Nkhata Bay, and the glory of Christmas, we headed to Lusaka for a CUSO meeting scheduled in early January, the last week of Christmas break. With perfect timing, the oil filter for the reconstructed Toyota had arrived just before Christmas, so Larry and David had the car roadworthy by New Year's Day of 1970.

From our arrival in late August of 1969 until our Lundazi Christmas four months later, we had lived and travelled in a world of small towns and family sized villages spread over wide-open savannah and tree-covered rolling hills. It was a world without power lines, telephones, or safe drinking water; a world without pavement, road shoulders or centre lines, stop lights, sidewalks or crosswalks; a world without garages, or tow trucks. It was a world of small, dusty shops with hand built wooden shelves that were full one week and bare the next. Meat and vegetables were either fresh from the market or tinned and imported from England, Denmark, South Africa or China. Petrol was made to flow by cranking a lever attached to one of the two battered pumps outside Mulla's store.

Grocery shopping meant planning ahead—figuring out how many tins of fish or beef would carry us from one month to the next between our trips south to Chipata, the capital of Eastern Province, or over the Malawi border to Mzimba or Mzuzu. During our first term, we depended on the "kindness of strangers," our neighbours, to provide transportation for heavy loads or trips out of town. They helped us learn how to adapt for shortages and glut, to make decisions about what to stockpile or not.

Many staff room conversations were about finding supplies.

"Mulla's has a new shipment of Danish margarine."

"Sonia saw cooking oil in that shop two doors up from the butcher."

"Too bad we can't eat Lifebuoy soap or live on Cinzano. They never run out."

Once we had our own car, we were ready to take part in the reciprocity of shopping. When we left Lundazi for our first road trip to Lusaka, we carried lists from Sonia, Dave and Joyce, Ben and Doreen, and David. It was our task to find basmati rice, sewing supplies, wine and car parts.

Larry drove the five hundred miles over two days. We both got international driver's licences before we left Canada, and Larry used his to obtain a Zambian licence. Without much discussion, he dissuaded me from getting one for myself. In Lundazi, the men on staff did the driving. At home, my dad always drove because my mom had never learned how to (years later she revolted and got her licence at fifty-five). When I look back, I am irritated with myself that I didn't drive in Zambia except in emergencies and then, still without a licence.

In theory, I was the navigator. The road had few junctions. The tricky part was crossing the bridge over the Luangwa River at a point upstream from the Mozambique border where FRELIMO (Mozambique Liberation Front) guerrillas were fighting the Portuguese colonial government. Armed Zambian troops set up roadblocks made of planks and petrol drums at each end of the bridge with the aim of preventing incursions from the battles in Mozambique. Their work was dull, so before we set off, David had warned us, "You can't predict their mood and you don't know if they have been drinking. Just keep extremely calm and be very polite."

After hours of driving on dead flat terrain, the road approaching the bridge took a steep, winding drop. The car's brakes were new, so we felt confident, but were uneasy about the sight of the six camouflaged soldiers waiting for us at the bottom of the hill with semi-automatics slung over their shoulders.

Larry braked and stopped at the roadblock. The burliest fellow dropped a cigarette on the ground, crushed it under his round-toed military boot then leaned into our car's open window, the barrel of his gun aiming for the sky, and asked, "Where are you going?"

"Lusaka."

"And what is it that you will be doing?"

"We are meeting with a group of Canadian teachers," Larry replied with deference.

"And are you having cigarettes?"

"I am very sorry, sir, but I do not smoke."

The guard stood upright and the gun barrel slipped 180 degrees to point at his feet. He must have felt we weren't worth the trouble and let us through.

A few hours later we were on the outskirts of Lusaka and for the first time since leaving Canada were on a paved road, facing an intersection with traffic lights. Pedestrians waited on the sidewalk for the light. Power lines ran over our head. On one corner there was a petrol station with pumps powered by electricity and next to it, a garage advertising repairs. We navigated the first intersection despite all the distractions and made our way to a restaurant where we met up with other Canadians who were in town for the CUSO meeting. Larry and I ordered a meal of stewed beef and vegetables on rice. After dinner, someone suggested we walk down the road to get an ice cream.

"Ice cream," I thought, "there's ice cream in Lusaka?"

I wasn't excited. I was worried and wondered, "What if it makes me sick?"

The only dairy we'd had for four months was Nestlé powdered milk, stirred laboriously into a paste then mixed with boiled, filtered water. Even then, it was lumpy and sickly sweet. I watched with fascination as the other CUSOs, who worked in Lusaka and the Copperbelt cities, licked their creamy cones as if this was the most normal thing in the world.

Larry sorted out directions to a grocery store on the way to Carol's house. She was a Canadian friend from our orientation in Quebec who had offered to put us up while we were in town. We found the store, collected our grocery bags from the back seat and locked up the car. The store's plate glass windows and doors were decorated with black metal burglar bars. Larry opened the glass entry door for me and stood back. Inside, I found a grocery cart and we walked down the rows and rows of well stocked metal shelves. An open deep freeze full of beef, chicken, goat, and fish like tilapia, chambo and bream lined one long wall.

"Look at all this stuff! Can you believe it?" Larry said.

He chose the fish and I found rice.

The store even had cash registers, old style for Canada, but space age compared to the compartmentalized wooden boxes shopkeepers used in Lundazi. Each cash register had a lever to open the cash drawer, much like the one we had in our family business.

Larry and I took our packages back to the car. We had paid attention to David's advice, "You don't leave an unlocked car in Lusaka for even three minutes. Each car is watched from somewhere in the street and everything in it will be stolen. You'll be lucky if the car is still there."

Larry opened the trunk where we had stuffed our luggage before shopping. He tucked in the groceries while I used the key to open each door, then I undid the steering wheel lock. Being liberal minded CUSOs, we didn't rail on about the crooked thieves, but rather talked rationally about the desperation created by poverty and said we didn't want to provide temptation for anyone. We were naive about the superb organization of the city's robbers, but never experienced theft in Lusaka. We were innocent of the Lusaka CUSOs' experience of being robbed almost weekly. Over time, we refined our routine of lock-up-and-hide-the-valuables to an art, and to this day I never leave our car unlocked.

We found Carol's apartment. She welcomed us and showed us where we would sleep. Once we had unloaded our luggage she invited us into the kitchen while she made a pot of tea. Her kitchen had a white enamel electric stove with black coil burners, almost like my mother's. Above the control panel were white glass salt and pepper shakers with perforated red lids. A black and red rooster decorated the pepper shaker and a red and yellow hen was on the salt. In a flash of disorientation, I was back in Canada. I thought of the cast iron, woodburning stove in our Lundazi kitchen and wondered, "How can you live in Zambia and have an electric stove?" All our efforts, adjustments and adaptations over the last four months seemed ridiculous and uselessly unfair. My heart clamped, my breathing froze, my vision telescoped, and I slumped to the floor fighting for air.

I remember Larry taking me to the car. Then I was lying on a bed in the emergency ward of the Lusaka hospital. I heard, "Stress?... panic attack...Valium," and I felt the needle.

I remembered the weeks of preparation for our departure from Canada six months before. One needle after another: cholera, tetanus, yellow fever, hepatitis B, measles, mumps, diphtheria, typhoid. At the same time, I was finishing up report cards from my first year as a Grade 3 primary school teacher and planning our low key wedding. Roberta, our school nurse, had listened to my timetable and said, "Let me get you some Valium."

A week before her offer, while I was waiting in the doctor's office for a cholera shot, I had picked up a medical magazine from the stacks of *Chatelaine* and *Maclean's*. A Valium ad, aimed at doctors, had the byline "Overeducated, unemployed: Valium" under a black and white photo of an attractively dressed woman, head in hands, sitting among the detritus of her children's toys and uneaten snacks. I was repelled. I thought the advertiser was making women look incapable and wondered what the ad was saying to doctors who were mostly men. I told Roberta, "No. I don't need that. I can handle it."

I successfully made my way through my long to-do list, including farewells to family and friends, flying in a plane for the first time in my life, and starting our married life in Lundazi.

To this point I was fiercely proud of everything I had learned and how well I had coped with tedious textbooks, October's slaying heat, silty drinking water, fly-ridden butcher shops, and leprosy afflicted tailors. It seemed that a Lusaka city life with electricity, running water and ice cream bore no resemblance to our rural Lundazi life of constant making-do. The final straws were the pieces of regular life from Canada in Carol's kitchen—the stove and the salt and pepper shakers.

The CUSO conference was dry and tedious, overshadowed by my embarrassment that a stove and a salt and pepper set had undone me.

The Russians Are Coming

In January 1970, at the start of our second term, news flashed round the school, "The Russians are coming." Zambia cast its nets internationally for teachers and this catch brought Russians to Lundazi. Correctly, they were Soviets, citizens of the USSR, but most of the teaching staff defaulted to calling them "The Russians." The headmaster told us, "You will find they have strong accents, but their English is clear enough to teach science and math. They are very well qualified in these subjects."

Speculation soared. They would be spies. They would be atheists. They would be Communists, unquestioningly loyal to their government. They would work subtly, insidiously, to create sympathy for communism. They would be stern and humourless. They wouldn't be able to control their classes. The women would wear babushkas.

Senator Joe McCarthy's frenetic search for Communists infiltrating American life had spilled north over the border and into my childhood. In the spring of 1957, just before Catholic News Month, Mrs. Black, my Grade 4 teacher, instructed our class to create a poster with a strong anti-communist message. "I will choose the best one and send it to the BC Catholic newspaper. The winner will be used for the cover of the paper. You could get a prize!" I wanted to win, and took my drawing papers home to work on. My parents objected to me creating something that was pro-McCarthy. Mom guided me to a more neutral image. I drew a fat globe and coloured it blue and green with my skimpy box of Crayola crayons. The globe had eyes and looked out through large, dark framed glasses like my father's. It rested on a banner that read, "See the world through the eyes of your Catholic press."

I didn't win a prize for this tame message, but I still remember Mom and Dad directing me away from a right-wing stance as proof that my parents once had more liberal ideas. Years later, fear did begin to dominate Dad's thinking and he defended McCarthy as someone who had the courage to tackle "Communist infiltration."

When I was nine the Russians launched a dog into space, and three years later in 1960, when I was in Grade 6, they sent a man. Sister Myra, my tall, electrically energetic teacher, paced back and forth in front of the blackboard, black skirt swishing, long rosary swinging from her waist, as she told us that the West had become soft and it was time for all of us to work harder to surpass the Soviets. They were technologically smart but spiritually bankrupt and uncivilized, as demonstrated by their leader, Nikita Khrushchev, who banged his shoe on the table at the UN. She warned us that the school curriculum was being revised to emphasize math and science so that we could catch and surpass the Soviets. However, I didn't notice any changes and math remained a mystery.

In October 1962, our whole high school was divided into groups and crammed into the few social studies classrooms equipped with televisions to watch President John Kennedy outline the immediate threat of the Soviets arming Cuba with long range nuclear missiles, and his plan for retaliation. Our teachers told us we were watching "history in the making" and dismissed us that afternoon with the expressed hope that we would still be alive and back in class tomorrow. After a sleepless night I returned to school to see our relieved but haggard looking teachers. My classmates had moved on to who was dating whom. We didn't realize that overnight the US and the USSR had shifted away from brinkmanship. Kennedy and Khrushchev had terrified even themselves by how close they had brought the world to nuclear annihilation.

In Lundazi, when we heard the Russians were coming, all our Communist stories were reawakened. We never did ask the Russians about the stories they carried into their first encounters with our school staff: capitalists who were emerging from being colonized or being colonizers. Larry and I had just finished reading the two volume set of *War and Peace,* not to prepare to meet the Russians, but because a book, especially a long one, was the best escape from the year-round, equal, equatorial nights that began, without variation, at six in the evening and lasted until six in the morning. The night before the Russians arrived, we closed the covers on the frigid Moscow winters of Tolstoy's novel. The next morning, which was sunny as usual, we walked up to the staff room with our heads full of snow and nineteenth century Russian nobility to meet the modern Russian strangers: Nadya and Volodya, and Nick and Nina.

Nadya was a few years older than I and a bit taller, about five foot six, but she thought in metric so that made her 1.7 metres. She was wearing a short, sleeveless, form-fitting cotton sheath dress and sturdy but stylish sandals, much nicer than mine. Her hair was a shiny black bob and she wore lipstick, something that only Sonia, the headmaster's wife, would wear for special events. Nadya introduced herself as a chemical engineer which she pronounced "kimikil" with a soft burr on the "g" of engineer. Her husband, Volodya, came from Alma-Ata in the Kazakh SSR. His blonde, brush cut hair stuck straight out of his skull. He had muscular hands and wide feet. In the two years we worked together we never succeeded in steering him onto politics. He wanted to talk about Western lounge singers—especially Tom Jones.

Volodya taught us how to make liqueur. Find a good clear glass bottle with a screw top lid. Stuff in all the fresh fruit you can find: papaya, mango, pineapple, guava, passion fruit—whatever is in season. Then mash it down using the end of a wooden spoon. Finally, fill up the remaining space with sugar, right to the top of the bottle and screw on the lid. Set the jar in the sunniest window of the house (in our house it was the window over the kitchen sink) and wait several weeks. The sunlight ignited the fruit and after a few days tiny bubbles began to form. A few weeks later, the fruit and sugar evolved into alcohol. This stuff was delicious. Volodya also did some distilling experiments in the science lab, creating alcohol so high proof I thought it was too dangerous to drink, so I stayed with the simpler kitchen window version.

When she arrived, Nadya was quite shy. In a letter to my mother I wrote about Nadya's quiet character, after I described her attractive dresses and nice sandals. I invited her to come to my place so we could cook together and trade recipes while she practised her English. She was like a new pet, and there was some competition among the other women on staff as to who would win her as their new friend. Soon Nadya claimed her own space. Her halting, book-learned English became fluent and her natural confidence and energetic nature emerged.

Nick filled the part our stereotypes craved—short, compact, intense, with a small pointed beard we knew was inspired by Lenin. Later we glimpsed a photo of Lenin in the entryway of his house, in the same spot that the Irish would hang a painting of the Sacred Heart. But Nick also avoided any talk that smelled of politics. His wife had accompanied him, but we didn't meet Nina the first day because she had already begun work as a midwife in Lundazi's small district hospital. She was petite, trim and doll-like but strong and firm in her opinions, as long as they were not political. Eighteen months later, she was one of the midwives who delivered our first son into the world.

The following term two more Russians, both single women, arrived. Olga, very serious, looked as if she would be happy in a babushka, while the other woman, Lina, was charming. However, neither of them was as fashionable as Nina or Nadya. The two women had to live in one house. They didn't appear to have a choice, and we didn't know if they had any connection before they arrived. The standard staff house had three bedrooms, so each had some privacy, but they shared their daily living space. Once they had settled in, they invited Larry and me for tea—not the familiar pound cake and black tea from a brown British teapot, but strong Russian tea from a small samovar placed on a table laden to feed multitudes.

There were lacy doilies on the settee and armchairs, matryoshka dolls on the fireplace mantle, and wooden trivets painted with wide, swift brushstrokes indicating stylized flowers. The deep maroon, patterned curtains were drawn shut, making the room feel dark and claustrophobic. The dining room table was covered with a lace tablecloth and there were plates full of cakes, cookies, tarts, candies and unknown treats. I wanted to try everything but wondered if I had the capacity. The cookies and cakes had a rich density. Many had cocoa in them. The women must have brought the cocoa powder from Russia and they were lavishing it on us. One delightful confection was a small, sweet, dark roll studded with nuts—almonds, I thought—but we hadn't seen an almond since we arrived. When I bit into the rich concoction, I realized that the women had bought peanuts from the market, roasted and sliced them into slivers, then inserted them in the bonbon to make it look like a lightly prickled hedgehog.

Larry and I ate with obvious enjoyment. When we were awash with tea, Lina, the one with a pleasant temperament, asked, "Can you guess what is in it?" She pointed to a cake. The answer: "Potatoes." To the cookies: "Potatoes." To the hedgehog roll: "Potatoes." To the sweets: "Potatoes."

I was overtaken with a vision from *Crime and Punishment* of long, bone-chilling nights, snow drifting outside over windowsills and thresholds, while inside, desperate, indomitable and manically creative women, deprived of all luxuries, created a hundred ways to use a potato. My view of the durability of the Russian spirit was formed as I ate this array of potatoes in impenetrable disguises.

The single Russian women kept mostly to themselves, but the two couples, Nadya and Volodya, and Nick and Nina, soon joined the foreign teachers for Friday night badminton games in the school's echoing dining hall. The hall did double duty. Chairs and tables were set up for meals, then taken down to open the space for assemblies. The tables were wooden with collapsing metal legs and were in constant movement through the day—legs open, legs closed, the locking metal rings clanging and clicking into place, metal thunking against the wood. Tables set, tables cleared, tables folded, tables stacked. Friday nights, after the tables were stacked, two badminton nets were strung across the two courts the teachers had painted on the floor. We sat out our turns on wooden benches under flickering white fluorescent lights and debated whether to play barefoot and risk getting glued down to the floor by students' discarded cornmeal porridge or keep our sandals on and risk a twisted ankle. It was there we picked up Russian phrases and were satisfied to learn that "Nyet" really meant "No" in Russian. The Russians tested out British slang. "Bloody hell" was a favourite. Nick explained with some embarrassment that the current Beatles refrain of "Ob-la-di, Ob-la-da" was an obscenity in Russian. Volodya shouted something that sounded like "trusi," Russian for "knickers" if Nadya took too deep a bend stretching for the shuttlecock. Since trousers and shorts were expressly forbidden for women in Zambia, the female staff always wore mini-length dresses and skirts.

In grade school I was always the last picked for the baseball team. I rarely hit a ball. Soon after we met, Larry tried to teach me how to play tennis. I started by hitting tennis balls off the outside of the gym wall at the school where I taught. I connected with about one in ten balls. Larry found my ineptitude astonishing but was impressed by my determination to keep practising and my conviction that I would eventually get it. In Lundazi I got my turn at badminton and never heard a hint of annoyance at my lack of skill. Anyone who put in the effort got to play. I had great persistence but miserable coordination. Twenty years later I met an optometrist who added a test for depth perception to the usual eye exam and said, "You can't play tennis with those eyes, can you?" "I can't?" "No, you won't be able to hit any moving ball with those eyes." My relief was exquisite. I still wonder how the world looks to those who can hit a ball with ease.

Volodya created a ping-pong palace in his front yard. First, with the help of his gardener, he erected an elaborate bamboo structure that covered most of his front yard. Then he planted morning glories by every bamboo pole. The season was right, and the green vines carrying blossoms like purple trumpets made their way up the poles, wrapped the trellis and travelled across the roof frame. Within a few months, he'd added a string of white lights to the green-wreathed gazebo.

He then built a ping-pong table and set it up in the gazebo so we could play during the day, shaded by the greenery, or at night, lit by the light bulbs, while we drank the fruity alcohol we had brewed on our kitchen windowsills. We learned that Russians liked badminton, ping-pong, dinner parties, tea parties, canasta parties and cooking, but they firmly avoided politics. The board game they enjoyed the most was Monopoly. Larry and I introduced both couples to the ultimate capitalist board game and the four of them were hooked. In a letter home I told my parents we were learning that people from supposedly hostile countries were just like us, and bemoaned the politics that kept us apart.

THE SCHOOL FARM

In many ways, Larry and I lived in different worlds within the school. With two years of teacher training and one year of teaching experience, I was able to link my work as a Grade 3 teacher in Canada to my new job teaching ESL to my First Form students in Lundazi. After Larry graduated with his degree in economics, he worked for a year driving a forklift as a longshoreman on Vancouver Island's Crofton docks. The job helped him pay off his student loans and he was able to save some money before we left Canada. We suspected CUSO had accepted us as a couple because I had a teaching diploma.

Larry faced his first classroom on the opening day of the September term: forty twelve-year-old first formers eager to improve their English. Larry's hidden talent, or Achilles heel, was his creative, purely phonetic, non-conformist spelling and random approach to punctuation.

On Wednesday of the first week, Weston, the boldest and brightest in the class raised his hand,

"Please, Sir, is *thier* correct?"

Larry paused, and in the gap, Samuel shot his hand up,

"Sir, I think it is spelled *t-h-e-i-r*?"

Elizabeth, tentative, waved her right hand,

"Sir, I am not understanding, what is *thair*?"

Larry said, "Ah! You are so smart. You have discovered my deliberate mistake. Samuel, you can come to the chalkboard and make the correction."

His three geography classes loved him. When he taught a lesson on glaciers, it was clear most of his students had never seen ice, much less a glacier. He marched each of his three classes down from the school and into our living room to examine the small freezer box and the tray of ice cubes in our bar-sized, kerosene-powered fridge. I am sure they also had a good look at everything in our sparsely furnished living room. Back in the classroom, Larry linked our ice cubes to glaciers and was rewarded with a glimmer of understanding in his students' eyes.

When I came home from my afternoon classes that day, I found our newly waxed floor stencilled with over a hundred muddy brown footprints starting at our front door and ending in puddles of melted ice cubes around our fridge.

In addition to English and geography, Larry taught one economics class: a dozen fifth formers (sixteen- and seventeen-year-olds) preparing to write the London School of Economics exam. He took over the group from Don, who was in the final term of his teaching contract. Larry, from Canada, and Don, from Australia, were both trained as economists, had both grown up on small family farms, and were both jokingly labelled as "colonials" by the British staff.

The economics class had an exam fee, unlike the other courses on the school curriculum. Some students had difficulty finding money to write the exam. Larry's godmother, Edie, sent him fifty dollars "to help a student in need." Larry used the money to pay a promising student's exam fee. The young man earned a scholarship, went on to study at the London School of Economics, and later became the Dean of Economics at the University of Zambia. This story came to us about five years after we left Zambia. It was one of those rare tales where a small, generous gesture blossomed into a benefit for the recipient and his country.

During our first term, Kenneth Kaunda, Zambia's president, arrived by plane, accompanied by dozens of bureaucrats and bodyguards in suits and black sunglasses. He came to officially open the school four years after it had begun enrolling students. The opening was a grand event, involving everyone at the school, administrators from the town, and hundreds of local people. Larry's task was to teach a demonstration economics lesson for the president. The students, pens in hand, sat alert and attentive, in their clean, pressed uniforms. Kaunda and his entourage filled the back of the classroom. Larry horrified the onlookers as he delivered a lesson on the economic realities of development assistance and the need for Zambia to repay its foreign aid loans. I wasn't there to watch the presentation because I was busy setting tables for the official banquet in the school dining hall. After Larry's lesson, Dave, who had observed the lesson, rushed over to the hall to find me.

"You might get your suitcases packed. Larry has just given Kaunda a lecture. He could be PI'ed. Larry's sure got nerve. What he said was right, but not what you should say to the president's face."

PI stood for prohibited immigrant. It meant immediate expulsion from the country and was the ultimate sanction for unruly expatriates. My heart jumped at Dave's story, but the celebrations continued and by day's end no one had knocked on our door with a summons. We thought Dave's reaction was overblown, but weeks later, when the January class timetables were being set up, we learned that economics had been cancelled throughout the country. It was now considered an unsuitable subject to be taught in Zambian secondary schools.

Besides economics, Don taught agricultural science, and he invited Larry to come for a look around the school farm. Soon Larry was helping to build a fence around the perimeter and talking with the students about their garden plots. Don encouraged Larry to teach agricultural science and take over the management of the school farm when he left.

Larry appreciated that Don put a lot of time into the handover. He left behind three years of lesson plans, notes, and a good collection of books on agriculture in the tropics. He introduced Larry to the researchers and agricultural extension agents in town.

Recently, Larry said, "It was such a relief to give up the English classes. The kids were better writers than me. Geography was not so bad, but the department head was always on a downer, a bit of an Eeyore. I've always been a hands-on kind of guy. The farm was a perfect fit for me."

When Don's contract was complete in January of 1970, Larry took over teaching agriculture for seven classes of First Form and Second Form boys.

Both boys and girls took science classes. The boys were directed into agriculture and technical drawing, metalwork and carpentry, while the girls took domestic science and typing. In the first term, when he taught English and geography, Larry saw that though the girls were bright and conscientious, many left school because they were called home to work on the village farm or because they became pregnant

Larry with agriculture students

and were expelled. "It broke my heart to see them go. They were the victims of the place of women. Boys were never kicked out of school for impregnating a girl."

The idea that girls would study agricultural science was outside the thinking of the Zambian school system, even though everyone acknowledged that women contributed the lion's share of labour in the village farming system.

From his second term onwards, Larry taught only boys. Although Don had left many resources behind, Larry felt the Zambian curriculum for agriculture was inadequate. There was an agricultural research station five miles east of the school, just across the Malawi border, funded by Britain and administered by British researchers. Among many projects, they raised contented, caramel-coloured Jersey cows with chocolate-coloured eyes. The cows produced rich yellow cream so thick it took only a minute to whip it into butter. We often took the short drive to the research station on the chance that we could buy surplus cream. In conversation with the researchers, Larry learned about an excellent agriculture curriculum developed for Malawi. With their help, he tracked down a copy and it became his bible for the next three years.

His students still didn't have textbooks, so he created dozens of illustrated charts with quirky drawings of farmers, pigs, chickens, rats, maize, peanuts, hoes and tractors. These served as on-the-wall books.

Larry continued Don's practice of assigning each student a garden plot. The school supplied seeds and manure for fertilizer. The boys chose what to grow, tended it or not, and decided what to do with their crop. Most grew leafy green vegetables or sweet potatoes that matured in one term. If the garden plot survived wandering goats and hungry students, the boys dined on their crop or sold it to the school kitchen.

Money in their pockets from the sale of vegetables kindled the entrepreneurial spirit in some of the boys. Larry helped them organize into clubs so they could work together on a project. Five boys decided to raise bees because honey had guaranteed customers. Larry introduced the boys to the beekeeper at the Ministry of Agriculture station in town. The beekeeper taught them to make traditional bark beehives. He showed the boys how to remove a four-foot-long cylinder of bark from a living tree to create the body of the hive. They learned how to make a cambium rope to hold the bark together. (The same way our driver had created a fan belt when we broke down on our first trip from Chipata to Lundazi.) Next, the boys used the cambium rope to weave a flat round cap to cover one end of the hive. They made a second cap for the other end, with a hole in the centre to allow the bees to come and go.

The Ministry of Agriculture office gave the boys knives to cut bark and wire to hang the hives in trees around the campus. The boys used the school farm's walk-behind Honda tractor and trailer to haul their hives and bee equipment. They borrowed ladders from the school to help them hang the hives in trees around the school, including one by our back door. We switched to using the front door.

Since the Ministry of Agriculture wanted to encourage fish farming as a protein source, one student decided to raise fish. He got fish from the NAMBoard (National Agricultural Marketing Board) office in town and raised them in the third settling pond of the school's sewage lagoon. Eventually, the boy waded into the lagoon to catch the mature fish. The water from the third settling pond was considered clean enough to flow back to the Lundazi River and then into the dam that held the town's water source. We didn't test this idea; we always boiled our water.

Larry hanging a bark bee hive

Larry worked with the boys to plant a variety of trees around the campus, but the project had mixed results. The students ate the fruit long before it was ripe, and the girls snapped off the young saplings to make brooms to sweep their dormitories. Looking back he says, "There was no harm intended. We were all working at cross purposes."

The school farm was about five acres and provided both demonstrations and training. The farm grew cotton, maize, groundnuts (peanuts) and green crops for fallow, set up in a four-year rotation. Pigs—only two at a time—and chickens were raised. NAMBoard bought the cotton crop and the money went into the school budget. At one time, the school's one-and-a-half acre cotton crop was the largest in the Lundazi area. The maize crop and the occasional pig went to the school dining hall.

Two hardworking men were hired to manage the farm and help the boys with their garden plots. They were like teaching assistants for the agriculture program, and like other school workers, were provided with modest homes for their families.

Support for the farm also came from January Mwale, a large-scale farmer south of town who supplied the school with cornmeal and vegetables. He and Don had become friends and after Don left, January continued to drop 'round to check on the school farm to find ways to help Larry and the agriculture students. Larry wrote home,

> January loaned us an incubator so we could hatch eggs and show the kids how chickens developed. The incubator runs on kerosene. I had seen lots of electric powered chick incubators when I was a kid, but I'd never seen one that ran on kerosene. I get eggs from Father Neiland, one of the Catholic White Fathers, and from the Protestant minister who teaches at the school. We need lots of eggs. There are seven classes and a chicken takes twenty-one days to develop. I fill the incubator and crack eggs open during class over a three-week period to show how a small red spot becomes a full-sized chick.

The school couldn't afford a tractor, so at ploughing time, Don rented one from the Tractor Mechanization Unit. The cost of owning and maintaining a tractor was far too expensive for small scale farmers. The Mechanization Unit rental scheme allowed them to hire a tractor and a driver when they needed it. The school took advantage of this plan.

In town, Larry met Karoy, who worked for the Zambian Tobacco Board. He was an Indonesian Dutchman, slim, short and wiry, with wild curly hair. His basic belief was that humans should only live in climates that would foster the growth of sisal. Karoy offered to loan Larry a tractor at ploughing time so he wouldn't have to wait in line for a rented tractor.

One term, with Karoy's encouragement, Larry had the kids grow tobacco on the farm, but some of the teachers, all smokers, complained, "Why are you letting the kids grow tobacco?"

His reply was, "I am trying to teach them how to make a living."

When Larry's agriculture students wrote their final exams at the end of 1970, they earned the highest marks in the country. Unexpectedly, the examining board in Lusaka accused Larry of cheating or prompting the students or somehow manipulating their marks. An invigilator was sent up and his students wrote the exams over again. Again, they scored the highest marks. They won the President's Shield, a national prize for the highest marks in agriculture. Larry and his students felt vindicated. They waited and waited, but the President's Shield, promised for display in a place of honour at the school, never turned up. A year went by. The students wrote their exams and for the second time they scored highest in the country. There were no accusations this time, but the hoped-for shield never turned up. The denial of the shield remained a mystery.

Twenty-five years later we learned that the school farm still grew vegetables to feed the students. It is Larry's hope that some of his students went on to become the farmers who provided food for their families and villages when Zambia's copper economy crashed in the mid-1970s. Today, small farmers in the Lundazi district provide twenty percent of the country's agricultural produce. Many of them will have studied agricultural science at Lundazi Secondary.

There is another possible legacy from the Lundazi school farm. Michael and Mark, our sons, teach sustainable agriculture at two different universities. For each of them, the heart of their teaching is centred in a student-managed organic farm.

FISHING

On a slow Saturday in February near the beginning of our second term, Larry fashioned three fishing flies from chicken down and feathers. He wanted to test them out, so we drove our reconstructed car to a dam north of town. There were several small earth dams backed by little lakes within five to ten miles of town. They had been built by the British colonial administration to catch seasonal streams and provide irrigation and water for the nearby villages. Many of the lakes had fish.

A dozen boys, who looked to be in the magic zone between six and ten years old, wrestled, shouted and splashed in the reservoir behind the dam's packed earth berm. Barefoot and shirtless, each boy wore threadbare khaki shorts. One, maybe a six-year-old, wore two pairs of shorts for modesty. The holes in one pair complemented the holes in the other. The boys had a metal laundry tub and some rusty tin cans. They switched between washing clothes and fishing. They piled the damp clothes into a metal tub and crammed their fish into rusty tin cans. The boys used worms for bait. Their worms worked. Larry's flies did not.

I had a book with me, but put it aside to watch the events on the dam. There was a footpath across the top of the berm, and throughout the afternoon clusters of children, men in twos and threes, women with clay water pots on their heads, skinny dogs, and even a cow with a calf, crossed from one side of the lake to the other. An elderly woman, with kerchiefed hair and a faded wrap skirt, tottered towards the dam, happy-drunk. The boys laughed at her, but as soon as she got near, they surrounded her and helped her cross. On the other side, she stumbled on, singing, and in response, the boys sang after her. Throughout the afternoon, they slipped from talk to song to chant. What sounded like a taunt was met with a chant and a few quick dance steps for punctuation. A minnow on the line prompted a song. Talk was either Chitumbuka or English. Song and chant were in Chitumbuka, but all these forms—dance, talk, chant, song, English, Chitumbuka—wove in and out, seamless and whole.

I thought that we were invisible or not noticed. No one looked our way or gestured in our direction. Then I overheard one boy explain to his friends, in choppy English, that he had finished Grade 7 and he wanted to enroll at Lundazi Secondary next year, so he would give the Mzungu—the White person—all his fish and then he could be in the new teacher's class. Later, as I picked up my book and folded the picnic blanket, the boy offered Larry his tin of minnows. Larry thanked him, but encouraged the boy to keep his catch.

I wrote my family about the afternoon and made a point that the slow pace of life in Lundazi was so much better than the rush of the life we had left behind.

> "The nice thing about sitting by the lake is that it was soooooo quiet. I could hear insects and birds, and people working and laughing on the far side of the dam. There were no sounds of engines—cars, trucks, tractors or planes.

I was striving for a Thoreau moment, but I was actually trying to convince myself that watching the boys on the dam did not make me miss noisy visits with my family, hugs from the three "Little Kids," or singing folk songs and Beatles tunes with my brothers.

PIGS

Ben, totally urban, educated by Jesuits in an upper class British school, philosophized himself into a corner where he concluded, if he was going to eat meat, he must be willing to raise his own animals and slaughter them. If he couldn't, then he felt he would be morally obligated to become a vegetarian. Larry, rural to the core, a survivor of a mediocre Canadian high school, grew up on a farm where his family had a large garden, raised chickens, turkeys, pigs and cows, and ate everything they produced. As the new agriculture teacher, Larry offered to help Ben raise livestock. Ben chose pigs for his experiment.

With the help of Bernard, an agricultural science student, Larry arranged to buy two feral pigs from Bernard's village. On the day of the pickup, a cast of thousands set off: Larry, Ben, Doreen and I, Dave and Joyce, and David. We drove two cars and David's four-wheel-drive Harvester Scout.

When we arrived at the village, I noticed an old woman sitting on the ground, her back erect as a ballet dancer's, her legs straight in front of her. Her hair was covered with a bandana, her legs modestly wrapped in an orange chitenge (a patterned cotton wrap). Her hands rested, at ease, in her lap. Her eyes acknowledged our arrival, but she remained still. Doreen, Joyce and I were wearing mid-thigh mini-skirts as we spilled out of our vehicles. Bernard was there to greet us, but his uncle, the owner of the pigs, had not yet arrived.

None of us knew what to do next. We were people of the clock. I remembered an Independence Day celebration in town, when we had seen ourselves parodied in a traditional dance. The Zambian dancers, their faces painted white and dressed in crisply pressed white shirts, white shorts, and white knee-high socks, stamped their feet with impatience, moved their arms in harsh, abrupt gestures and repeatedly checked their large, paper-cut-out watches.

The village was quiet. The air smelled of smoke, sweat and dust. A few chickens, heads jerking back and forth, chased insects. The old woman watched us, impassively, with no obvious curiosity. Larry and Ben double checked their watches and Bernard reassured them that his uncle was on his way. Twenty minutes may have passed, but it felt like an hour. I examined a wooden rack about four feet high, standing by the door of one of the rondavels. It was made of poles cut from the bush and functioned as a dish rack that held a metal washing bowl and two blackened enamelled pots above the reach of children, dogs and chickens. All five rondavels in the village were constructed of poles and mud, and roofed with thatched grass. A tan coloured dog, ribs prominent, flies aligned along its eyelashes, slept beside the door of one house. Two children, four or five years old, chased each other into the bare swept areas between the houses, near the dish rack. They stopped and stared at us and we looked back at them. The small girl wiped her runny nose on her arm. The boy pointed at us and squealed "Mzungu! Mzungu!" Then he bent over, picked up a stick, and poked the dog's ribs until it yelped, got up and ran away, tail between its skinny legs. The old woman's eyes followed the dog.

When Bernard's uncle appeared, he sauntered towards us. The men greeted each other, shaking hands, holding them longer than British men would usually allow. Larry and Ben had learned to make a small bow over the clasped hands, then give a final, slower shake before releasing their grip. The women were observers while the men negotiated the deal. By this time Joyce had given up and went to wait in the car, but Doreen and I hung on and waited for the pigs. The young boy reappeared and shooed the pigs with the same stick he had used to prod the dog. Doreen jumped into the air as the pigs shot past her, heading for the long grass. We all ran about, dodged dogs and children, darted through the grass and grabbed armfuls of air. Finally, Bernard and his uncle caught the pigs, bound their feet with bark twine and trapped them in the box in the back of David's four-wheel drive.

Larry and Ben built a pig palisade in Ben's backyard. They collected saplings cleared from the school farm and bamboo from the dam near the river below the town. They dug the upright poles into the ground to make a circular enclosure. After supper, Larry and Ben alternated a daily run to the school kitchen and loaded up the leftovers into pails: cold, lumpy nshima and the scraps of vegetable stew that the kids found inedible. The pigs squealed with gusto when the food fell from over the edges of their palisade like manna from heaven. They feasted better than any Zambian bush pig in the country. Over the next few months, two more pigs joined them. One sow had a litter of five piglets which Ben and Larry sold off to the school kitchen, but they kept the largest pig, a huge grey-skinned one with coarse black hair covering its wide body. When the pig began to dig away at the base of the pen, threatening to uproot the walls, its time had come.

The pig ate its last meal on a Friday night. Larry, Ben, David and Dave sat in our living room, drank beer, and psyched themselves up for the next morning's slaughter.

When I was a kid my dad had kept pigs, but he had them slaughtered by the butcher. My uncles hunted deer then hung and dressed them on a makeshift tripod in our backyard. I also knew the true meaning of "running around like a chicken with its head cut off," having watched our headless hens jump off the chopping block and run all over the yard spouting their life blood, before they stopped abruptly and keeled over.

I knew what was involved in butchering and I didn't want to be around. I left the men in the living room. They finished their beer, blustered and made pointless jokes to distract themselves from the fear of the task they had set themselves. I had never allowed my brain to make the link between the live animal and the meat on my plate. Since coming to Zambia I had learned how to pluck, gut and butcher a chicken, but Bedford always dealt with the transition between the live birds we bought at our back door and the carcasses he set on the stainless steel drain board at the edge of our sink.

When I was about eight, my cat dragged an injured baby rabbit into the house and presented it to me. I felt I must put the bunny out of its misery and filled a bucket of water—but I could not bring myself to drown it. After several long arguments with myself, I took the soft animal out into the field and laid it down in the long grass. A few hours later, the cat brought it back to show me—this time he had finished the job. Fifteen years later, I had no desire to be part of the pig to pork event.

Mzungu dance

My memory of the butchering is spotty. I crossed the path and watched as Larry and Ben roped the pig's legs. That was enough. I decided I had lots of marking to do, went back to our house and chose to work in the space furthest away from the sounds of the pig pen. The squeal of the pig penetrated our walls, then, there was merciful silence. There were no freezers on the school site, so Larry and Ben divided the fresh meat among the staff that afternoon. The East Indian teachers declined. I remember a pink chunk with grey skin still attached. I don't recall eating it.

Doreen had decided to film the event with her small, Super 8 movie camera. It took months for the film to travel from Lundazi to England for processing and back again. When it finally arrived, the pork was a long-ago memory and the pig pen walls were gone, marked by a very fertile patch of ground in Ben and Doreen's vegetable garden. (They had reverted to buying meat in tins or from the weekly town butcher.) We watched the film in the AV room where we first watched Tom Mix and his backwards cowboys. The grainy, jumpy film leapt around Ben and Doreen's backyard, jittering over the pig palisade, then it focused on the men roping up the pig's legs. Even though the film had no sound, I could hear the terror-filled scream of the pig again. I shut my eyes.

NYIKA PLATEAU

In April 1970, at the end of the second term, we took our bush-scavenged, reconstructed car on the first of many journeys into northern Malawi to explore the Nyika Plateau, a landscape that would enfold us and live on in our imaginations. The road, sometimes gravel, sometimes dirt, took us through the tung tree plantations of the Viphya Plateau. We stopped on a height of land to admire the trees that ran for miles in orderly rows. I thought of gentle Francis Fortin, my great-grandfather, who built what became the guest bed in my parents' upstairs room. He was an artist who used a chisel. He carved stylized oak leaves into the headboard; leaves I traced with my fingers when I was a child. When the bed was complete, Great Grandpa Francis had rubbed tung oil from Malawi into the wood grain to create a shining finish resistant to dirt and scratches. He did not know he would have a granddaughter who would remember him when she stood under a tung tree in the Viphya Forest of Malawi, five years after his death.

We descended the plateau, following the road around groups of grey volcanic plugs over a hundred feet high, like round-shouldered, sleeping elephants rising out of the earth. There were few cars on the winding road, but there were dozens of carts loaded with wood, pulled by pairs of oxen with bony haunches. Goats slept in the centre of the road and ignored cars, carts and pedestrians. We slowed down as we drove by groups of women walking with bundles of firewood balanced on their heads. When they heard the car, they moved to the side of the road, but we still covered them in clouds of red dust.

Our first night, a hundred miles into the journey, we slept at the Mzuzu rest house. In the morning we continued north, through the almost-not-there town of Rhumpi where three sparsely stocked shops offered Fanta, Coke, sugar and tinned margarine. Rhumpi was the last stop for petrol, so we filled the tank and both jerry cans before we began to climb the escarpment. We left behind the world of villages, farms, schools, government offices and beer halls as we climbed to eight thousand feet. This land was too high and too cool for crops. Archeologists have found evidence of old foot paths and overnight resting places marked by the charcoal remains of small fires, but there are no traces of sustained human settlement on the plateau.

The road led us into Nyika National Park. Its rolling hills, grass-green and bracken-brown, were accented with splashes of heather-pink. Zebra, eland and impala moved in herds, hunted by solitary leopards. Wildflowers grew in profusion, with colour combinations that defied my ideas of what a flower could be.

Before Independence, the British colonial government had built Chelinda Camp in the park—four cottages in the scoop of a small valley—and constructed a dam to supply water and a village to house the workers who attended to the travellers who came to stay in this pristine paradise. Around the cottages and the workers compound were young pines and eucalyptus, planted as a forestry experiment in the 1950s.

In the stand of pine trees, a few hundred yards from the cottages but hidden from our sight, was the compound where the cooks, game guards and maintenance people lived. There was a petrol pump, and a store for the workers to get limited supplies, trucked one hundred miles from Mzuzu. This compound was out of bounds to travellers and a place where money, influence or white skin would not provide access. If you forgot salt or cooking oil you did without—or the cook improvised without. There were speculative stories about what would happen if you ran short of petrol but Larry, ever the Boy Scout, never took the chance and we always carried extra. Travellers could live the fantasy of pristine isolation and oneness with nature, supported by those who lived behind the screen of trees.

The interior of our two-bedroom cabin was cool and austere. There were no frilly cushions or dust catching knick-knacks. Every item was functional. Next to the window that overlooked the dam stood a wooden table with four chairs. They were built in the same style as our Lundazi government-issue furniture. Two armchairs and a settee, cushions covered in sturdy, faded chintz, were grouped around the stone fireplace, the only source of heat on chilly July evenings. The two bedrooms had two single beds each. "Oh, the British," we sighed in mock horror. "How did they ever reproduce?"

We hadn't yet found a double bed in our travels through Zambia and Malawi. Larry kept the trunk of our car equipped with rope, two full jerry cans, a spare tire, patching kit, tools, tarp, random car parts, loops of wire, flashlight, candles, matches, a canvas water bag and our first aid kit. He went out to the car, dug out short pieces of rope and once again lashed the legs of two single bed frames together.

The bathroom had a deep tub and a small sink. To use the toilet required slimness and agility, because it was in a separate cubicle so small that the open door barely cleared the edge of the toilet bowl. A pump brought water up from the dam to an outdoor water tank supported on a brick frame built over a fire. From there, the piped water ran, steaming hot, directly from the tank into the cottage. A hand-lettered sign warned everyone to stand clear of the tank because the water would often boil, then geyser from the overflow valve on the top of the tank and splash onto the walkway.

Off the living room was a small, inefficient kitchen. The once-pink wall behind the cast iron woodburning stove was brushed with feathery patterns painted by years of soot and smoke drifting up the wall. A wooden counter butted up to the edge of the rusty sink. One tilted shelf held basic place settings for four. A stack of blackened, battered cooking pots sat on the floor next to the stove.

As in other rest houses, a cook made our meals. It was our responsibility to bring all our own food for a three-day stay, right down to the salt and pepper. Before dawn, the cook started the fire beneath the water tank so that we had hot water for bathing when we woke. He also lit the fireplace for us to enjoy in the evening.

Edward was the cook for our cabin. At first, he startled me because, even with black skin, he bore an uncanny physical resemblance to my own brother, Ed. The resemblance ended there. Each time I spoke to Edward, he cringed. His every move was apologetic. After I gave him our food supplies and explained what we wanted to eat, he clasped his hands together, bowed his head and backed into the kitchen, "Yes, Bwana. Yes, yes Madam." I guessed he was in his early thirties, and I wondered if growing up in a British colony had formed him into a cringing man who worked hard to make himself unobtrusive and nearly invisible. He was an excellent cook despite the minimal kitchen equipment.

Thirty years in the future, our convoluted fortunes brought us back to the Nyika and back to the same cabin. Edward, now in his sixties, was still there, still the cook. He didn't recognize either of us, middle-aged and one of the hundreds of guests he had served, but he greeted us with the confidence of one who has made his place in the world and knows his own worth.

Near the cabin's fireplace was a bookshelf with a few books for bird and plant identification, and a collection of guest registers. These records, with their blue-lined pages and brown paper covers, went back to the early 1950s when the cottages were built. Guests recorded their names, home base, date of visit, and comments on their stay. We deciphered the signatures of the Leakeys, the archeologists who described humanity's origins in Tanzania's Olduvai Gorge. The names of men famed as big game hunters, such as Norman Carr, were also there. When we returned to the cottages over the next four years, we liked to find our own signatures and the comments about our visits. Along with the other guests, we recorded sightings of herds of reedbuck, roan antelope, zebra and the occasional bush pig. We became part of the history of transient humans who passed through this Eden for two- or three-night stays.

The cabin's purpose was to provide warmth, food and a safe place to sleep. Once we satisfied those basics, we headed outdoors to wander, hike, or drive the hills in search of game, flowers and birds, or just to experience the open, uninhabited landscape. There were no poisonous snakes on the Nyika. The altitude and the cool temperatures combined to banish malarial mosquitoes. In Lundazi, our fear of malaria and snakebite hummed, a barely suppressed undercurrent, through our lives. In the altitude of the Nyika we let go the double threat, but didn't think to fill the gap with leopards.

Each morning after breakfast, Larry and I drove out into the hills looking for animals. Zebras grazed on the slopes or gathered at the height of land, silhouetted on the line between earth and sky. Pneumatic-limbed gazelles sprang out of the valley, leapt across the road and skimmed the hood of our car. Stolid, heavy-horned roan antelope roamed in large herds, ignoring us. We pulled off the road and wandered down into the dips looking for wildflowers. I knew nothing about the rare orchids that grew there but was curious when we spotted small groups of older British women (at least in their forties!) who wore sensible sun hats and searched purposefully for flowers. I saw what looked like stalks of pink gladiolas, and nearby, arched wands with pink petalled bells that reached over my head. Later, in the harsh climate of Winnipeg, I became a passionate gardener and learned that gladiolas and dierama or "Angel's fishing rod," as well as more than two hundred types of orchids, grew on the Nyika Plateau. I regret my ignorance, but at that time I saw only unfamiliar but intriguing flowers.

On one trip in our second year, when I was just beginning to show my first pear-shaped pregnancy, carrying the son who would have a career devoted to plants, I wandered off from the spot where we had parked. I drifted from one small discovery to another—a flower, a lichen, a bristly seed head. I lost my orientation to the car and when I looked back up the hill, saw Larry, a shape on the horizon line above me, waving his hands frantically. "What's the fuss?" I thought, and began to climb slowly up towards him. He was calling something, but the breeze blew his words adrift as he shuffled sideways down the slope towards me and I pulled my slow, round body up to meet him.

"A leopard has been stalking you for the last ten minutes." I looked back, down into the valley, but saw nothing, just soft brown heather colours muted by a grey sky. I felt no danger and didn't believe there was any, excepting the fear on Larry's face.

Night was the time for leopards, and the smaller cats, servals and civets. Sometimes we arranged a night drive with an organized group and a pair of armed game guards. We rode in a large open-backed truck fitted with tiered seats, with a spotlight mounted on the hood of the truck to pick out animal movements in the bush. Other times, when we travelled with friends, we crammed into a car or small truck and headed out on our own, equipped only with flashlights. One night there were six of us in a Datsun pickup, two of us in the cab and four in the open box at the back. This was a chilly night under the Southern Cross, miles and miles from streetlights, a night with no moon, no campfires, just stars—stars in their full, icy white, ancient glory.

The truck's engine growled in first gear. The headlights lit the road a hundred yards ahead and provoked a fluster of wings as clumsy nightjars flew up from their nocturnal dust baths in the middle of the roadway. Our flashlights searched the bushes to the side of the vehicle and caught the circles of reflective cool blue eyes watching us. The flashlight beam picked out a hyena crouched over a carcass. My stomach clenched in revulsion at the unbalanced body. Its powerful muscled front quarters pivoted on its smaller hindquarters as the hyena ripped into its meal. When George, one of our fellow travellers, turned and swept the beam from one side of the truck to the other, two pairs of yellow eyes flashed back at him a few yards behind the tailgate.

"Oh my God!" He jumped up and hammered on the roof of the cab, then bent forward to shout into the driver's lowered window. "Leopards. Get going." We couldn't outdrive leopards, but they didn't speed up. They followed us and kept pace with the truck until we turned off the main road and headed for the cabins. And still, I felt safe.

Because I felt no danger, some mornings I would step out of the cabin, down two steps and onto a crunchy gravel path that led up to the pine plantation. I liked to take my guitar up to the woods, where I found a place to sit inside the first row of the plantation. I strummed "Blowing in the Wind" and "My Favourite Things," and imagined myself as understudy for Julie Andrews in *The Sound of Music*. When I ran out of memorized songs, my silence defaulted to listening: a clang of metal from the workers' compound, a woman's voice on the wind, the breeze above me, and then birdsong. When I looked around, the pine trees spoke of Scotland and a world that thought in orderly lines. The trees were tall but slender trunked, still young and open enough to let in the sunlight that splintered, shattered and shimmered as it passed through the clusters of green needles. The ground was covered with a slippery scattering of dried needles that had turned russet and gold.

The Nyika was the place I learned to savour solitude and silence. As a child I had lived on high alert in a crowded, often fraught household of eight; then I'd withstood the intensity of university, followed by teaching thirty-three eight-year-olds in the mini circus of a primary classroom. At the edge of the pine forest I breathed in the clear air and tasted the beginnings of peace.

Lundazi's savannah, Luangwa's rift valley, Nkhata Bay's shores, and the Nyika's rolling hills were the landscapes of our young adulthood—our new independence and our developing sense of capability—where we grew proud of our ability to improvise, work and explore in conditions that our Canadian peers considered dangerous.

Into these places, we carried the unexamined, earliest impressions of our childhoods: the relationships and the sensory experiences that had shaped our certainties about how the world worked and felt. Africa upended our certainties about people and things. It gave us a fresh set of indelible "first times," potent new memories, and the richness of a powerful second childhood that Larry and I could share with each other. We learned red soil, cicada songs, and rain on dust. We found that friendship crosses boundaries of nationality, politics and race. We experienced the evil that flows from fear. Underpinning the newness and change was the land and, for me, the Nyika was the gentlest of African mothers.

From our Nyika cabin I could walk to the west, away from the pine forest, past the small reed-ringed dam and beyond, where the world opened into sensuous, undulating hills, marked only by the scratch of a dirt road tracing the rise and fall of the plateau. The memory makes my heart expand with longing. I am still pulled to that landscape, imprinted on its horizon line, with the urge to fold myself into its valleys.

I can feel its shapes in my body. The line of the hills repeated the contours of a reclining hip and thigh, the curve of the calf, the scoop at the base of the neck where it meets the clavicle. Later, when I met the high, hard and haughty grandeur of the Rockies, I remembered the Nyika, and how it carried my eye through the dips and rises that flowed with the comfort of an unmade feather duvet.

Years later, I struggled to explain to Mark, our younger son, the deep magnetism of that place. "Mom, weren't you a toddler in the foothills of the Rockies? Don't you think you are imprinted on those hills?" A lovely notion, but my early childhood was spent first on the flat of the prairie outside Edmonton, then in the mountain canyons of Yoho National Park. When I passed through the foothills, on the way from the prairie to the mountains, maybe the rolling hills caught me then.

A Malawian game guard on the Nyika told us that travellers would look at the hills and say, "It's just like the Scottish moors" or "the Welsh hills of Brecon Beacons" or "the Sussex Downs" or "the Chilcotin." I believe it is a maternal landscape that reminds us of the safety of our first explorations, nestled against our mother's reclining body, before we pull ourselves up to balance on her hip, then topple happily back onto her thigh.

THREE C GIRLS

Three C Girls were the butt of staff room jokes. Someone always had a story about the girls' inept behaviour or naive responses. The implication was this group of girls only had a secondary school placement because there was a quota to fill. As the new kid on the block, in my first term Three C Girls became my homeroom class. We started every day together and I taught their English lessons.

Three stood for Third Form (equivalent to Canadian Grade 10 and C was their rank when the Third Form marks were averaged). Three A was the top form academically, Three B was middling, Three C was near the bottom—but Three C Girls were lower still, and they were the only all-girls homeroom.

I took to them like Joan of Arc rescuing kittens. The year before in Canada, during my first year of teaching, I realized my heart went out to the odd ducks and stragglers in my primary class as puzzles to be solved. I would lie awake at night dreaming up solutions. For my first English lesson with the Three C Girls, I chose a love story from a Zambian magazine I had found in Lusaka during our orientation. The girls adored it. Some pretended to swoon. Prisca rolled her eyes in delight, "Oh, Madam!" I felt I was off to a wonderful start and would soon vindicate the girls' reputation in the staff room. Within a week, I hit the wall of no resources. There were no more magazines. Our school library had only two shelves of novels, most of them beyond the girls' reading level. The English supply cupboard was stocked with dry grammar books filled with schematic charts of sentence patterns such as: adjective/noun/verb/adverb. I realized the other teachers scrambled from lesson to lesson, in effect, writing the textbook the night before. I fell back on the dull grammar texts.

A year into our contract, a small miracle happened. Leonard, who taught English to the fourth and fifth formers, was on holiday in Tanzania when he met another ESL teacher, who introduced him to a beautiful series of East-African themed textbooks for teaching English as a second language. Without the yet to be invented internet or even telephones, we depended on chance meetings and serendipity to help us find good teaching materials.

A second miracle happened. Leonard brought samples of the books to show Brian, our headmaster, who, without hesitation, authorized the purchase of the new texts for the whole school. It seemed an eternity before they arrived. I can still picture the tidy, tightly packed cardboard boxes, hear the pen knife as it sliced through the gummed brown paper packing tape, and the rub of the flaps as the boxes opened onto coloured covers—maroon, green, blue, rust and orange—one colour for each year from First Form to Fifth Form. The books had pleasant black line drawings to accompany stories of African children playing soccer, feasting with their village and even getting into mischief. There were lesson plans, questions, quizzes, and thoughtful assignments, all set out in a logical learning sequence. Pure luxury!

But those books were too late for my time with Three C Girls. I taught using the tedious grammar charts, but supplemented them with journal writing, letter writing and a classroom newspaper—the things that had worked with my Grade 3 students back home. I tried to adapt them for girls of fifteen and sixteen, pulsing with energy. They rolled up the waistbands on the blue skirts of their school uniforms to raise them a half-inch above the maximum allowable "miniskirt" length. The top buttons on their white blouses were always undone. They claimed the blackboard nearest the door, labelled it "Flash Corner" and filled it with school gossip, some in English, some in Chitumbuka or Nyanja, so I could only guess at the messages they giggled over before homeroom every morning. I accepted this as multilingual literacy.

A few of the girls had skin that was lighter toned, evidence that they used the skin-lightening cream Ambi, a toxic brew that kills skin pigment cells. I was shocked when I overheard the girls talk about their desire for lighter skin. I wrote to a friend in Canada and asked her to send me copies of *Ebony*, the Black American news and fashion magazine. The magazines arrived two months later and the girls loved them. They cut out the fashion photos and pinned them all over the bulletin board at the back of the classroom. From my position in front of the class, I looked over the heads of my students and realized that none of the glamorous faces on display were actually black. As a result of years of racial mixing, the Black American women's skin tones were various shades of café-au-lait—just the colour my students aspired to, the colour that Ambi skin cream promised them.

I didn't think of the incongruity of a White woman instructing her students to be proud of their black skin. Even though I was White, my grandfather had been a defeated, dirt poor farmer during North America's Dirty Thirties and I felt that gave me some link to the girls' impoverished rural backgrounds. However, I was born in Canada, carried a Canadian passport, grew up in the prosperous 1960s, and had a university education. I was convinced I was not a racist, but I was oblivious to the fact that I carried many advantages by accident of birth.

I assumed a secondary school education, denied to them before Independence, would free the girls from village life and open possibilities for them that their mothers never imagined, but I had no clear vision of what their lives might be. I was only five years older than most of them and immersed in my own adventure.

Most Three C Girls dreamt if they learned the boring grammar patterns, mastered math and excelled in domestic science class, they could live in Lusaka, wear beautiful clothes and marry a civil servant.

From her seat near the end of the second row, Maiwass stared out the classroom window, chin in hand and smiled dreamily.

"Maiwass," I said, "have you finished your journal editing?"

"Madam, you have stopped my dream. I was imagining my husband and my house in Lusaka. You are not fair."

Lizzie didn't want to wait for the dream. She had Ambi-light skin, was movie-poster beautiful and found ways of adjusting her uniform and arranging hair ornaments that made the boys, and even the male staff, turn their heads. Occasionally, shiny black cars owned by government officials would arrive at the school, and important looking men would spend time with the headmaster, the deputy headmaster, or the boarding master. Our neighbour, Ben, said sometimes a car would return at night, headlights off, and park outside the girls' dormitories. Ben said he saw Lizzie come out to

Three C girls

chat with the driver of the car. She might even open the rear door of the car, step in and ride away to spend time with the important men who had come to do school business during the daytime and personal business at night. I didn't let myself hear these stories, but three years later, after we had left the school, a final story reached us. Lizzie had died of diseases given to her by the men in the black cars.

The students talked of "the vd that kills you." We explained the effectiveness of antibiotics to treat these ancient diseases, unaware yet that something viral was travelling through war zones and truck stops. It would be ten more years before it arrived in San Francisco and was given a name. I wonder if that is what found Lizzie.

The boys taunted the girls of Three C. "You waste the space. Girls do not need school." Bertha pushed back. She scowled at them, "Iwe! Choka!" (Chitumbuka for, "Hey you! Get out!") and turned away. Head down, intense, Bertha worked hard in every class. She ignored Flash Corner and the other girls' chit-chat. Bertha graduated from Lundazi Secondary and went on to the University of Zambia. We heard rumours that she had become a civil servant or possibly a lecturer at the university. Recently I did a search and found her name on several papers and publications relating to transportation policies in Zambia.

Into my second term of teaching I decided, without question, that the practice of streaming students into classes based on their marks defeated the ones at the bottom of the list and made the top A stream group cocky and smug.

In the staff room I argued, "We need to break up the class system among the students!"

The Brits teased back, "Oh, it's the egalitarian Canadian...."

I countered, "After all, they have already been selected by marks from the top three percent of the country. Why should we bring them here and divide them up further? We turn them into successes and failures before they step into their first lesson."

To my surprise, Sonia, head of the English department, took me seriously, "I'm sure they would all be better off if we built the class lists without reference to the students' marks."

It helped that she was also the headmaster's wife. We decided that we could divide the classes randomly and label them with the names of different colours. We devised a plan to interview the prefects and student leaders before the end of the term about the cultural meanings of different colours.

We asked, "Which colours tell that a person is important or powerful? What colours relate to chiefs and headmen? Are there colours that mean witchcraft or death or illness?" The students consistently said that yellow, red and black had powerful attributes, so those were the colours we chose to avoid.

When the April term break arrived, Sonia and I went to Mulla's Hardware at the end of the shopping street and bought tins of house paint. We mixed them into colours with neutral associations—greyed blues, greens, maroons and browns. It took us a week to repaint every classroom door. Then we went through the class lists and sorted the names in each form into groups of forty students for each homeroom. We assigned them each a colour, such as First Form Green, First Form Blue, and First Form Maroon rather than First Form A, First Form B, First Form C and so on down the alphabet. We used the colours for each form from one through to five.

Then we took our colour coded class lists to the timetable crew. Larry had joined Ben, Dave, and David, who constructed the school timetable each term. They took over the technical drawing classroom and taped together large sheets of white paper to construct an even larger sheet that covered one wall. They drew a giant grid over the whole sheet and used coloured pins as moveable tools to help them create a master timetable based on forty students in each class, forty lesson blocks a week, and forty minutes per lesson. The sciences got double blocks. The headmaster provided information on the staff who were about to complete their contracts and leave. He gave the timetable crew the names and subject areas for incoming staff. The boarding master did the same for the students, listing who would graduate and who would arrive in the new term. Then the men co-ordinated students, teachers, subjects, classrooms and time frames. Sometimes Doreen, Joyce and I walked up to the technical drawing room and brought them lunch or tea. The four men worked with the concentrated seriousness of teenaged boys solving a Sherlock Holmes mystery. It would have been a perfect job for a computer, but the technology for personal computers was five years into the future. However, no one expressed any regret that the job meant they had to work together for at least a week of every term break holiday.

When Sonia and I handed them our class lists labelled by co-lour instead of grades it didn't concern them at all, because the labels made no difference to the overall system.

When our May term with de-streamed classes was underway, the geography teacher, Ray, expressed his frustration and disappoint-ment at the even nature of each class. He could identify the stars within a class, but he couldn't pick any one class as superior to the others.

Three C Girls were no longer the punchline of jokes. They were interleaved with their age mates behind the muted rainbow of co-loured classroom doors.

A New Way of Seeing: Canada

It was early November 1970, the day's classes were done and most of the teachers sat around the staff room tables waiting for the headmaster, Brian, to arrive and the staff meeting to begin. We marked notebooks, chatted, or read the mail that had just arrived in a backlogged bundle: blue aerogrammes with stamps from around the world, white envelopes with business letters, and out-of-date newspapers.

Beside me, Nadya had spread out the weekly edition of a Moscow newspaper. The Cyrillic script turned every story and headline into a complete mystery. Only the black and white photographs provided a few clues.

Half-heartedly, I was reading through Fourth Form English essays. Nadya flipped over the page of her newspaper and I saw a photo of a soldier with a round helmet, standing at the top of a short rise of stairs. The building behind him looked like it was built in the 1800s. He held a rifle at an angle across his chest. A group of children looked up at him from the bottom of the steps. One boy mimicked the soldier's stance.

Oh dear, I thought, the USSR has invaded some country and is bullying the local population and terrifying children. I wonder where it is. But I won't ask.

I wanted to honour Nadya's resolve not to talk politics. I glanced away and tried to focus on the unmarked essays. Nadya continued reading, then she pointed to the photo, turned to me and said, "It's Canada."

"No," I said.

"Sure," she said. "It is telling about an organization called the FLQ. The picture, it is Montreal."

"Really?" I said.

"Yes. A man is dead."

What she said seemed impossible. Three years before, in the summer of 1967, I had lived and worked in Montreal during Expo 67, a world showcase of art, music, architecture, and international cooperation. I had fallen in love with the joie de vivre of Quebec, the home of my ancestors since the 1600s.

In late November, three weeks after Nadya had told me that an unnamed man was dead in Quebec, the October 1970 edition of Canada's major news magazine, *Maclean's,* arrived in our mailbox. I learned that the FLQ (Front de libération du Québec), a group inspired by the independence movements in Africa and Asia, wanted to free themselves of the "agents of imperialism." They wanted to lift off the "English yoke" that controlled business in Quebec. They believed that violence was justified to achieve their goals, and they instigated 160 violent acts, including bombings and robberies, in their short history. On October 5, 1970, they kidnapped James Cross, a British diplomat. On October 10, Pierre Laporte was kidnapped, and then killed a week later. Prime Minister Pierre Trudeau invoked the *War Measures Act,* which permitted severe restriction of civil liberties, including arrest and detention without charge. (James Cross was finally released in early December.)

By the time *Maclean's* arrived, the FLQ incident had been forgotten, buried under the more current international news exchanged in the staff room. I was embarrassed and still disbelieving and did not want to talk about it again. In my picture of the world, soldiers and guns were synonymous with the USSR and the USA, not Canada. I began to understand why Nadya did not want to discuss politics.

Building a Village

Parasitic flatworms lived in slow-moving water. The drug cure for a worm infestation called bilharzia was brutal, but if the parasite settled into the intestines or urinary tract, the disease was debilitating and for life. Swimming was only for the foolhardy and we carefully avoided stepping into streams, rivers, ponds or dams.

David had a solution. Soon after our arrival, he began to build a swimming pool. With the help of Dave, Ben, and his gardener, he excavated a rectangular hole, six feet deep, in his garden. They lined the hole with bricks, plastered them into place and created a small pool, long enough to allow three strokes and a turn. David bought a pump and a filter and kept the water clean, except when he got distracted by another project, then green slime colonized the water's surface. All around David's yard, his gardener built the tallest, thickest grass fence on the school compound, to make a private space and to screen us from our students, who hovered nearby and tried to pry peek-holes in the wall of grass.

How did we appear to our students? When I watched a clip of a forty-year-old cine film shot around the sparkling pool, the shaky moving pictures looked like a trailer for a glamorous 1970s beach party film. A dozen voluptuous, bikinied women (teachers and nurses in another guise) lay on grass mats or lounged on flimsy deck chairs, while tall, thin, unevenly tanned White men in boxer trunks (teachers earlier in the day) wandered about smoking cigarettes and fixing pool pumps, filters and water pipes. Two toddlers stumbled between the bodies. I sat on a reed mat, eating a melon slice and wearing a bikini I had sewn for myself from patterned blue and orange terry towelling lined with worn out pillowslip fabric.

During the month-long midterm breaks, we left the screened-in pool to revisit the game parks of the Nyika Plateau, or the Luangwa Valley, or to swim in the clean, government-tested, bilharzia-free water of Lake Malawi. Others went further north to Tanzania, Kenya, Mauritius and the Seychelles or south to Botswana and South Africa. Our students packed their belongings into suitcases and fabric-wrapped bundles, sang as they boarded buses and travelled home to their villages. They left behind electricity, running water and three meals a day.

When we set off on an adventure, we depended on our wits and the stuff we carried, knowing there were no garages and only occasional, unreliably stocked petrol pumps in small settlements. Cell phones were still the stuff of science fiction and Dick Tracy comics. We often travelled in convoys of three or four vehicles. We headed into the bush on dirt roads, tracing lines on unreliable maps, our cars loaded with food, rope, spare parts, and jerry cans full of petrol. Once, these ropes pulled our Toyota out of a deep runaway stream that had washed out the approach to a small bridge. When the car was back on solid ground, Larry, Ben and Dave crawled under the car to repair its undercarriage. Each breakdown metamorphosed into a victory, a celebration of mechanical creativity.

The men honed their skills for these adventures back home in Lundazi. The closest garage for car repairs was in Chipata, a hundred and twenty miles away. The men ordered and shared thick repair manuals with line drawings that illustrated how to remove and replace malfunctioning parts for each make of vehicle. On the weekends, three or four men would stretch out beneath a Toyota or a Peugeot, or dig around under the hood (which we learned to call a bonnet). They lined up parts on a clean tarp in the precise order illustrated in the manual. At the end of the day, they retold the details of the repair step by step or groaned over a disastrous blow-up caused by an incorrectly installed spark plug. I would listen with half an ear, and found the details somewhat amusing but mostly boring. I was blithely unconcerned about the threat of breakdowns miles from any outside help. My father and grandfather were excellent mechanics and I assumed "guys" knew how to fix things and would do so happily.

Larry and I carried a blue nylon tent from Canadian Tire, a gift from his parents. It had aluminum poles in telescoping sections, yellow nylon tie-downs and orange plastic tent pegs that we replaced with metal spikes. We needed sharp spikes to hammer into the hard, gravelly terrain if we had to pitch our tent at the side of the road. Around 4:30, after a day of travel, on our own or with others, we'd look for a flat spot to set up camp in time to cook a meal before the precipitous sunset. Larry always dug a narrow channel around the tent in case of rain, even in the dry season, because he had perfected his camping skills in the wet woods of BC's west coast. One morning, the dust around the tent was pricked out with the usual marks of insect, lizard and bird tracks, the record of the previous night's small travellers, but that time, they were overlaid with the deep paw prints of a lion. We had heard nothing in the night.

The rutted dirt roads took us through open savannah forests filled with trees we could not name or understand. Light filtered through their open umbrella-shaped canopies and fostered the understorey of unfamiliar vines, bushes and grasses. Meandering paths wound through the forests. Once in a while, a shady space under the trees was filled with the blocky shapes of cattle, tended by three or four young boys in ragged khaki shirts and shorts. They provided a reason for the twisting paths. Whenever we saw boys and cattle, the forest would soon open into cleared land, family fields of rustling green corn and a cluster of round, thatched-roof rondavels. We might see a woman pounding hard white kernels of corn into gritty flour for her family's evening meal. She would stand straight-backed, feet planted on the bare-swept earth next to her home, as she raised a wooden pestle more than half her height and hammered it down into a deep wooden mortar. A skinny dog slept nearby. Chickens scratched, then flustered up as we drove by, billowing red dust. We considered ourselves benign explorers, not invaders. We speculated that some of the villages we passed had never seen a White person. Sometimes a young child would point our way, cry and run in terror.

How did we look as we drove by on our adventures in our Toyotas and Peugeots, built in Japan and France, imported on ships, shipped by rail and powered by petrol from the Middle East? The villages we passed were close to self-sufficient in food, with seeds saved from year to year, oil from pounded peanuts, sweetness from wild honey, and occasional meat from their cattle and chickens. As we passed, we created indefinite and unsettling desires. Once a teenaged boy ran after our car, shouting. "Take me. Take me with you.

Here there is nothing for me. Take me." At term break, our students returned to villages like these, and after a month, they came back to the school and the promises of the education offered by their European teachers.

Once, on an excursion into northern Zambia near the Tanzanian border, we met evidence of a fingerprint of history that pre-dated even our parents' lives. Our travel companions were Dave and Joyce. We were lost, an easy thing to be. Dave decided we should stop at a village with half a dozen grass-thatched homes. One rondavel stood out. It was traditionally built, of stick lath and mud plaster, and had a newly thatched roof, but it was oval and twice the size of a regular circular rondavel.

A grey-haired man wearing a khaki shirt and worn, grey trousers stepped out of the oval house. He chatted with Dave then gestured an invitation to follow him inside. Minutes later, Dave returned and called to us, "You have to see this!" Larry, Joyce and I followed him into the house. A carved wooden clock hung on the wall. Its pendulum counted the seconds and its face registered accurate time. An oak side table displayed four rose-patterned, English bone china teacups. A small shelf held seven books, including Shakespeare's sonnets and a leather-bound copy of Goethe in German. Was it possible this man had served in the colony of German East Africa during WWI? When the war was over, had he remained there and worked under the British when they formalized control of the area in 1922 and named it Tanganyika? His English was formal and courtly. Did he speak and possibly read German as well?

His home was meticulously tidy. He honoured items the Brits and Germans would each consider symbolic proofs of their civilization: Goethe and bone china. He carried stories inaccessible to us.

I thought we were unique, inquisitive and open-minded because we risked living in another culture far from our home comforts. We didn't recognize how the wealth of the West allowed us freedom to choose an adventure rather than a regular job. The old man had tasted other cultures, by accident of history rather than choice. Maybe his need for work took him north into East Africa, an area of competing empires. When he returned home to his village, he brought the essence of what he had discovered and admired in a foreign land. He displayed the books and other keepsakes in his home in the same way I treasure the Zambian woven grass baskets and carved wooden bowls on my hearth today.

When we left Zambia and transitioned back to our Canadian lives, we learned new phrases like "culture shock" and "reverse culture shock." I sometimes wondered about our students and how they adjusted to moving back and forth between their home villages and their European-style school. I also wondered about the man with his china teacups and wooden clock.

In 2002, thirty years after Lundazi, Larry and I travelled together on an agricultural exchange between Canada and Malawi. We found ourselves once again in the market town of Mzuzu, one of our long-ago weekend destinations, about a hundred miles from the school.

On an agricultural research station outside of Mzuzu, I met Margaret, a petite Malawian woman with a PHD in agronomy from a British university. We stood to one side while the important men talked together at the edge of a demonstration plot of hybrid corn.

She told me she had high blood pressure from the stress of her work.

"I always have to work twice as hard as those men. But when I am very tired and need a rest, I go back to my village on Lake Malawi, near Livingstonia. They have nothing—no electricity, no running water. When it is dark, we sit by the fire and we laugh and laugh, and we sing. We are so happy together."

Margaret could say this because she was a Malawian woman. I would not presume to say it. It might sound romantic and patronizing if I said that African village life offered satisfying simplicity. But I had experienced the truth of it, in moments camping when I was a child: a tent, a campfire at night, roasting marshmallows and singing silly songs. At those times, the tensions of our complex family life dissipated into the warmth of an August night, replaced by cricket songs and the shimmering rustle of ponderosa pines.

A few months after the conversation with Margaret, another Malawian colleague, Teddy, arrived in Victoria as part of the agricultural exchange, and stayed with us. His first question was, "I need to see your village." We took him to Cowichan Bay near Larry's childhood home, but Teddy said, "This is a town, not a village." We drove him to the site of Larry's old family farm and that gave Teddy more satisfaction. He explained that the village stands for origins and roots;

the place you return to once you have tasted city life. It is the place that explains you.

In the years when Lundazi was our home, Zambia's border encircled a land of villages. At that time, I wasn't aware we too were building a village together with those we taught and travelled with. As we navigated our days at the school and explored the tantalizing, unfamiliar landscape, we were building a village of the heart. A village we return to in memory, stories, visits, phone calls and emails. A village we still hope might explain us.

A NEW WAY OF SEEING:
COCKROACHES AND COCA-COLA

Doreen and I sat on the edge of the dusty concrete slab that was my front porch. Our miniskirts wrapped us at mid-thigh, so our legs were slanted, angled together for an approximation of modesty. From the girls' dormitories, a stone's throw away, we could hear soft chatter and random joyful shouts, "Aieee-eee!" Clusters of girls in twos, threes, and fours wandered by on their way to Lundazi township to explore the single row of small shops. They wore their school uniforms, the top two blouse buttons undone and, as usual, their skirts hiked above their knees. Some girls balanced small bundles of fabric on their heads. They would unfold the fabric and use it to wrap up their purchases when they found the right skin cream or spool of heavy thread for plaiting their tight curls.

Doreen's straight blonde hair curved under her chin. She sat perfectly balanced, her right elbow propped on her knee, her forearm perpendicular, supporting the hand that held her cigarette. I thought of her as a woman who was calm and curious about everything. In contrast, I felt boringly pragmatic. I couldn't fathom her love for Muffin, her Heinz 57 dog. Muffin's mouth hung open in a trusting grin and her bulging brown eyes oozed adoration for everyone. Her uneven, tawny hair stuck out in all directions and shed promiscuously. Muffin was an extremely fertile, continuously pregnant bitch, who popped puppies every six months. The township was full of her spiky-haired offspring, running free. I had no sympathy for that dog.

Unlike me, Doreen had a great tolerance for cockroaches in her kitchen. The previous Friday she had invited us to dinner and promised a diversion from our usual diet of stewed beef, rice and local greens. By candlelight she served a salad of seedy watermelon, peeled grapes and raw bacon while cockroaches skittered across the dining room table, dropped onto the floor and crunched underfoot. The meal was edgy and fascinating, flavoured by Cinzano vermouth mixed with Mazoe orange cordial. I enjoyed the intimacy of the four of us, Larry and me, Ben and Doreen, eating in the darkened dining room, faces warm with candle glow and the heat of the waning dry season. But the next morning, grumpy with a headache, I wondered what Doreen and I had in common. I knew raw bacon was unsafe and I was proud that my kitchen cockroaches were under control.

On our porch a few days later, Doreen and I shared a bottle of warm Coca-Cola. I remembered our CUSO orientation when the field director told us we should brush our teeth with Coke if we didn't have boiled water. Coca-Cola would never give us diarrhea. The thought of Coke and foamy toothpaste still makes me nauseous.

Doreen drank her half from the scratched, blue-green glass Coca-Cola bottle, embossed like the ones I remembered from childhood. I sipped mine from a chipped orange enamelled tin cup with a blurry "Made in China" stamp on the bottom. We sat back and watched Muffin stretched out in the middle of the dusty path, soaking up the afternoon sun. The smoke from Doreen's cigarette made lazy loops.

It was near the end of our first year. I was no longer writing "Gee whiz! Wow!" letters home, letters packed with superlatives and dramatic details about fire ants cleaning out the math teacher's house, the chameleons that tottered back and forth along our grass fence or the lion shot near the government offices. At this precise moment, I knew deep down I would never share a warm bottle of Coke with a friend in Canada. There would have to be two bottles. They would be cold; there would be ice cubes; there would be spotless clean glasses to drink from. We would sit at a clean, sanitized, Formica-topped table in an air-conditioned restaurant.

On a Lundazi afternoon, Doreen and I shared that sweet, warm luxury. The bubbly fizz burst on the roof of our palates and tickled our noses. The air was so still it could not be felt. It wrapped us in perfection, neither too hot nor too cold. We sat together in comfort, enclosed in a space extracted from time, without expectations or plans.

BETRAYAL

Larry and I began to feel we had a special bond with the Russians, especially Nadya and Volodya. Later we wondered if the four of us felt a link because we came from vast countries whose identities were formed by long, cold winters and drifts of snow. It was a romantic notion because both Larry and I actually grew up in Canada's anomaly, the benign southwestern corner of BC. Some of our grandparents had settled on the Prairies, so we could claim to have winter in our genes. What we were certain of was that we wanted Nadya and Volodya to travel with us to share the rolling landscape we had fallen in love with on the Nyika Plateau. As our friendship grew, we invited them several times to come with us. Each time, they quietly declined.

Finally, after we pressed them to reconsider, they said, "Our visa does not allow us to leave the country. But that is OK with us. The Luangwa Valley is very close by and we can see many animals there when we wish."

For a while we let the idea rest. However, I came from a family where no one accepted "No" for an answer. Roadblocks were just challenges to get around, argue with, or reshape. Both my parents knew how to get their way—Dad by bluster and loud argument, Mom by tactful cajoling with a little injection of guilt. Plans changed constantly around our house because someone was always thinking up a better idea or because another opportunity came up. From what I'd learned at home, I had no doubt that there was a way to get around the silly bureaucratic order that prevented our friends from enjoying the beauty that awaited them on the Nyika. As Canadians we were not permitted to travel to South Africa, but many CUSOs inserted a loose sheet of paper for the border crossing stamps then destroyed the paper when the journey was over. We never went to South Africa, but we knew it was possible if we wanted to.

We studied a map and learned the Nyika game park paid no attention to political divisions. It straddled the border of Zambia and Malawi. I decided we had found the perfect solution. Nadya and Volodya could travel with us to the Zambian side of the park. A closer look at the map showed one hitch—the road to the Zambian rest house went through Malawi for a stretch of ten miles before it swung back again into Zambian territory.

In March of 1971, we took the map to Nadya and Volodya.

"Look, the park stretches into Zambia and there is a rest house on the Zambian side. The road crosses the border here, then turns back again at this place. Only villagers use those crossings. You don't have to worry about getting a stamp in your passport. Besides, the road runs for just ten miles through Malawi and then we are right back into Zambia again. We will be in Malawi for only twenty minutes."

Finally, Nadya and Volodya looked interested. I couldn't understand their hesitation. I didn't know what they could be worried about. This was the 1970s. I believed we lived in a world of scientific progress and international understanding. By the time I had finished my Grade 11 history course, taught by my beloved Mr. Andres, a Mennonite pacifist, I was convinced of the futility of war and conflict. I thought if I had figured that out at sixteen, I was sure important world leaders, much older than I, understood that international cooperation was the answer to the world's problems. My adolescent conviction that we were in a new age of peace ignored the simmering war in Vietnam, a small country far away. By the time I began university, the prevailing youth culture declared history as irrelevant in the present-centred, forward-looking excitement of the 1960s. In Lundazi, now that I was twenty-three, I had first-hand experience that our supposed enemies were no different than we were. I was sure our friends had nothing to worry about. The Russian embassy was five hundred miles away in Lusaka and no one would ever know if they drove in and out of Malawi for ten miles.

Nadya and Volodya decided they would take the risk and come with us for a weekend trip. And so, on a Friday afternoon, as soon as our last classes were done, the four of us began our journey, travelling in our Toyota Corona. We headed north of town parallel to the border for an hour then veered towards the border crossing. We were surprised to see a border guard. But he was bored, and happy to have some business. He only asked, "What is your occupation? Where are you going? When will you return?" He didn't ask for any papers.

Larry put the car in gear, and we pulled away. "There, that was easy wasn't it?" I chirped. A muscle twitched in Volodya's jaw. I tried distracting the two of them with silly stories and school gossip as we drove the ten-mile stretch in Malawi territory. The next border crossing, back into Zambia, was just a sign at an unmanned post, even easier than the first one. When we began to climb the escarpment's switchbacks, Volodya's jaw relaxed.

The Zambian side of the park had one rest house, unlike the collection of cabins we were familiar with on the Malawi side. The house stood on the steep slope of a hill and its screened-in porch looked down into the lush and jungly Chowo forest. We were the only guests in our house in the trees and we saw no one else during our two-day visit except for the quiet, unobtrusive cook who lit the fireplace and created meals from the food we had brought with us. The building was constructed in the 1950s, with four double bedrooms and a spartan communal sitting room. Hot and cold running water was noted as a special feature.

The cook told us about the local version of the Loch Ness Monster, "Please. Bwana, Madam, we are having a lake, a small lake, but it is deep, very deep. At the bottom is living an animal, very large, very dangerous."

When we woke on the first morning there was the briefest kiss of frost on the grass. The air was cool and misty as we walked into the forest. Vines dropped like trapeze safety lines from far over our heads, where monkeys bickered and invisible birds trilled and warned their friends of danger. Blue butterflies drifted, slipping past our outstretched fingers. By mid-morning the sun placed shifting hotspots of light on the trail and warmed the air.

In the afternoon, we took the car and explored, driving slowly on winding, minimally maintained dirt tracks. About four o'clock, we reached a dead end in the road. We stopped, turned off the engine and stepped out into silence accented by the burr and click of insects and random distant bird calls riding on an easy breeze. Together we walked to the edge of the escarpment and looked down the direct drop of hundreds of feet. The four of us stood and looked east across the Great Rift Valley and caught a glint of Lake Malawi miles away. We were so high over the valley that we could have been birds. The treetops looked like broccoli crowns. There was not a single hint of human activity anywhere we looked. No smoke rising, no lines for roads, no hum of planes or cars. The slanting golden afternoon light shone through monumental cumulus clouds that rose up from their level lead-grey bases into brilliant mounds of blinding white. Behind us, leaves with names unknown to us chattered in the breeze, but you could imagine they were the voices of poplars or aspens. The tall, lush trees around us carried the luxurious blue-green of home, not the acidic lime-green of thorny savannah trees. Despite the great drop before us I felt safe and on familiar ground. I whispered to Nadya, "It feels like home." She and Volodya had been speaking softly to each other in Russian. "I just said the same thing to Volodya. It feels like home."

This was one of the rare moments in my life when I was filled with an intuition of the essential rightness of things. For a breath, the four of us shared a connection, a vision, a common sense of home. The problems of getting to this place seemed trivial and the effort worthwhile. We had so wanted to share this taste of paradise with them. That moment still holds. I can see the valley, hear the clatter of the leaves and my heart remembers the companionship. That I hold, despite all that came later.

On the second morning, after breakfast of fried eggs, tinned Danish bacon and slightly charred British style toast cooled on a rack, we packed for our return. Volodya proudly signed the guest book in Russian, checking first to confirm that his was the only message in Cyrillic script. Our return and the border crossings were uneventful. Nadya and Volodya did not seem as edgy when Larry drove the short road section on the Malawi side. We arrived in Lundazi on Sunday afternoon and headed home to lesson preparations.

Larry and I were relieved that everything had gone without a hitch. I felt triumphant at having found a way to circumvent a silly rule. School swallowed us up again and we only had time for quick hellos as we exchanged smiles with Nadya and Volodya in the staff room. Another weekend arrived, but they were busy. The next week Volodya seemed strained when we crossed paths on the way to our classes. He said that Nadya had a great deal of marking to do. It was a relief when one evening about two weeks after our return, he knocked on our door. We welcomed him with overly enthusiastic warmth, but he said he didn't have time to stop for a beer.

Volodya asked, "I need to write a business letter. Could I borrow your typewriter?"

"Of course, of course. You're welcome to use it here. Or do you want to borrow it?" Larry said.

"It is short. I can do it quickly."

Volodya sat at our living room table which was covered with our next day's lesson plans. He typed for a few minutes and rolled the paper out of the platen.

"There, it is done. Thank you very much. Now, good evening. I must go."

Volodya stood up and left immediately. Larry and I both felt like the air had been sucked out of the house. Something was wrong.

The next day we heard that Volodya would take the five-hundred-mile drive to the Russian embassy in Lusaka as there was some business to settle. He had been granted a week off because of the urgency of the task.

A typewriter has its own mechanical, staccato personality. Its pre-cast, reversed letters, held in a concave fan, wait, alert on their metal stems, for the levered action of a keystroke. A bit of dust in the eye of an "o," a knick in the tail of a "j," or a slight twist in the supporting stem of an "m" makes a characteristic mark on a document as the keys strike through the inked ribbon. The ribbon itself, whether worn or new, also leaves a telltale trace in the intensity of the ink impression or microscopic threads of shredded fabric.

A typewriter puts its fingerprints all over a letter. A letter had been typed on our typewriter and mailed to the Russian embassy. The letter detailed Nadya and Volodya's trip to the Nyika Plateau, across the Zambian border and through Malawi to the Zambian rest house. After Volodya received a summons from the Russian embassy he said nothing about it, but he went to staff members with typewriters and asked if they would allow him to type a short letter on their typewriter. When he typed his letter in our living room, he created a sample of our typewriter's peculiarities that matched the letter received at the Russian embassy in Lusaka. He explained this to us when he returned from Lusaka. He didn't accuse, just described what had happened. Our confusion and shock may have eased his suspicions, but it did not resolve the question of who wrote the letter or how that person got access to our typewriter.

I was a muddle of disbelief, denial and despair. How could this have happened when I thought we lived in a reasonable world, almost a new age of enlightenment? We were well educated and rational. We had crossed the border of lifetimes of prejudice, discovered the common humanity of a people once held as enemies and found new friends. Now we were suspected of betrayal.

For weeks the questions and speculation swirled within us and around us. Who wrote the letter? Did either of us loan the typewriter to anyone? Who had a key to our house? A silly question since there were only twelve different keys for all the doors on the campus. Each key had a number stamped on it: K1, K2, K3, up to K12. These keys looked like a child's fairytale illustration—a cloverleaf shaped head, a round shaft and a notched square at the business end. Keys were distributed depending on which one matched the lock to your house, classroom, or storage cupboard. There were several copies of a master key that opened every door on campus, the classrooms and the private homes. Depending on a person's level of responsibility in the school it was possible to hold a master key permanently or to borrow one for a limited time. A locked door was a formality that was universally observed among staff and students. Theft was non-existent within the school community but common in the town where the small shops needed barred windows.

"Who?"

The question was asked in small groups just outside the staff room or behind closed doors. Besides ourselves, Dennis, who lived in our house before us and might still have a key, was also a suspect. During the previous midterm break, we had attended a CUSO meeting in Lusaka and were told, very hush-hush, that Dennis was a spy for the South African government and we needed to be careful what we said around him. The notion of spies seemed fantastical to us. The rumours in Lusaka seemed to bear no connection to our quiet neighbour. For what purpose would he turn in the Russians other than pointless spite? There was much calculation involved in this scheme of betrayal—I had considered Dennis more of a drifter than a planner.

Nadya and Volodya pulled back and kept more to themselves. Their zest dimmed and our relationship became more formal. I was too young to identify the symptoms of grief, but experienced them in vague fatigue, distraction, and an inability to settle. I read in the afternoons when Nadya and I would have played at baking Russian cakes or adapting ingredients to make something that resembled Nanaimo bars. We had bright, brief chats in the staff room. I was so uneasy and concerned that she might suspect me that I didn't think of what it felt like to be in her position. She and Volodya had no choice but to continue working and socializing every day with the unidentified person who had betrayed them. They never explained how their embassy had responded, but we assumed they were being monitored. We avoided mentioning our weekend trips to Malawi to pick up brown sugar, tinned beans and sometimes, even chocolate. After a few weeks the wound closed on the outside, but it remained raw on the inside. Other things took our attention. There were problems developing with staff relationships—and I had a growing distraction of my own.

BABIES

In September 1970, a year into our contract, CUSO mailed a health warning to its female volunteers. "The birth control pill, C-Quens, causes cancer in lab dachshunds. If you are using it, discontinue and find another choice."

I thought back to our CUSO interview in the spring of 1969. The panel included a nurse and her twelve-year-old nephew. She had brought him along for the experience. When the interview seemed to be complete, she had taken my elbow and steered us to a space between a felted room divider and a grey filing cabinet. After checking to see that her nephew was out of earshot, she had whispered, "Now, tell me, are you using reliable birth control?"

I didn't answer because I thought her question was presumptuous and nosy.

"You must under no circumstances consider having children while you are there," she said.

"But we don't know where 'there' is yet," I said.

"You can't imagine the dirt, the diseases, the parasites, the infections. You cannot subject a child to that."

I had focused on her brassy hair tint and decided she was too old to know anything. I was sure the entire continent of Africa was full of women with babies and that Larry and I could make our own decisions, thank you.

I hadn't taken the nurse's lecture seriously and I felt vindicated because we were surrounded by pregnant women, babies and children in Lundazi. The Ashworths, a British couple in their thirties, (middle-aged, in my eyes) had arrived from England with three. Most of the staff were twenty-something. Ben and Doreen were the first expatriate couple to start a family, followed by Dave and Joyce and then the Danish couple Hans and Lisbet. A new Welsh couple, Ralph and Jo, became pregnant soon after their arrival. Veronica had six children, and the wives of the East Indian teachers each had two or three youngsters and more on the way.

At twenty-two, I was part of the first wave of women in history who could control their fertility by taking a daily pill. It had become legal in Canada in early 1969, just before we got married. When I tossed the packets of C-Quens bubble-sealed white pills, I didn't quite believe I could become pregnant.

There were no other options available in Lundazi, or anywhere in Zambia. The concept of birth control was abhorrent to most men, and a Zambian man who learned, or suspected, his wife had attempted to control her fertility could beat her.

Doreen, Joyce, Jo, Lisbet and I, each in our time, went to the district hospital for a pregnancy test. Instantaneous, blue-bar tests were unimagined. One week later I returned for the results, and a brief meeting with the Ceylonese doctor, Djury Singham, who said, "You can go home and be happy." He sent me for follow-up blood work with a tall paramedic who took the blood sample with such gentleness and skill, I didn't feel the needle going in or out of my arm. I think of him each time I need blood work done, still hoping I will meet his match. His pale brown nails glowed in contrast to his deep black skin, and healing emanated from his hands. As a child I had been compelled by the stories of Jesus laying his hands on sightless eyes or withered limbs. As an adult, I yearned for that gift when my own children were ill. When I placed my hand on their distressed bodies, I wished I could relieve the fever, the chill, the cramp, or the migraine. The paramedic with healing hands had kindled the hope that such things were possible. After the blood test, he sent me home with folded paper packets full of prescribed vitamins and minerals. I went in every two months to see a midwife for a blood pressure check and a "How are you feeling?" Sometimes I chatted with Dr. Djury for a few minutes. Ultrasound had not been invented.

What I had in common with the new mothers at the school was that each of us experienced our first pregnancy and birth without the presence of our grandmothers, mother, or aunts. We didn't hear their voices because the closest telephones were in Chipata, 120 miles south. Their support came in blue tissue aerogrammes and many small brown-paper parcels filled with books on childbirth, blue and white circular tins of diaper rash cream, knitted wool booties in neutral yellow, cotton vests with silk ribbon ties, and blue and pink capped safety pins.

The parcels created a tangible link to home and family, but what I didn't realize was that Larry and I already carried the maternity stories of our mothers, grandmothers and aunts. As older siblings, we each had our own unexamined experiences as caregivers to brothers and sisters. Our vague new sense of ourselves as parents was a crazy quilt of unacknowledged, subterranean influences.

My French Canadian great-grandmothers and grandmothers bore ten, eleven, or even a baker's dozen children from their twenties until their early forties. Larry and I were the results of the post-WWII baby boom where families of four were an average size. Among Catholic families like mine, six or eight children were the norm. Larry's family of five boys and three girls was unusual for an Anglican family, but his mother, Phyllis, loved babies.

Phyllis raised eight children to adulthood but lost another five to miscarriages. She was often a single mom when Larry's father, Norm, worked for months at a time in logging camps. Phyllis managed babies, toddlers and active boys and girls while she kept a small farm running, with chickens, pigs, cows and a large vegetable garden. As second eldest, Larry had farm chores and helped with babysitting. He enjoyed young children and easily entered their world of wonder.

My mother sustained herself through six pregnancies with the poetic images of Bliss Carmen, Joyce Kilmer and Wordsworth: roses, lace, and sunlight through trees. On the windowsill over the sink, she propped up historical romance novels while she washed dishes, cooked, organized and mothered us. She read the *Ligourian,* a Catholic magazine filled with articles on the blessings of large families. My reading addiction drove me through several issues, but I saw a mismatch between the sweet stories and Mom's life: her fatigue, varicose veins and her chapped hands that bled when she ran cloth diapers through the wringer of the washing machine. The way she and Dad didn't speak for up to four electric days in a row.

As the big sister, first in line of six children, babies became familiar territory to me. Tom was born when I was two and I got a "big sister" gift—a chocolate bar and a sheet of paper dolls to cut out. When Mike arrived a year later, my mother nearly died of a hemorrhage, but I was protected from that knowledge. Five years later,

Eddie was born. Mom joked, "I created a five-year space by using the Church-approved rhythm method—a calendar and a baseball bat." I overheard this when I was nine but didn't understand it.

Olive, my mother's mom, died of a stroke five months before Eddie was born. Mom was keeping her fourth pregnancy a secret because Olive, unlike my Catholic grandmothers, was adamant that three children were enough. She had birthed three children then miscarried twins. After her loss, she moved into her own room and there were no more pregnancies.

I desperately wanted a sister. Two years after Eddie, Theresa arrived, followed by Pauline thirteen months later. Then we were done. We fell into two groups, The Big Kids and The Little Kids. By age eleven, after Pauline arrived, I considered myself an expert in bathing and diapering babies. I could sweep, wash dishes and set the table with one hand while gripping a baby on my hip with the other. I longed to escape to read *Little Women, What Katy Did* and *The Five Little Peppers and How They Grew* but reading had to happen while I was rocking babies. At first, I sat on a chair with one hand balancing the book, the other bouncing the handle of the navy blue baby buggy. Gentle rocking failed to satisfy any of The Little Kids for long. Pauline, as an infant (and later as an adult), wanted the most action. I tried to stand and push the buggy back and forth with the book balanced on the handle but that didn't work because rocking and reading made me slightly nauseous. I got a six-foot piece of sturdy elastic, wrapped it round the buggy handle and sat on a chair. I gave the buggy a solid kick and sent it shooting across the room. When it whipped back with a jerk, I kicked it again. That kept Pauline happy so I could immerse myself in *Little Women* and console myself that the trials of Jo, Meg, Beth and Amy were worse than mine.

Throughout my school days there would be stretches where I stayed home partly because I was prone to long-lasting head colds and partly because I was needed at home to help with The Little Kids. In high school, I turned it into a kind of game to see how many days I could miss and still get an A. One week away was no problem but two weeks was too much.

In Zambia, I discovered that little girls between the ages of nine and twelve wore their brother or sister in a fabric sling on their backs while they carried on playing their games. The baby was comforted by the sound of their sister's heartbeat. Later, the baby would be returned to its mother to nestle against her back and hear her larger heart beating.

Soon after Pauline was born, my father's parents, Eduardina and Alfred came to live with us for a few months while Alfred received medical treatment. At Christmas that year, Grandma Eduardina and I were sitting in the living room by ourselves. The sun shone through the window behind her and lit up the blue brush strokes on the Virgin Mary's cape. At Mom's request, I had painted a crèche scene using poster paints and I was pleased I had filled the whole window. In my painting Mary held an oval bundle while Joseph stood beside her. They were enveloped in long shafts of light from the six-pointed star in the top left-hand corner. When Grandma spoke, her English was simple, hesitant and soft because she hadn't learned to speak it until she was sixteen. Quebecois French permeated her words. She was the softest person I have ever touched—skin like warm, pliable, pizza dough. Dad told us that during the Depression she rubbed her hands with bacon grease from their homegrown, home-slaughtered and home-cured pigs. The grease protected her hands from the harsh red carbolic bars of Lifebuoy laundry soap and the fine grit of dust storms that sifted through the visible and invisible cracks in the walls and windows of her sod house.

I'm not sure how our conversation began, but it took a turn that confused me. She told me how desperate she felt when she became pregnant for the eleventh time. Her story didn't fit the myths about family I had grown up with: the tales of my grandmother who coped with every deprivation and challenge the Prairies threw at her; Sunday priests who praised the mothers who welcomed every child as a gift from God; and the *Ligourian* magazine at the back of the church which extolled the wonders of large families. (Mom and Dad had a stack of copies in the living room.) As Grandma spoke, I felt like I was pummelled with feather pillows that knocked the breath and belief out of me. She said, "I cried and I cried. I cried for nine months. I did not want another baby."

Several years later, soon after I began university, I was alone with Aunt Delphine, my slim, beautiful aunt with the Nefertiti profile. My aunt was my mother's younger sister and playmate in their perfect childhood of dolls, tiny tea sets, and frilly dresses with matching hair ribbons. My aunt the painter and the potter, who wore brilliant silk scarves to hide the bruises around her neck inflicted by her husband's rage. My aunt with eight children who said to me, "How would my life have been if I'd had fewer children?"

"But who would you do without?" I said—a line of my eight cousins filed quickly through my mind. At the same time, a wide empty space, tinged with disbelieving panic, opened. "How can she say that?" I wondered, even though I already envisioned myself with only two children because I didn't want the lumpy, blue varicose veins that mom and Delphine covered in makeup and elastic stockings. Mom had a daily routine where she lay on the double bed with her feet up the wall to reverse the flow of pooling blood in her legs. After a few minutes, she pulled on her heavy elastic stockings. She started at her toes and rolled the tightly compressed fabric over her heels to the top of her thighs, then attached the stocking with garters.

Two of my father's sisters, who did the right thing and married Catholics, chose abusive alcoholics and tended broods of eight and ten. The one sister who married a Protestant in a "mixed marriage" had only three children. When I was nine, our family travelled to join Dad's family in Dawson Creek, where one of his brothers would be ordained a priest. One afternoon, cousins Vicky and Donna and I slipped under the long, checked tablecloth and crammed ourselves around the centre post of the dining room table. We had just settled when the aunts came in. They brought their tea, pulled back the chairs, sat down and began to talk. We were ringed by stubby heeled, black shoes that laced up just below the ankles. Sensible shoes built for durability and economy. Some legs ended in white ankle socks and some were covered with carefully darned elastic stockings. One pair of feet wore slippers. They traded stories of childbirth, hemorrhoids, broken sleep, fatigue and babies' fevers. I heard my mom say, "Having two children is just playing house. After three, you have a family." The conversation intensified, accompanied by clucking and *tsk, tsk* sounds directed towards the anonymous selfish women who had only two children. Then one aunt accidentally kicked me—we were discovered under the table and chased out of the room.

My Aunty Joy, married to Mom's only brother, Lawrence, had just two children. I longed to live in her spacious house because it seemed calm, tranquil and orderly. I also knew she was a Protestant and that Lawrence had "left the Church" to marry her. From Sunday sermons I knew that "left the Church" was a powerful phrase, laden with sorrow, loss and disbelief. I loved Lawrence, the best of uncles, who liked jokes and played Swing music on his clarinet, or accordion, or piano. When I was eight, I also suspected that he played Santa Claus at our Christmas celebrations.

Aunty Joy worked in a pharmacy before she married Lawrence and that gave her extra powers to bandage a cut or to apply just the right amount of calamine lotion to a sunburn. Without words, I also knew that being a pharmacist's assistant and a Protestant meant she knew how to have just two children. When she became pregnant with her third, I was shocked. I thought, "Only Catholics can have more than two kids." She upset my spiritual certainties.

A New Way of Seeing: Evaristo

Evaristo Phiri, one of the few Zambian teachers on staff, taught history. He was about fifty, spare of build, lanky and languid in his movements. By coincidence, in the first term of 1971, Evaristo and I both taught night school in town and met randomly as we walked to and from our classes.

At night school, I taught English as a Second Language to men who would never find a place in secondary school. They worked for local government as clerks, messengers, or janitors. Our classroom was a government office, large enough to hold a dozen people. Oil lamps hung on metal hooks drilled into the ceiling. Their light was skim milk pale. The pitted blackboard, mounted on a wobbly easel, crumbled the chalk so quickly the floor was covered in snowy dust by the end of the class.

I felt I was in a sentimental movie where the passionate teacher comes to Africa to teach grateful, driven students. I have never before nor since taught anyone so dedicated. Their eyes never left my face. Each of the men was polite, respectful, and listened with intense concentration. Their belief in English as the unquestioned key to a better life was so strong I began to feel like a fraud, unable to deliver their dream.

After class I walked home in the dark. My flashlight spilled an oval of yellow light in front of my feet, the Southern Cross shone above me, and the dark shapes of trees and low buildings filled the periphery. A whiff of tobacco smoke and the hot red spot of a cigarette tip told me Evaristo was heading home too. Sometimes he walked beside me for a while. I learned he was a rambling philosopher. "We are created equal, but it is always war, war, war. We do not learn."

I didn't wonder about his story, where he came from, how he got an education, or why he became a teacher. His presence gave me comfort, made me feel settled and at home. It took time for me to realize he reminded me of my French Canadian uncle, Alec. He smelled like Alec, moved like Alec, and talked like Alec. Had he been a soldier like Alec?

One night he saved my toes. I was walking home wearing open-toed sandals, scuffing up dust and looking at the stars. I heard, "Hmph!" and Evaristo materialized beside me, his flashlight beam steady on the ground in front of me, where a six inch black scorpion arched the curved lance of its tail over its back, just a hand's breadth from my toes. I blurted "Oh!" and stepped back. Evaristo drew on his hand rolled cigarette and its red tip brightened. We walked side by side for a few minutes before he veered off towards the beer hall.

I began to realize our human variations of character are universally shared.

THREE LETTERS: HOW I SPENT
MY CHRISTMAS HOLIDAY

"Dear Tom," I wrote to my brother during Christmas holidays at the end of our fourth school term,

> In some ways nothing ever happens here. Sometimes six of us will sit down for beer or tea in the late afternoon and realize we have absolutely nothing to talk about except school. In other ways it's like watching a drop of pond water under a microscope—a small world with lots going on.

I wrote about our attempt to sleep in on the first day of the holiday. Bedford had travelled to see his family in Chitipa and we didn't need to be up and alert for his early morning start. But not all the students had gone home yet, and at seven in the morning there was a knock on the door. Wayson, one of Larry's Bee Club students came to tell Larry that he and his friends had cropped a large beehive the night before. Did Larry want to look at the honey?

Both of us decided to get up. We ate the remains of our last box of corn flakes and then went to check out the honey harvest. On our way, tall, angular Bill, the new American teacher, stopped us to ask advice. He said his hens had stopped laying and his rooster had become impotent. As we talked, three students walked past and Bill called them, "Come on over. I'll take your picture." Bill pretended to take dozens of shots using a broken camera. The boys posed and hammed it up. Then Bill opened the back of the camera and pulled out a long snarl of old movie film. At first the boys examined it seriously, then one of them shook his head and said, "But Sir, you have cheated us," and everyone collapsed into laughter.

We said goodbye to Bill and found Wayson and his gang with their honey. Larry pronounced it fine work, and the boys gave us a chunk of honeycomb. They planned to sell the rest in town.

Hans and Lisbet walked past. They invited us back for coffee as it was now midmorning. We drank coffee, ate honeycomb, and pretended the wax was chewing gum.

I ended,

> Larry went off to play tennis before lunch. In the afternoon he built water troughs for the chickens at the school farm. Later in the day we stopped for tea with Ben and Doreen.

To my thirteen-year-old sister, Theresa, I wrote another aerogramme.

> We had a party here last night. The first sweet corn was ready, so we had a feast of that along with meat loaf and rice salad. Then we played canasta and the guys drank beer. We taught the Russians how to play Monopoly, and they are still crazy about it.

I went on,

> Sonia is having a party and she asked me to bring a pizza. I bought the olives in Ndola (seven hundred miles away), and the tomato sauce in Malawi. Ben is bringing the cheese from Lusaka (five hundred miles away). More than pizza, the things we crave and can't find anywhere are Miracle Whip mayonnaise, Kraft peanut butter and Heinz ketchup.

At the end of the same Christmas holiday, I wrote to my parents,

> Sonia and I painted a dingy classroom to brighten it up. Dad, I'm sure glad you taught me how to paint a wall. I'm the only one on staff who knows how to go from prep to cleanup. When the painting was done, Larry and I drove to Malawi to get the car fixed. After that we went south to camp at Salima on Lake Malawi.

I described how we sat on the beach and watched square-sailed boats that made me think of Christopher Columbus's ships, carrying their cargo of dried fish packed in six-foot reels wrapped in plastic, sticks and twine. The next morning, we rented a canoe with another couple and paddled out to an island two miles offshore.

> We found thousands of cormorants, fish eagles, grebes and kingfishers. What a glorious whirr when they took off! When we pulled the canoe onto shore, we disturbed twenty green-scaled monitor lizards, each about six feet long. I felt like I was Charles Darwin arriving in the Galápagos.

Then I reminded my mom of our first Christmas party in Lundazi the year before, and how the story had spread and many people wanted to celebrate together again this Christmas. I planned a way to host thirty guests. David agreed to collect turkeys from Chipata once more. Joyce offered the ovens in the school kitchen. By Christmas day the guest list had ballooned to sixty-eight and we ended up serving dinner in the school dining hall. The turkeys didn't have enough ice on the long trip from Chipata and they were slightly off. Everyone seemed to have a great time though, and no one got sick, but I didn't get a chance to sit down and eat anything. Larry told me he would drag me off to Malawi next Christmas if I tried anything like that again. We could not know that we would in fact spend the following Christmas in Malawi, as far away as possible from Lundazi, the school, and everyone in it.

I closed my letter home by listing, in mock horror, a week of dinner invitations every night of the week leading up to the beginning of the new term. And so, at the zenith of adventure and camaraderie we began to talk about extending our contract.

TRANSITION

When the school year began in January 1971, we had completed four teaching terms and had two more to go before our two-year contract would expire in August, around the same time as our first child would be born. Our letters home reflect our ambivalence about returning to Canada. (There is nothing there to hint that I was concerned about travelling with a newborn.) We had some romantic ideas about homesteading and asked our parents many persistent but vague questions about the price of land in northern BC. My grandparents and great-grandparents had homesteaded in Quebec and on the Prairies. Larry came from a line of farmers in England, documented back to the 1600s in the Vale of Evesham. My personal farming experience amounted to planting flower borders for my mom, weeding my father's tomato plants and a year of managing our vegetable plot in Lundazi. On the other hand, Larry had grown up on a small farm and was finding the work on the school farm deeply challenging and satisfying.

We were still interested in the stories of farming communes developing in Canada and wondered if living in one of those would be a natural extension of our close-knit Lundazi community. We had always lived with many people, first in our large families, followed by university dorms and then the school compound. However, these imaginings came to nothing concrete and Larry abruptly shifted his thoughts to Papua New Guinea where CUSO had just opened a new program.

Our CUSO field director, Sam, came through Lundazi and stayed with us. Over dinner Larry said, "We've been thinking we're not ready to go back home yet. Papua New Guinea sounds interesting. What can you tell us?"

I listened, becoming more and more disturbed, thinking there was something wrong about bouncing from one personal adventure to another when we were just beginning to develop some roots in Zambia. I cradled my expanding belly and burst into tears, "I really don't want to do that."

Sam said, "Maybe you will be able to think about this more clearly once the baby is here and you aren't so emotional."

I was furious, but just sat and steamed. I hated being seen as emotional and illogical, but it was not the first time my unacknowledged true feelings erupted and broke through what I thought was my usual rational self.

A few days after Sam left, I said to Larry, "We've talked about staying on, renewing our contract. That would give us three years, like the Brits. I could teach part time like Doreen and Joyce did after their babies arrived. Bedford could help babysit. I feel like we are just getting started in some ways. We're having such a good time and we're only just beginning to connect with some of the Zambian staff, like Chris Zulu, for instance."

Larry was willing to consider the idea, as we had no solid option for a return to Canada.

"Well, it means I could see some of my students finish their projects and graduate. Wayson and the Bee Club are working really hard. Now the farm is staffed, we can expand the cotton crop. I'm not really sure about Winterstone, our new ag teacher, but maybe he just needs more time to settle in."

We considered the idea for a few months, and in April 1971 we decided to extend our contract for one more year.

At the end of each term a few teachers finished their contracts and left. The staff, once predominantly British, slowly shifted to a more international mix, but the gaps were always filled, and over the school break, new teachers arrived. Writing home, I listed a tally for the start of our fifth term.

So, the new teachers are:

A Norwegian couple. The wife, Astrid, plays the guitar.
A British couple with a four-month-old who never stops screaming.
A single guy, Pierre, French, super shy.
Winterstone, an agricultural specialist, British, older.

When I wrote the list, I could not anticipate that Winterstone would slowly reset the social structure and tone of the school. Everything we valued about the staff community would disintegrate over the next six months.

In another letter, I note that we started the term with eleven nationalities on staff, but I don't mention the Zambian or South African staff. To me, "nationality" meant "foreigners" like us. As we taught alongside the handful of African teachers, I feel we were mutually respectful, but we confused and often bemused each other. Larry and I were sure we had a better education than they did, and we were still confident that we had much to offer. We had a growing, tentative relationship with Chris Zulu, who was our age. At the time, we didn't think we were segregating ourselves, but we had developed our close friendships when the staff was still predominantly European. It wasn't until our last term that the balance between expatriates and Zambians began to shift, when several newly graduated young Zambians joined the staff. This was in line with the government's plan that foreign contracted teachers would fill the gap while young Zambians undertook teacher training. A few years after we left, the recruitment of European teachers dried to a trickle. Our opportunity to live and work in Zambia as teachers took place within a very narrow window of time.

While we were struggling with our decision whether or not to stay, many of our British friends, including Ben and Doreen, as well as Dave and Joyce, were planning their return home to England, to master's degrees, mortgages and urban living. We didn't really think about what it would be like after our friends were gone.

Graham, single, was another of the new British teachers. He had straight, lanky hair and a slight build. At twenty-one, he replaced me as the youngest person on staff. We enjoyed a shared taste in music, and he was excited that my brother Tom was writing and recording songs back in Canada. Tom had just cut a 45 RPM record with two of his own songs and he mailed us a copy. We didn't have a record player, so Graham brought his around and we listened together. I gained at least one week of fame on staff for having a musical brother with a sound similar to the Beatles.

Pierre, the quiet young Frenchman with only basic English, had chosen teaching over military service in France. The French military made his choice as onerous as possible by sending him to English speaking Zambia instead of any one of the French speaking former colonies in West Africa. We would cross paths with him on the way to and from classes or in town, but he was always alone. Once in a while I wondered what it would be like to be on my own teaching at the school. I felt momentarily sorry for the single men, Graham and Pierre, but never for David who was always launching into a new project.

The new couple with the screaming four-month-old added a new tone to the community. They talked incessantly about how much money they were going to make, a topic that had never come up socially or in the staff room. They were openly terrified of Black people and germs. The mother, who did not teach, kept the baby indoors all the time.

Winterstone's reputation as an experienced agricultural expert preceded his arrival. He had worked in Tanganyika (before independence) and The Gambia. Even though Larry's students had won the President's Medal for the country's highest marks in agricultural science, Larry still felt keenly his lack of teaching qualifications and the sense that he was flying by the seat of his pants from day to day.

Larry asked Winterstone over for a beer soon after he arrived. When he came to our house Larry welcomed him and I stretched out my hand, Winterstone didn't take it. Set off balance, I exclaimed brightly, "We've been really looking forward to your coming." His raised eyebrow and impassive face left me feeling like an enthusiastic, untrained pup.

Within weeks of his arrival, many of the single men, including Graham, began to constellate around Winterstone. Drinking became the purpose of their social life rather than a side story. In the staff room, he was a sardonic raconteur of tales of the "good old colonial days." I wondered if he was the sort of Brit that CUSO had warned us against a couple of years before.

Although he looked like an old man to me, twice my age at 45, he was attractive in a way: well-tanned, slim, with dark hair. He usually wore a white open-necked shirt with the sleeves rolled up, the shirttail tucked into his khaki trousers. His movements were economical and slightly languid. I never saw him smile. He could have been a stand-in for Humphrey Bogart on the set of *The African*

Queen. He was rumoured to have a wife in England who cared for their disabled child.

After Winterstone arrived, Graham began to distance himself from us. I overheard Winterstone teasing him about the mixed blessing of using the slippery interior of a fresh cut papaya for sexual release. "No shame, no shame, just healthy bodily function."

Winterstone also made Pierre the butt of jokes about the superiority of England compared to France. He threw in digs, carefully within earshot, about Pierre's lack of masculinity, as proved by his choice not to serve in the military.

Late on Friday and Saturday nights we could hear Winterstone and his young acolytes singing, swearing and stumbling their way home from the bars. I listened with disdain from my full nest of coupledom and impending motherhood.

Change and transition gave an unsettling edge to the relationships on staff. We knew that Ben, Doreen, Dave and Joyce, our closest friends, had one more term to go. David gave no indication of leaving but through Karoy, he was making new connections in town and we didn't see him as often. Brian and Sonia planned to remain until December, two more terms, so the administration would be stable for most of our contract renewal. Our connection to Nadya and Volodya was still tense in the aftermath of our trip to the Nyika but we hoped it would mend. Ralph and Jo, recently arrived from Wales, were also expecting a child and that gave us some common ground. Once our decision to extend our contract was made, Larry became engrossed with the harvest at the farm and I was overtaken by pregnancy.

In May, the beginning of what would have been our last term, Larry wrote a note to his parents, one that carried more foreboding than we could possibly imagine.

> The social set-up of the school is getting a bit stinky in some corners. There is an anti-headmaster group that loves to complain. Along with a few other couples we've refused to join in the squawk and the result is we are getting cut off from some groups. Oh, lots of staff are leaving in August, so that will change things (actually, most of the non-complainers are leaving).

PREGNANCY

Of the two doctors in Lundazi, Dr. Djury Singham was admired for his passion, compassion and competence. The other doctor, a rotund man, did not fare so well in the stories that flowed through the community and defined the reputations of the two men.

Dr. Djury was about five feet six, fine boned and extremely slim. His hair was wavy black, his skin deep olive brown, and his eyes dark, intense, and piercing. The midwives told us he worked relentlessly, throwing himself into the Sisyphean task of staunching the never-ending flow of need. Patients came to the hospital on foot and by oxcart, often as their last option. Preventive medicine was unheard of and intensive, critical care was the norm.

Tess, the Irish midwife said, "He keeps going by taking 'uppers.' Then it's 'downers' when he gets too wired. I'm afraid he's going to do himself damage."

In his cramped private office the windowsill was lined with protective icons: a statue of Buddha, another of a blue-robed Virgin Mary, a small crucifix, a prayer wheel, a black rosary, Ganesh the elephant God, and Shiva balanced in front of the wheel of creation and destruction. It jarred my sense of how spiritual things were ordered. I thought I was open-minded about different paths of belief, but I saw them as separate expressions that led to a common goal. It had never occurred to me that a crucifix could sit side by side with the Buddha, or that a person in distress could access many paths and appeal to multiple rescuers, redeemers and restorers at once. One reason Dr. Djury may have felt the need for powerful support was because he had come to Lundazi as a family practitioner and had no training in surgery. Early on, I wrote a note home describing how he had to become a surgeon by trial and error, but by the time we arrived he was quite skilled and hardly lost a patient. Based on the stories I heard from the midwives, I trusted him completely long before I needed him as my doctor.

I was determined to not fuss about my pregnancy because the Zambian women who filled the world around me, but with whom I had minimal contact, did not fuss. Larry told me about the wife of a school farm worker who rose at dawn, walked to the hospital, gave birth to her third child and was back in the field hoeing by late afternoon. I thought about my grandmother, Eduardina, who birthed eleven babies in her sod house on the Saskatchewan prairie.

About a year after our arrival, Joyce gave birth to Helena, and Doreen to Zoe. Joyce pushed through pregnancy and into motherhood with her crisp, British, no-nonsense approach. Doreen smoked and told quirky stories of pregnancy and childbirth that she found amusing, tales of children born with extra fingers, conjoined toes, or vestigial tails. I was horrified. Throughout her pregnancy, Ben and Doreen continued their feisty relationship peppered with creative insults and jabbing repartee, augmented by Doreen's repeated complaint that she felt "like a cow." There were no dreamy earth mothers around me. Like the other European mothers, Doreen and Joyce carried on working, supported by "house boys" who took on washing the terry towel diapers or "nappies" when their babies arrived.

In February of 1971, when I passed the three months mark, I wrote,

Dearest parents, you are now prospective grandparents.

By the time I wrote home I had decided not to follow the usual expatriate pattern of moving south to the larger, better equipped hospitals. I continued,

We'll make history in Lundazi because I'll probably be
the first European woman to have a kid in the Lundazi
hospital. Dr. Djury assures me the hospital will be in
good shape by then.

In Lundazi, the expatriate women left when their due date approached. Some flew home to Europe, but most trusted the hospital in Chipata or Lusaka and stayed nearby with friends until their baby was born. I decided to stay in Lundazi. From the sound of my letters, I was impatient with the idea of waiting around in another town for an indefinite number of days or weeks. I planned to teach up to the last minute, settle into motherhood in the one-month term break and return to part-time teaching in September, with Bedford for support at home. Dr. Djury also assured us that Larry could be present throughout my labour and the birth. Lundazi's first time British fathers, Dave and Ben were present at the birth of their firstborns at the hospital in Chipata. Back in Canada, this was still a radical choice, promoted only by hippies and back-to-the-landers.

I wrote to my mother and assured her that all would be well,

> This has to be the easiest place in the world to have a kid. The British women won't tell me horror stories (too understated). Doreen says it was no worse than a bad period cramp. Joyce says it was just terrifically hard work. Lisbet (Danish) said she didn't know it could be so nice. The African women have their babies between breakfast and lunch. Bedford's wife was out in four hours. If anything unexpected happens, a midwife with fifteen years' experience lives next door.

Doreen loaned me Dr. Grantly Dick-Read's *Natural Childbirth,* published in 1942. In 1948, the year I was born, Dr. Dick-Read was hounded out of Britain for his radical beliefs. He moved to South Africa, where he refined his ideas by observing traditional African births. It seemed appropriate that I should read him in Zambia. I studied the charts and illustrations that explained how to change breathing patterns during labour, short and quick at the top of the diaphragm for sharp pain, deeper for the space between contractions. The variations in pain and breathing were illustrated by zigzagging lines that changed in sharpness and intensity of ink.

Wasn't I afraid? I suppose ignorance is bliss. I had memories of the births of five siblings. I knew there were some problems, but as my mother's mantra was "Everything will turn out all right," I reasoned that the whole human race had got here by being born, and there were babies being born in grass thatched homes as far as my imagination could reach. Lundazi's little hospital was tidy and squeaky clean. I knew all the midwives. I thought Dr. Djury could walk on water.

I felt healthy and energetic for nine months. In that time Larry and I had travelled with Nadya and Volodya to the Nyika, flown to Dar es Salaam for a CUSO conference and visited the island of Zanzibar. There was only once I felt constrained. On the beach at Mombasa, Larry said no when I wanted to go on a snorkeling tour. He felt that hauling myself in and out of a boat might be dangerous. I was six months pregnant, but just beginning to show. I sulked on the beach while he went to watch fabulous tropical fish. I still think I could have gone.

We were sure that there were no dangers for us or for the child we were calling "The Kid." Tess, one of several midwives, told me proudly that the hospital had just acquired a hand-held aspirator that could be used to clear out a baby's congested nasal passages after birth. The aspirator, a pair of forceps, and an oxygen tank were the only pieces of equipment in the maternity ward. No drips, no fetal monitors, and no epidurals. I re-read Dr. Dick-Read about the ease and wonder of natural childbirth. I was confident that my experience as the big sister would carry me through anything.

Before Liam, my first grandchild, was born, I was able to follow the progress of his growth by consulting websites that compared the baby's growth with the sizes of various vegetables and fruits. At week seven he was the size of a blueberry; week twelve, a plum; right through to a watermelon just before he appeared as a boy. With Michael, I had a few pages of simple line drawings of a small gilled creature with enormous eyes who grew into a compactly curled-up Buddha with an expression of detached contentment. His thumb was in his mouth, and his feet were crossed at the ankles even though he was packed upside down into a tightening uterus, unaware of his imminent entry into the booming, buzzing, confusion of life. I had great difficulty connecting the line drawings to my own interior. When the fluttering began at four months, I could finally believe that something was happening inside me. Then I put lots of energy into sourcing clothes, blankets and diapers.

At first, I thought I would keep my pregnancy a secret as long as possible, but that didn't last. I told Doreen and she loaned me books on natural childbirth. Veronica, the deputy headmaster's wife, who was expecting again, asked me outright if I was expecting and we traded maternity dress patterns. Then I told Nadya and Sonia. From then on, my letters are relentlessly upbeat and sound like I'm organizing equipment for a military campaign.

> The local shops have plenty of baby soap, talcum powder and baby lotions, but I do need:
>
> 3–4 yards of fabric for sheets
> 2 light blankets
> 1 cotton backed rubber sheet
> 1 dozen cloth diapers
> 6 undershirts
> 2 pairs of plastic pants
> 2 baby stretch suits

These items were listed in letters I wrote from Dar es Salaam en route to the CUSO conference during the April spring break. On a side-trip to Zanzibar we found the perfect wicker baby basket. Our plane ticket said that luggage for babies travelled for free. At check-in, on our return from Zanzibar to Dar es Salaam, I handed over the baby basket, which was stuffed with clothing and a delicate Tanzanian reed fish trap that resembled the traps crafted by native fishermen on BC's west coast. The airline staff looked at the basket and said, "Where's the baby?" "In here," I said, rubbing my belly. A pause, eyebrows raised, then laughter. "All right then." The basket went through for free.

When we landed in Dar es Salaam that night the basket didn't come off the plane with the rest of the luggage. Larry looked out the open door of the airport arrivals area and saw our plane with its luggage bay doors open and our basket sitting on the edge of the bay. "That's it," he said and then he ran across the tarmac, jumped into the belly of the plane and grabbed the basket. That was in the age of innocence before airport security.

En route home through Lusaka, I bought a few baby bottles, rubber nipples, a bottle brush, bibs and diaper liners, all documented in letters home. Doreen offered to sell me her daughter Zoe's baby buggy and diaper pails. She asked her mother to send me diapers from England. British "nappies" were made of thick, looped terry towelling, highly absorbent but difficult to get used to after the thin Canadian-style cotton flannel diapers that needed multiple folds to soak up moisture. Those nappies lasted for years, serving both our sons, and finally ended up as floor rags.

A friend from Ndola sent more used baby items. I loved the idea of collecting baby equipment from all over the world. For my birthday, Larry ordered an electric blender / hand mixer / coffee grinder, with a bowl that I could use for making baby food. This machine also satisfied Larry's love of multiple-use gadgets like Swiss army knives. David brought the blender back from England when he returned from leave there.

We assembled a baby basket. I wrote,

> Dear Mom, we made a kid-bed today. The basket is made of reeds and tree bark. I made a mattress from a piece of foam rubber cut from an old school mattress. The mattress cover is made of brown khaki material given to the school by the Red Chinese when the school opened. I lined the basket with a white cotton Tanzanian kikoi cloth that has a woven purple and yellow striped border. The sheets are second hand from Germany (from our Ndola friends). Larry refinished the stand, which came originally from England and has been used by six babies already. Now it looks like we are ready to play dolls.

My due date kept changing. I wrote home,

> Oh, the doctor says August 24 or July 29 and I say August 7 and the midwife says August 10, so take your pick. I haven't actually talked to Dr. Djury. I heard the dates from Nadya who heard it from Nina (a nurse and midwife) who overheard a conversation at the hospital etc. etc. You can't do anything in this town and keep it private.

Jo, the new home economics teacher from Wales, was expecting just a few weeks after me but she had decided to travel two hundred miles south to the larger hospital in Katete. I wrote home,

> We hardly ever talk to each other about it because she is being all delicate and fainty about it and I am be-

ing tough and growly. It's just a different approach, both cover-ups for the same feelings I suppose, but she thinks I am hard-hearted and callous, and I think she is wishy-washy. So much for giving each other moral support.

On July 25, all the final parcels from the grandmothers arrived on the same day. In a thank-you letter, I wrote,

> We had a great time unwrapping everything. Larry untied all the knots carefully to save every bit of string. We'll iron out the burlap and I can make a wall hanging from it.

BIRTH

I taught until midmorning July 30, when the contractions started halfway through an English lesson on how to write a business letter. That day I wore a blue and white tent-shaped dress that was stretched to the limit. I turned from the blackboard and faced forty teenage boys ready to talk about the different choices for salutations, "Dear Sir," "Dear Madam," or "To whom it may concern," when one student raised his hand, "Madam, you look *somehow....*" I was startled that I was so transparent and that he was alarmed at what he saw. I excused myself, walked to the office to tell the principal that I was done for the day and went home. Riding the energy surge before going full on into giving birth, I finished sewing a nightgown to replace my ragged one.

When Larry finished his classes, the nightgown was done. We drove the mile across town to the one storey brick hospital surrounded by a field of trampled dry grass. The head midwife, Mrs. Mfune, assigned me a bed in the maternity ward. As I expected, I was the only White woman in the room. The other women looked toward me, but no one stared, they just went back to their own business, resting or chatting to each other. Lisbet, the Danish midwife, suggested we walk to get things moving again. We went outdoors to walk around the hospital and across the field of spiky, lion-coloured grass. A galvanized standpipe with a tap stood straight up in the middle of the field like a three-foot-high flagpole. A collection of bricks was laid out in a two-foot square under the faucet to break the flow of the water and minimize mud. Around the field were clusters of bricks laid out in groups of three like a peace sign or a Mercedes hood ornament. The bricks were used to hold a cooking pot over a small fire kindled with sticks and dry grass. The hospital was free to everyone, but it had no kitchen facilities, so the patients' relatives cooked meals for them in the field. I took in all those details calmly, but I was impatient for

Dr. Djury Singham

something to happen. It was not the first time in my life that waiting seemed a waste of time. "It doesn't hurt," I said to Lisbet. "Oh, don't worry," she laughed and even her laugh was Danish accented, "It will!"

The maternity ward held sixteen beds, eight down one side and eight on the other. The beds were on high metal frames, the mattresses almost hip height. Mine sat at the end of the row, near the entry door, shielded for privacy by the only tri-fold screen. The labour room was about twelve steps away, out the door and along the open veranda shaded by a corrugated asbestos roof. On one side, the veranda looked out onto the field. On the other side, doors opened off to the labour ward, the day clinic and small offices. Women sat on the veranda, resting their backs against the brick pillars, relaxing, holding their full, round bellies and chatting with the relatives or friends who stood by to assist them or cook their meals.

When my contractions strengthened, Lisbet settled me into the only labour room, a room large enough for a narrow bed and a table in the corner. Cupboards, made of wood and painted white, hung on the walls. One black oxygen tank stood in the corner. My mother had told me that within a day or two of labour she forgot the pain, couldn't recall it even when she tried. She said this was a protection for mothers but also, "It's a bit of a trick to ensure the propagation of the human race, otherwise there would be no more people." The books I read had not described what a contraction actually felt like, and, thinking back, it is difficult for me to remember. I dove down into darkness, breathed, counted, and pictured the jagged rhythms of the chart lines in Doreen's book. In the gaps, I was able to relax and found it unbelievable that another one could possibly come again. I was aware of Larry behind me and a midwife beside me. Sometimes it was Tess, sometimes Nina, or Lisbet, or Mrs. Mfune. Almost every time I resurfaced into the afternoon light there was a woman on her knees washing the floor. Each time it was a different woman—with a different multicoloured chitenge wrapped modestly around her hips and knees—who scrubbed diligently and listened to me. I realized that the entire cleaning staff was taking turns to wash and rewash the floor as they monitored my performance, compared it to their experience, and tried to discern if White women laboured the same as Black women. Once, a chicken skittered and scrabbled through the open door and shot under my bed. It squawked as the kneeling woman swept it out the door. Soon that bird would be stewed in a pot, balanced over the three-pointed brick stars out in the field, to provide another patient's evening meal.

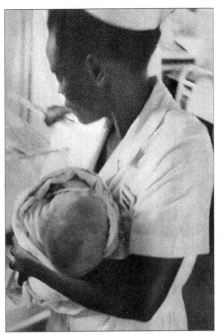

Mrs. Mfune

As the clamping down grew stronger, I was aware that someone had closed the door to the labour room, but in the short gaps between contractions I heard voices outside and the clink of glass that reminded me of beer bottles. Then came the long moments where I thought, "I cannot possibly bear this anymore," followed by another and another and red-hot searing and then my baby was there. I heard a metal weigh scale clank near the end of the bed and the voices of three midwives clustered together. Out on the veranda, a cheer. The chink-chink of beer bottles meeting in a toast. Voices called out, "It's a boy." Dr. Djury came in for a few minutes, pronounced both of us sound and disappeared.

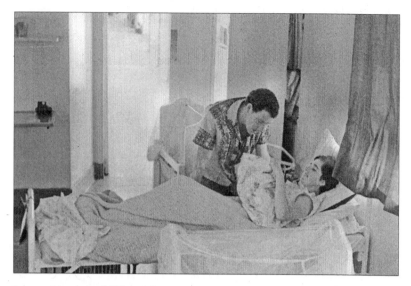

Larry, Mary and Michael

Later, Larry told me two dozen of the teachers had gathered outside the ward. They sat on beer crates and waited for Michael's arrival. Many of them were travelling down to the Luangwa Valley game park that night. As soon as Michael arrived, they cheered, downed their beer, hopped into their waiting vehicles and drove the ninety miles of unlit washboard switchbacks down the escarpment to the game camp. Mrs. Mfune said it was time for me to move to the maternity ward. Earlier in the day I had seen a Zambian woman walk from the labour ward to her bed in the maternity ward. I pulled myself up into a sitting position and swung my legs over the edge. Larry helped me get my feet on the floor. I stood for a moment and then I fainted. There were no wheelchairs, so Larry manoeuvred me into a lawn chair he had brought from home and slid me along the concrete floor from the labour room to the maternity ward. Out on the veranda, two Zambian women lay on canvas cots in the middle of their labour while another one paced up and down between contractions. I don't know which one took my place in the labour room.

In the maternity ward everything about my bed was white—painted white metal frame, white sheets and a thin white blanket. Because it was the cold season, Larry brought a pink cotton blanket from home. (The blanket was a wedding present and it lasted until both our sons left home.) Michael's crib was wood, painted white, short and narrow to fit a newborn but tall enough to make it level with my bed. It was like the cradle I remembered from an illustration for Sleeping Beauty, where the ends swept up to a wooden rod that supported a small mosquito net.

Under every mother's bed except mine was a woven grass mat where each newborn's grandmother slept. These were the grandmothers who gathered in the field outside the hospital to cook cornmeal porridge, boiled greens and even chicken stew. Larry brought me dinner from home, but my excitement cancelled out my hunger. He didn't seem to mind that I just took distracted nibbles of the food he had prepared. Together we did what new parents do and watched our baby sound asleep under the fairytale net. Our world was now a small bubble, with me enclosed in my narrow bed, Larry hunched over the wooden cradle, and Michael cocooned in his blue, lamb-patterned, flannelette blanket sent from Canada. At about nine o'clock, when the ward lights dimmed, Larry left to go home to sleep. Through all the hours of labour while I dove down into pain with my eyes squeezed tight, making red fireworks bloom behind my eyelids, I craved unbroken sleep, sleep without contractions. But that night I was alert, wide awake, unable to believe I was a mother. I stared at a tap dripping slowly into a scratched enamel sink that hung off the wall at a slight tilt, a few feet from my bed. A dented aluminum pot, one baby bottle and a yellow bar of Sunlight soap sat on the sink drainboard. I became aware of the other women. Some, like me, had delivered, and others lay on their backs waiting for their mountainous bellies to erupt. Under the beds, the grandmothers slept or tried to sleep on the hard concrete, with the foreign sound of the hospital generator humming across the field. I wondered if they missed the sounds of cicadas outside their own thatched sleeping huts. Near her head, each woman had a bundle of what I guessed were cooking pots and food wrapped up in a piece of fabric. I tried to imagine my round, pudding-shaped, French-Canadian grandmother cooking me tourtière in the field then trying to fit under my bed.

Mrs. Mfune, the head midwife, arrived pushing a rattling, four-wheeled trolley filled with pills, paper cups and charts. She was almost as thin and wiry as Dr. Djury. She was about thirty-five and I thought she was old. I remember her long, slender fingers and her white, starched, sharply folded cap. Her uniform made crisp, crinkly sounds as she bent over and handed me a paper cup and two pink pills.

"This is for you, Mrs. Bomford."

I swallowed obediently. These were the days when I still trusted pills.

"So. How are you?" (Abrupt stop after "*So.*" Rolled "*r.*" Uptick on "*you.*")

"All right. I guess. I think I want to breastfeed him, but I brought a baby bottle just in case. Is it time to feed him?"

"You do not give him that, isn't it?"

Her English was layered on top of Chitumbuka, her first language.

Mrs. Mfune picked up my baby and placed him in my arms. She matter-of-factly opened my night gown, tickled my baby's lips and enticed him to suckle. Now I was a mother, not just a competent big sister.

"See you do not need that one. The bottle. It is no good." She straightened up, satisfied, as Michael suckled.

At the opposite end of the ward a woman moaned softly. She lay on her back. Her right arm, full and muscular, covered her eyes. This was a woman who chopped wood, pounded grain and hoed corn. I guessed this was a woman who wouldn't come to the hospital unless she feared death more than European medicine. She moaned again, turned her face to the wall and her whole frame abruptly released itself into sleep or unconsciousness.

"Aahh!" said Mrs. Mfune. "That one. Mrs. Banda. She is very bad. Two babies by the stomach and both dead. Do you know Caesarean? She's very sick. Very sick."

I understood that the woman had needed a Caesarean section to deliver her stillborn twins.

Mrs. Mfune lifted Michael's hand and waggled it. "You can be very happy with this strong one. He is looking just like Mr. Bomford." Then she leaned over the trolley handle and wheeled the cart to the end of the ward. My world closed to my baby's kneading fist and searching mouth. Then I fell asleep.

When I woke, Mrs. Banda's mother, the bereft grandmother, stood next to her daughter's bed trying to give comfort. The daughter's moaning grew louder. Mrs. Mfune came through the door at the far end of the ward. She and the grandmother bent over the bed.

Mrs. Mfune left and returned ten minutes later with the doctor, the doctor whose name I have chosen to forget. Dr. Djury had finally gone off duty. The other doctor stood several steps from the bed, arms crossed. He spoke to Mrs. Mfune who replied and explained something with her hands. He grunted and she left. She returned a few minutes later pulling a black, bullet-shaped oxygen tank mounted on an unstable cart whose wheels kept jamming. The doctor stood, unmoving, arms crossed, and watched her. I had the impulse to get up and help her but didn't want to faint and complicate things. When Mrs. Mfune managed to steer the tank over by the bed the doctor muttered orders. I watched her put the mask over the woman's face. The doctor didn't approach the woman and didn't touch her.

I was propped up on my pillow. I tried to close my eyes because I felt like a voyeur. In the low light it was like watching a tableau in sepia played out at a distance. I opened my eyes again and the doctor was gone. Mrs. Mfune and the grandmother leaned over the woman's bed. Mrs. Mfune stood back and her shoulders dropped. She reached over and removed the oxygen mask. The grandmother raised her hands over her head and let out a cry. She turned and walked down the aisle between the beds, pulling at the fabric of her chitenge skirt wrap. She passed my bed on her way out the door as if we inhabited different worlds.

I closed my eyes again. I did not want to believe what I had seen. I had ridden safely through the birth of my first child—never really fearing that anything could go wrong, but the woman at the end of the ward had lost her twins and her life while my baby slept on beside me.

Outside, a deep moan began to rise, accompanied by muffled drums. Through the doorway I saw a line of mourners, women and men, chanting and swaying to the subdued drumming. They passed the foot of my bed, moved down the ward and filled the aisle. They circled the woman's bed. A dozen women in worn-out dresses, with orange, lime green and purple skirt wraps patterned with shields and the president's portrait, swayed and keened in yelps and octave jumps. Men in worn khakis drummed as they walked. I smelled the dust, wood smoke and sweat carried on their bodies.

I rationalized that she had come in too late. Few rural women came voluntarily to the hospital to deliver their babies. The majority who

The mourners

came were the ones already in serious distress. My thoughts were silenced by the drums, the ululating wails and the shifting, rocking bodies lit by the bare, dimmed light bulbs dangling from the ceiling. I felt immobile, as if there were a gauze scrim between myself, the Lucky One, and the Unlucky One. Mrs. Mfune stood against the wall and watched the mourners. She looked fragile, her dark, slightly bowed legs silhouetted against the whitewashed wall of the ward. The crowd flowed around the bed so each person could look at the body and intone, "Ahhh!" One woman, large with pregnancy, lifted her hands, dropped them, shook her wrists and wailed. Eventually Mrs. Mfune gestured, and the crowd turned as one body, one heart, held together by the dulled drum beating, and filed out of the ward. The room went silent, vacuumed out. Just before I fell asleep, I heard Tumbuka voices exchanging goodnights outside in the dark.

In the morning, the blue curtains by my bed drifted into the room, billowing and falling back on a soft breeze that rustled the mango leaves and carried in the dry dust smells of an African winter. The light reflected off the white cradle where Michael slept, knees tucked in and bum in the air. I picked him up and he nursed. The bed at the end of the ward was empty, newly made with fresh white sheets. The black oxygen tank with reluctant wheels was gone.

At the end of the week a crowd of men gathered outside that doctor's house and hammered the cowhide skins of their drums steadily and relentlessly. The doctor was accused of leaving Mrs.

Mfune to handle the oxygen tank on her own, of standing back and not even touching the mother who died. He left town and Dr. Djury remained as the one physician for sixty thousand people.

Larry arrived early and brought cereal topped by strawberries from Nadya's garden. I told him what had happened in the night, but there was no lingering evidence of the chanted grief in my sunny corner. Erik, our Danish neighbour, came to say hello. Erik was tall, very quiet and filled very little space. He was a good photographer and regularly recorded school events. I noticed he had a tiny camera with him, but I didn't give it much attention. Two days later when I was back home, he knocked on our door and offered us black and white prints of the hospital, Dr. Djury and Mrs. Mfune, and ourselves as new parents consumed with amazement. Those photos still trigger gratitude towards Erik whenever I look at them.

We took our baby home the afternoon of his second day and began to create our new family. The school term was nearly finished and someone took over the teaching duties I had totally forgotten about. I slipped happily into breastfeeding. My childhood memories of scrubbing baby bottles sealed that choice. I knew next to nothing of the benefits of breast milk for the baby, but I decided that since it was "natural" like "natural" childbirth, it must be a good thing. My main concern was trying to establish a feeding schedule. Larry's mom sent her well-used copy of *Dr. Spock's Baby and Child Care* from the 1950s, where I read about the need to get the baby on a structured feeding schedule as soon as possible, because a lack of routine at the start of life could lead to a spoiled child and dissolute worker. After a week of frustration, Michael's and mine, I took him to the clinic and asked Mrs. Mfune, "What I should do? He is so hungry after two hours I can't make him wait for three hours. That is what Doctor Spock says is best."

"But madam, this child, he knows nothing of clocks. You feed him when he is hungry."

Her reply captured all the struggles I had experienced trying to live between two cultures. I was reminded again of the traditional dance that mocked the Mzungus—the White men. All the traditional dances except the Mzungu mockery were fluid, electric, dramatic, erotic. The traditional costumes were made of skins, feathers, bells, bottle caps, and re-imagined rags. But for the Mzungu dance the men painted their black faces white and wore pressed white shirts and shorts, and white knee-high socks. The men's huge paper wristwatches and rigid steps backed by a drummer's sharp, mechanical rhythm mocked the controlled spirit of the colonial administrators.

When I dropped Dr. Spock's Western-style feeding charts and followed Mrs. Mfune's awareness of a baby's natural hunger cycles regardless of his culture or colour of skin, Michael and I were both happier. When he cried in the night, I searched with my fingertips for a match to light a candle. His eyes followed the flame. In his twenties, when he explored photography, he often captured images of the small white-gold and blue flickering heart of a candle flame wrapped around its black, calligraphic wick.

A New Way of Seeing: Palms

When Michael was five days old, Mr. Nayar knocked on our door. He was a short, dark, soft-spoken man, one of our math teachers. In his singsong (to my ear) Punjabi accent he said, "Would you be wishing to have the astrological reading for your new son?"

"Oh. Oh." I stuttered, "Please come in."

He sat with Larry while I went into the kitchen to make tea and thought fast about what I would say to him. My dad had forcefully forbidden fortune telling, tea leaf readings, Ouija boards and deciphering palms, because those things would invite the devil's power into our life. My mom blithely agreed that the Catholic Church frowned on such things, but there was no harm in tea leaf reading. When she was a senior student at St. Anne's Academy in New Westminster, she had a Russian girlfriend whose mother, an aristocratic escapee from the Russian revolution, served tea in the afternoons from a samovar then read the girls' fortunes from the leaves that settled in the bottom of their china cups.

I decided while waiting for the kettle to boil that Dad worried too much. I would follow Mom's lead, and so I accepted Mr. Nayar's offer, in the spirit of courtesy and curiosity.

When we finished the ritual of drinking tea, Mr. Nayar gave us a small piece of paper with symbols and script I couldn't understand.

He said, "When your son is sixteen you will take this to a qualified astrologer. He will read it then. It is not good to push a young child towards his destiny. He needs to be of some maturity before he hears his reading. But if you wish, at this time I could read your palms for you."

I thought of the British expression, "In for a penny, in for a pound." I looked at Larry, he nodded, and so we agreed to look into our future.

Mr. Nayar took Larry's hand first and studied his palm. He looked puzzled, then apologized, "I am sorry. I must concentrate. It is difficult for me to read a white hand. There is little contrast in the lines. A dark hand is easier to read."

I found his comment startling and refreshing. It was the first time anyone on staff had spoken directly about the colour of our skin, the most obvious difference each of us carried, the mélange of hues from palest white, through tans and browns to black, the colours each of us lived inside. Mr. Nayar's honesty stayed with me even longer than the shock of listening to him start at the beginning of Larry's life and accurately describe the details of his childhood illnesses, accidents and injuries as they were laid down in the pale skin of his difficult-to-read palm. I felt slightly off-kilter that our hands were deficient compared to darker palms. I became uncomfortably aware of a previously unacknowledged, unheard voice inside me that had quietly assumed white was best.

Mr. Nayar rested my open palm on top of his own. There was a light intimacy to his gesture. We had never touched before, not even to shake hands. My skin, a soft mix of pink and yellow underlaid with the hint of blue veins, didn't offer any contrast in the lines that revealed life, heart and fate. I noted that the skin of his soft brown palm darkened in the creases and provided strong, definite life lines that told a clear story. He took a moment, ran his index finger over my pale palm, then cupped my hand and bent it slightly to enhance the lines he was ready to decipher. I don't recall what he said about our futures—he said nothing of the turmoil approaching in the coming months. What I do remember was a certain relief and lightness that no divine or demonic retribution followed. The sky didn't fall, the devil didn't appear. Instead, a gentle human exchange occurred. For the first time, I could appreciate and wonder at the mystery held in the lines of our palms.

FATHER ZELLER

Father Zeller shone. In my life I have met only three people who carried such a warm glow that I wondered if they might be luminous in a darkened room. Father Zeller's face was open, his eyes clear—without wariness, calculation or defensiveness—the adult face of a well-loved child. He was Swiss, and I pictured him growing up in the high, clean blue air of the Alps, like Heidi, my favourite childhood character.

In late July, when Michael was four weeks old, Larry started talking about Michael's christening and who would perform the ceremony. I had entered marriage determined that religion, with its hidden traps, barbs and convoluted rules would not sit as a barrier between the two of us. We had chosen Father Ryan, the Catholic chaplain from our university, to marry us in my family's parish church. We couldn't use the tiny Anglican church of Larry's childhood that stood near his family farm because it had been hoisted up and trucked one hundred miles to Port Renfrew a few years before. We adapted the basic Catholic ceremony to include readings from Saint-Exupéry's *The Little Prince*, "It is only with the heart that one can see rightly. What is essential is invisible to the eye." And from Margery Williams' *The Velveteen Rabbit*, "By the time you are Real, most of your hair has been loved off, and your eyes drop out and you get loose in the joints and very shabby." A few years later, the Church declared these kinds of adaptations were "non-scriptural" and were no longer allowed.

Before the ceremony, Larry signed the pledge that he would help bring up our children as Catholics—there was no other option if we chose to marry in my childhood church—but I didn't think that a promise under pressure counted.

For a few days I resisted Larry's wonderings about a christening. Did I want to burden our son with the complexities of a religious denomination? Larry, I was to learn ever so slowly, held more to tradition than I did. Despite his political opinions, which my parents considered near-communist, he enjoyed ceremony, respected the institution of the monarchy, honoured the soldiers of both World Wars and took promises seriously.

Every missionary we knew in the vicinity of Lundazi, except one, was a Catholic priest. Reverend Denny was a Presbyterian pastor working for the Church of Central Africa Presbyterian, in a direct line from the mission founded by David Livingstone on the shores of Lake Malawi. The Reverend and his family were recruited from Northern Ireland, and his sympathies seemed to lie with the Orangemen and other anti-Catholic factions in the Irish Catholic battles with Protestant England. I was not so rebellious against my own heritage as to turn to the other side, so if Michael was to be christened, it would be baptism in the Catholic Church.

Father Zeller taught RK, or religious knowledge to the Catholic students at the school. His main work was that of parish priest for the Catholics of Lundazi township, and he lived next door to the church. He would ride to the school on his small motorbike, teach his classes, then return to his work in town. He didn't hang about the staff room or socialize much with the staff, but everyone respected his calm, almost serene presence. He would greet us as he strode across the campus wearing his grey safari suit—a short-sleeved shirt with useful buttoned pockets over loose cotton trousers. He always wore socks with his sturdy European woven leather sandals.

I liked Father Zeller's warmth and gentleness, so we decided to ask him if he would baptize Michael. He agreed, but then we asked, "But could you create a baptism service where everyone on staff would feel welcome? You know them all: the Buddhists, the Hindus, the Anglicans, the Christians and the Muslim Zambians, even the Russians?"

"Yes," he said.

We asked Doreen to be godmother as I was already godmother to her daughter, one-year-old Zoe. Ben, who had hated his harsh Jesuit schooling, said he wouldn't come. The Russians also apologized in advance.

The three photos we have of that day show a spare, simple church interior lit by arched windows of plain glass. The walls are painted with colours pulled from the Zambian flag. The sanctuary has a soft, orange-tinted glow and the walls in the area for the congregation are a light green. Orange in the flag symbolizes Zambia's soil and mineral wealth and green stands for its lush green grass in the rainy season. The walls are highlighted with paired stripes of red and black—black for the people of Zambia and red for their struggle for freedom. I didn't understand these connections until recently when I studied the photos to spark my memory of that day. The altar is made of two-by-fours, painted black. The baptismal font is a large clay pot, made by a local potter, and it sits on a low table covered with a scrap of tree-patterned fabric I had left over from our living room curtains. Given Michael's future life with plants, the trees seem a good omen.

In the photo, Father Zeller wears a white robe that drifts above his ankles and exposes his trademark white socks and leather sandals. Over the light robe is a white tunic with a slightly crooked hem that reaches mid-calf. The sun falls on his left side and lights up his face and garments. The tunic is like a storybook embroidered with the symbols I was familiar with from my childhood: three interlocking circles representing the Trinity and eternity; a cross above wavy lines for water, life and baptism. On a white stole draped around his neck is the early Christian symbol for Christ made of the Greek letters chi and rho, looking like an X overlaying the tail of a capital P. There is also a stylized flower with the petals resting on the Trinity triangle and the stitched Latin words in square, capital letters: IN NOMINE PATRIS, ET FILII, ET SPIRITUS SANCTI. In the name of the Father, the Son and Holy Spirit.

Despite eight years of Catholic school, I didn't know at the time of Michael's baptism that those particular words had to be spoken aloud by the priest in order for the baptism to be valid. At twenty-one I did know that Larry and I were able to marry in a Catholic ceremony because Larry had been baptized as an Anglican. I did not know that it was these specific words spoken in both the Anglican and Catholic rituals that made his baptism real in the eyes of the Catholic Church—so he did not have to become a Catholic in order for us to marry in my family's church.

The last detail I notice about Father Zeller's garments is a rosary that hangs around his neck. It is much larger than the personal rosaries I recall from my childhood. Those could be held in the palm of your hand. Father Zeller's has white beads and its wooden cross rests in the centre of his sternum. The rosary raises contradictory emotions in me, along with memories of tedium. I can still feel myself propped against the back of the church pew, kneeling on the padded red church kneeler, rosary dangling from the seat in front of me. I knew the drill. Repeat the Hail Marys in groups of ten, take a break, say an Our Father and start over again through five cycles of repetition as lethargy pulled me into near-sleep and the sun shone outside. By the age of twelve I started to see the ritual and the symbols as ends unto themselves that distracted from the simplicity of Christ's teaching to love one another. Recently, a friend not raised in the Christian tradition, surprised me by describing her awe of European cathedrals. She explained how the statues, the incense, the stained-glass images, all told stories to pre-literate people and how these were the visual reminders and teaching points of their faith. I can see now that Father Zeller wore these things with sacred intent, displayed for a community of pre-literate people living in an oral, musical tradition. Today, priests do not wear rosaries around their necks. Pop stars like Madonna wear them or just the cross minus the beads, dangling between breasts or swinging across muscled pectorals. I wonder what power the cross will have when no one remembers a rosary. I admit to a sense of disturbance recently when my niece used tiny pliers to pick apart old rosaries and transform them into earrings. I realized that a sense of the sacredness of some objects still rests within me and might explain why my great aunt's rosary from her prairie convent school days in the early 1900s sits on the windowsill over my desk. It is tangled up with other treasures: stones, beach glass, seashells, and the bleached skull of a crow.

We thought that Father Zeller was very old, probably one of the oldest people we knew in Lundazi, but the man in the photo might be in his late forties. In the photo he is shorter and stockier than I recall. I remembered him as taller, slimmer, more ethereal, closer to Dr. Djury in build. The two occupy a space of near saintliness in my memory: Dr. Djury fills it with burning intensity and Father Zeller with glowing serenity.

Doreen, hair pulled back in a ponytail, wearing her perennial sunglasses and a short yellow sundress, stands beside Father Zeller and holds a burning candle. Larry and I, as honoured parents, are seated at the front on folding green plastic lawn chairs. Our guests are on wooden stools. Included in the photo frame are Astrid, one of the new teachers, and Veronica. There is a glimpse of the face of one of the East Indian teachers and someone with sideburns, maybe Duncan.

In the last photo, Father Zeller is leaning over Michael to give him his name, Michael Kondwani Bomford: Michael the light-filled archangel; and Kondwani, which means "Let's be happy" in Chitumbuka, chosen by Bedford as Michael's African middle name. His last name, Bomford, represented generations of farmers, some long rooted in England, others spread across the Commonwealth.

After the ceremony, Ben and the Russians joined everyone back at our house for tea. It was the biggest crowd we'd had in our home since the first Christmas when we had squeezed two sittings of Christmas dinner into our living room. It was also the last gathering at our house. We didn't know—couldn't imagine—that it was the end of the peaceable kingdom. Within days, Ben and Doreen, and Joyce and Dave were about to set off, each couple in their road-worn station wagons, for a land and sea return via South Africa and India to their homes in England. New staff would replace them. We would stay to see the players in our world change and our vision of our peaceable kingdom shatter. When we were all squeezed into the living room and the tea and beer were flowing, Father Zeller arrived. He accepted a mug of tea, stayed standing, and chatted quietly. Then he waved goodbye, stepped out through our bamboo fly curtain and returned to his life in town.

THE DEBT OF WATER

When Michael was about seven weeks old, we took him on his first trip south to Chipata. We needed to stock up on groceries before the term began again in September. Our list included an array of things, from fragrant basmati rice in its dusty hessian sack to four-ounce cans of tinned pilchards in tomato sauce. We carried only one other shopping list—David needed some bolts and AA batteries.

As always, Larry drove. When Michael was awake, I sat him on my lap and when he was asleep, I lay him in his travel bed in the back seat. It was a usual sunny day in early September as the cool season waned and the heat hinted its return. Many trees were leafless, and tall, tawny grasses waved dry, bleached seed heads. The road was its usual rutted, orange-red corrugated gravel. For a while we followed a grader that scraped up russet clouds with its slanted blade. We cranked up the car windows and pulled past the roaring machine, but the rusty dust sifted through the vents. I untwisted the cap on our white plastic water bottle and moistened the corner of a flannel blanket to clean Michael's face and hands. The sight of water reminded Larry and I that we were both thirsty, so we shared the remainder of our bottle of orange Fanta and ended up with sticky hands, which we cleaned by dampening the edge of the small blanket again. By now we were sixty miles from home. We had sixty miles to go, with about one cup of water left that we both wanted to drink, and it had just become obvious that Michael needed a diaper change. It was well over another hour to Chipata, on a road with no towns, no villages, and no services of any kind. We drove on. While Michael was happy to breastfeed and didn't care that he was smelly, we became desperately thirsty.

A few miles on, I saw a small, arrow-shaped sign attached to a stick pointing off the road to the right. I turned my head and read "Kawinga Mission" as we passed it. A few hundred yards further,

Larry braked, stopped and U-turned. We went back and turned off the main road onto a winding one-vehicle track, following the contour lines between leafless, spiny bushes that scratched and clattered along our Toyota's fenders and doors. Five minutes of cautious, slow driving brought us to a group of buildings: three basic houses built of concrete blocks, a shed with corrugated asbestos roofing, a structure that could serve as a classroom or a church space, and a large galvanized water tank raised up on a platform about fifteen feet off the ground. We stopped and got out of the car. I carried Michael on my hip and, feeling like an intruder, tentatively walked around one of the houses looking for the front door. I heard soft, young voices. In the shade, around the corner of the house, two boys, about five and seven years old, were crouched over a game in the dust. A series of holes the size of soup spoons scooped in the dirt were dug out in a pattern like a large egg carton. Each child took turns dropping little stones into the holes and counting, then the other boy dropped his stones in, took out some of his partner's stones and moved on to the next hole. It looked like a cross between Snakes and Ladders and Chinese Checkers.

The younger, pale boy, had straight hair the colour of dry season grass and the older, dark boy, had tight-twisted black hair. They leaned in together, their shoulders brushing comfortably as the young one reached to move his stones. They shifted back onto their heels, looked at us, then turned away and kept playing.

We found the front door of the house. It was open and Larry knocked. I heard flip-flops, then, a woman appeared. She looked a few years older than me and wore a sleeveless, washed-out cotton dress. Her straight, light brown hair was tucked behind her ears and she had a pleasant, no-makeup face.

"Well, well. Hello, hello. Welcome. Welcome. What can I do for you?" British accent, not posh.

"I really don't want to bother you, but we're on our way to Chipata and we've run out of water. We just didn't realize how much we needed for three of us. Could we borrow some?" I hitched Michael up on my hip by way of explanation and tried to hide my embarrassment at my lack of planning.

Asking favours did not come easy to me. My Grandfather Charlie had drilled into me, "Pay your bills on time and don't ever be in

Mary and Michael

a position of owing anyone." He was the most generous of souls, but you could not do anything for him or give him anything. His daughter, my mother, quoted Shakespeare, "Neither a borrower nor a lender be," and made sure we did not beg sweets off neighbours or wheedle presents from our grandparents. At this moment, thirsty and sticky-handed, I didn't think of the absurdity of asking to "borrow" water.

"Come in, come in."

The woman waved us in and invited us to sit. Her living room was similar to ours: concrete floor polished with the usual red floor wax. Metal door frames, designed to frustrate termites, led to the bedrooms and a kitchen. There were easy chairs and a simple wood-frame settee holding foam rubber cushions covered with a faded geometric print that matched the sun-bleached curtains. On the wall there were two pictures: one of an English countryside featured breeze-blown apple blossoms floating on a sparkling stream; the other a Zambian tourist poster of an elephant head-on, tusks raised, trunk erect. A closed bible rested on a doily covered round wooden side table. I sat on the edge of the settee bouncing Michael up over my shoulder while Larry sat back into one of the easy chairs. The two boys' voices chattered on in Chitumbuka outside the window. It was hard to tell which voice belonged to the Zambian child and which belonged to the English child.

The woman came back carrying three glasses of water on a wooden tray. Three cookies, the kind that never ran out in Lundazi's shops—round, beige biscuits stamped with curlicues, sandwiching bright yellow icing—sat on a blue, chipped saucer. I babbled on, apologized for the imposition and explained how we'd left behind our extra water jug. She brushed that aside and asked, "How old is he? Such a strong little man." I asked if I could change him. She showed me the washroom and gave me two well-worn towels. I lay him down on the blue one and damped the edge of the beige one in the sink. The water that flowed over my hands and wrists, and the suds from the thin, yellow cake of soap were pure luxury.

The cookies and glasses of water waited until Michael was freshly diapered and tucked into the wedge of the settee beside me. While we drank the water and ate the biscuits, the woman sat easily with us as if she had all the time in the world. When we stood to say goodbye, I said, "I'm so sorry we can't repay you."

"But you don't repay me. You just give it to the next person."

Over the next few days I thought about what she had said.

We had become accustomed to the closed loop of the school's exchange system: flour borrowed, flour returned; dinner invitation accepted, a meal returned; shopping lists exchanged. I had Grandpa's example of always giving and refusing to receive.

I began to see the possibility that generosity, acceptance and gratitude could be an open, flowing economy, free of balance sheets and obligation.

I did not need to be concerned about debit and credit cancelling each other out for a balance of zero, nor about controlling generosity. Instead, I could pass it on without calculating its next move.

RIOT: SEPTEMBER 1971 TO NOVEMBER 17, 1971

For years afterwards, I glossed over it if anyone asked. I minimized its impact and jammed it concisely into a nutshell, "There was a riot at the school. Some of the staff blamed us for starting it along with the students. We moved to Southern Province and began one of the best jobs of our life."

The September term of 1971 began quietly. Larry was intensely involved with his teaching, his students and their projects at the school farm. I worked part time, teaching three classes a day. Bedford looked after Michael while I taught, and I scheduled my lessons so I could take the five-minute walk home to breastfeed Michael. Bedford's cousin, Peter, who worked for the Danish couple, Hans and Lisbet, minded their newborn son, Seka. Peter had helped Hans and Lisbet choose Seka's name, which meant "let's laugh" in Chitumbuka. Every morning, Monday through Friday, Bedford and Peter settled the two very blonde babies, Michael and Seka, into their pushchairs and walked through the school campus to visit the other "house boys" and check out the small details of Lundazi life: the chickens, the dogs, and the progress of vegetable gardens.

As we devised new routines for home and school, we were surprised to miss some of the old ones. After Dave left, we realized that he had been the constant catalyst for social get togethers, and no one filled that gap. Larry missed the rapid-fire repartee with Dave and Ben. I didn't recognize, until she left, how much Doreen had been part of my day. I missed how she would pop over to show me odd things—a dead beetle with metallic wing covers that reminded her of cloisonné—or how I could knock on her door to get a translation from a British cookbook, "Why is this called flapjacks when it looks like oatmeal squares, not pancakes?"

A very quiet, single Brit moved into Ben and Doreen's house. We rarely saw him, not even in the staff room. Three new Canadian CUSOs, a couple and a single woman, joined the staff. These four replaced Ben, Doreen, Dave and Joyce. As a new mother with two years of Zambian experience, I felt they were young and naive. What I didn't recognize in myself was that I was feeling detached from the school and preferred to be at home with my new son.

Our connections with the Russians were warming, but still cautious. David was independent of Winterstone's group and spent most of his social time in town. Sonia and Brian would complete their contract in December, the end of the term. In preparation, Sonia stopped teaching and spent her time preparing for their departure. Many of our everyday, taken-for-granted friends had disappeared or changed.

I tried to visit with the mother who feared germs and Africans. Her child was almost one year old. When I brought Michael over, she rushed me inside and slammed the screen door to keep out insects. (There were very few insects except during the rainy season.) As I left, when the short, awkward visit was over, the woman screamed at me for my lackadaisical, uncaring, dangerous parenting. "How can you leave your baby with that uncivilized Black man and let him drag your child around the schoolyard. There are filthy wild dogs everywhere. They might have rabies. And you don't know who will touch him, where their hands have been."

Early in September, after a weekend of drinking, the other agriculture teacher, Winterstone, forgot to check the temperature on the incubator and a clutch of chicks died. After that, he began to whistle softly in the staff room the tune of the WWI song, "How Ya Gonna Keep 'em Down on the Farm (After They've Seen Paree)?" He diverted a substantial portion of the agriculture budget into the purchase of test tubes, which he donated to the chemistry class. "To real science," he said. "What these kids really need are accounting skills and commercial skills to get them out of the villages and into the cities."

Conversation between Winterstone and Larry had become increasingly tense and unproductive since his arrival eight months before. Even more unsettling than Winterstone was the dramatic arrival of Leon Holsey. As I left my afternoon classes I would sometimes catch a glimpse of him striding across the campus in a full length blue and white batiked West African traditional robe. Holsey, a Black American, taught history.

Within days of his arrival the staff room buzzed:

"The man has an avocado coloured fridge and stove. Why would anyone want ugly green appliances?"

A few days later, Duncan, another history teacher, gloated:

"My house boy tells me Holsey's appliances are a joke. None of them work. They are American; they won't run on the school's wiring system. He'll have to get the standard white British models if he really wants appliances, but they won't be much use of course. Hasn't he got it figured out that there's no electricity except in the evenings? What does he think the kitchen wood stoves are for? How useless will an electric refrigerator be when we only have power in the evening?"

The students supplied more fodder for the rumour mill and Grant reported:

"The kids are talking. They say that Holsey travels to nearby villages on the weekend and hands out wristwatches and American dollars."

The teachers asked more questions. Suspicion grew. Coffee breaks became the opportunity to update and analyze Holsey's actions.

"Where did he get the money to ship those appliances here? Is he rich or does he have funding from some American group with deep pockets? What's he really here for? Who does he actually work for?"

Holsey's history classes were loud and raucous. Some teachers swore they had seen him teach the kids the fisted Black Power salute, "Say it loud, I'm Black and I'm proud." His accent was Baltimore-tinged. He avoided contact with the White teachers. He traced his roots to West Africa and claimed he had the right to wear West African traditional garb. His outfit was unlike anything worn in Zambia, a country with seventy-two different languages and dozens of different tribal cultures. He seemed to consider Africa one country, a unified embodiment of like-minded peoples. He told our students they were downtrodden victims of colonialism and imperialism and it was time for them to wake up to their plight.

Larry overheard Holsey confront the Zambian staff for wearing what he called "colonial" clothing: shirt, tie, and sports jacket. Holsey ran up against Manyinda, the deputy headmaster, the heir apparent for the position of headmaster when Brian's contract would end in December. Manyinda was much shorter than Holsey. He was also proud, short-tempered and often fell into rages. Holsey argued with Manyinda and called him an Uncle Tom, a reference to the character from Harriet Beecher Stowe's novel *Uncle Tom's Cabin.* During the American civil rights movement, Uncle Tom became the symbol of a Black man who made himself subservient to the White masters.

All these details are cobbled together from third party stories and overheard snatches of conversation. The truth is, wrapped in motherhood and English grammar lessons, I never spoke to Holsey the whole time he was there. Then on November 17, after an especially loud session with the senior level history class, he disappeared. The next evening, the lights went out.

RIOT: NOVEMBER 17

At just past seven in the evening on November 17, I headed across the road from our house to Chris and Amy Zulu's place three doors down. I swept the pale yellow oval of my flashlight beam back and forth over the gravel, on the alert for scorpions that roamed the road after dusk. I had taken only half a dozen steps when, from across the campus, I heard the hum of the school generator shift to a dying drone. The lights in the classrooms and dormitories and in every house along the street faded out. The silence was punctuated by small exclamations of crickets.

Chris Zulu had invited me to visit. He said his wife, Amy, could show me how to cook the wild mushrooms that had popped up everywhere after the first rains. Several times since the beginning of term, Chris had stopped at our place after school. We drank Mazoe cordial and ate lemon biscuits from Mulla's store in town. I don't remember what we talked about—our students? school? soccer? maybe our families? Michael seemed aware of our conversation and babbled along, easing awkward pauses in our adult talk. These times were our first social visits with Chris, even though we had worked together for two years and lived on the same street.

Of all the Zambian staff, Chris was the most urbane, the one who seemed slightly more Western than the others, the one most interested in having these visits and conversations. The Zambian teachers wore dark trousers, sports jackets, and white shirts and ties when they taught. The White male staff, except for the headmaster, wore short sleeved shirts—some made of African fabric—and light khaki trousers. The Zambians dressed in respect for the role and the Europeans dressed to show their freedom from meaningless formality. Chris stepped on the bridge between the two positions. He wore a sports jacket, but occasionally took off his tie. Chris's invitation was my first to the home of a Zambian teacher.

I stood still about halfway across the street, moved the flashlight's beam around my sandalled feet and waited for the lights to come on. I was both excited and hesitant about my visit to Chris and Amy's home, but I wanted to see the familiar glimpses of living room interiors restored, the shadows on curtains, and the clutter on front porches revealed before I took another step. Out of the dark, I heard the babble of many voices from further down the road, close to the homes of the headmaster and the deputy headmaster.

My body turned to the sounds near the deputy headmaster's home and I saw flickers of orange light. I blinked and the flickers turned to flames. I turned again and my flashlight beam found the entrance to our driveway. I ran and my sandals crunched on the grit. The voices burst into shouts as the grass fences around the deputy headmaster's house exploded into flame. I heard the clank of our front door as Larry opened it and said, "Get in here quick. The kids are marching on Manyinda's house."

I bolted inside, straight to Michael's basket in the corner of the living room and lifted him up, even though he was asleep, and clutched him to my shoulder. Larry took my flashlight and together we went from window to window trying to get glimpses of what was happening outside. Close to Manyinda's house, orange flames licked upwards and dissolved into apricot grey smoke. Silhouettes of teenage arms and legs, backlit by the fire, leapt out from the solid shapes of bushes. Somewhere glass broke, feet pounded past our house, and sharp voices called from every direction. Larry lit our kerosene lamp. The blue-white flame wobbled on the cotton wick and cast shaky shadows. I lay Michael back into his basket, where he looked around, solemn but silent. Larry and I went through the house, methodically lifted up the foam mattresses from the beds and propped them against our windows. The idea of leaving simply didn't occur to us. Our car sat useless in the driveway because its battery had been stolen the previous night. We suspected the fellow who ran the school's generator. He regularly borrowed car batteries when the generator's starter battery failed.

When the mattresses were in place, I took Michael into the bedroom and propped him on a pillow on the floor. I sat cross-legged beside him, picked up my guitar and began to sing "Blowing in the Wind." I had taken part in many sit-ins at university and had watched hours of black and white TV coverage of the US civil rights protests. I knew the routine: protest, sit down, sing. Uprisings and guitars were inextricable. I sang to calm Michael and myself. Larry went outside to try to figure out what was happening, then came back inside to check on us. We looked at each other across the dim bedroom, determined to not be afraid.

A loud explosion. The tear gas looked like low, drifting smoke and it seeped in through our windows. I had seen tear gas on the TV news, but didn't know its throat-constricting smell. Now we wanted to leave, but we could not walk into that choking air with a four-month-old infant. As we tried to imagine what to do next, a car pulled into our driveway. Someone jumped out and called us to come, but neither of us remembers who it was. It hadn't occurred to me that anyone would look after us or that there was anywhere to run. I wrapped Michael in a big wool blanket and made a monk's cowl around his face and mine to capture a bubble of clean air. Larry opened the door, led us outside into the drifting grey gas and bundled us into the car. As our rescuer drove, the cylindrical white beams of the headlights captured the dark shapes of students running, the shine of buttons and belt buckles on the uniformed policemen posted at every intersection, then the empty road that led to the police station in town.

I sat in the front seat, Michael on my lap. He leaned into me, his small body held rigid, his wide-open eyes looking up at mine. My eyes were hot and itchy. I wanted to cry but crammed down the urge. My fingers rubbed at the rough wool blanket which was still saturated with the caustic smell of tear gas. I could still hear the pop-pop of gas canisters in the distance. My world closed down to a circle encompassing Michael and the rough wool of the blanket. I wasn't even aware of Larry.

Our rescuer pulled up to the police station where most of the staff were gathered. When I stumbled out of the car, Michael's blanket slipped, and I struggled to wrap it tight around him again. Fear blocked the fact that someone had cared enough to come find us and bring us to safety, but when I looked at the crowd standing in the shadows beside the station, I couldn't identify anyone. I saw only clusters of anonymous white faces. The lenses of the ones who wore glasses reflected white circles of cold light from the car's headlights. I sensed no welcome, no relief, no concern. Even as we walked towards them, my gut told me that, as the last to arrive, we had fallen outside the members of the tribe.

Maybe what I felt was my own fear, and theirs, reflected back at me. I wanted someone to rush forward, someone to wrap me in warm hug, someone to tell me everything would be all right. No one moved.

After that I have only fragments of memory. The dark blue dress I wore that night. An uncomfortable couch. No toothbrush. No diapers for Michael. We spent the night in town at the home of Karoy, David's Dutch friend, who had a spacious staff house provided by the Zambian Tobacco Board. There were other teachers there, but I have no memory of who they were.

We left Karoy's at sunrise. The temperature was already twenty degrees Celsius and climbing. Bedford was at the house when we got home, ready to look after Michael as if it was an ordinary day. We washed up, brushed our teeth and arrived at our scheduled classes for the first period. Many desks were empty. A few windows were broken. Outside, at the corner of each classroom block, stood a policeman in khaki shirt and shorts, black belt, polished round-toed boots, black calf-high socks, brimmed cap, and a semi-automatic rifle over his shoulder. Inside, my students sat slumped and sullen, eyes fixed on their desktops while I taught the structure of an essay. At the end of the first hour of the sham class I received a message—teachers should gather for an urgent staff meeting. The armed guards would remain while the students stayed in their classrooms. A few looked up, eyes dull, they asked no questions, made no objections. No one answered my questions. No one said anything about the night before.

Around the edges of the staff room, some teachers sat on chairs and some slouched on the worn-out couches. Others sat at the tables made of sheets of varnished plywood supported by brown tubular metal legs. From my table I looked out the window and saw the armed guards that held our students in the classroom blocks.

Brian, as headmaster, took his position at the front of the room. Manyinda, deputy headmaster, wasn't present. Brian asked for suggestions as to what action the school should take. Silence, followed by the buzz of side chat, then the geography teacher said, "We can take advantage of this and get rid of all the troublemakers in the school. We can clean them out of here. We can start circulating a list—everyone can add anyone they think is a rabble rouser."

I looked out again at the police, standing motionless in the rising heat, positioned to attack. I didn't wonder where they had all come from and I wasn't amazed that the small, sleepy town of Lundazi could supply so many uniformed armed men. I hadn't learned to ask those kinds of questions yet

One teacher raised his hand shoulder high and called out the name of a Fifth Form student. Another one took his pen from his pocket, flipped a sheet of printed foolscap over to its blank side and began to write. One more kept track as some of the teachers called out the names of every student who had defied them. The list gathered momentum. Six. Ten. Twenty-two names.

My mind drifted back to my ten-year-old self watching a Perry Mason show, the popular lawyer series on early black and white TV. Mason had defended an obviously guilty murderer and I asked my dad why such a smart lawyer would waste time on such a bad man. Dad carefully explained the concept of "innocent until proven guilty." I looked away from the window, focused back on the meeting, and opened my mouth.

"You can't prove all those kids started the riot. It isn't fair to accuse them just because you are irritated with them for other reasons."

The names kept coming. Fifty-four. Seventy. Ninety-nine. The list was complete at one hundred and ten. One in eight students were named and expelled, including those with leadership potential who weren't shy about challenging authority. Each went on the whim of a teacher who decided the student was a troublemaker and deserved expulsion. Some students were ready to write their exams and graduate after five years of high school. Others were about to complete their first year. They were the select cohort of the first Zambians to have access to secondary school. Chris Zulu sat to the side, silent throughout.

As I came out of the staff meeting, I was challenged by Denny, the religious education teacher, the Northern Irish Protestant I usually avoided because of his dogmatic, anti-Catholic views on the Irish Question, "You have broken ranks. You have betrayed your fellow staff members."

Later in the afternoon I joined those who gathered at Astrid's to dissect the riot. Earnestly, naively, I still defended the terrified students who had come to us late in the morning, after the police allowed them to leave their classrooms. I described how twelve-year-old Simon sheepishly told us he had run away from the riot and straight into the sewage lagoon as he fled in the dark. No one paid me any attention. Shoulders hunched up and turned away from me. Groups of twos and threes sat together, elbows jammed down on knees as hands chopped downward gestures, punctuated by the smoking tips of cigarettes. I responded by talking faster. I defaulted to my mother's tactics in the face of disaster: scramble for the positive signs, "It wasn't all the students. Some of them were as scared as us."

Astrid had had enough.

"I think it's time you went home now."

She opened her kitchen door and firmly steered me out by my elbow.

As damages were assessed and compared, it became clear that our house was one of several left untouched—no windows smashed, no fences burned. Within a few days I realized there was a second list, an unwritten tally of staff suspected of collaborating with Holsey to incite the students to riot. Our names were on it. One Russian couple and a Black Guyanan had stayed in their houses. They joined us on the list.

I told myself I didn't care. I folded myself into looking after Michael. Larry spent more and more time at the school farm.

In the staff room: silences. Glances slid away when I approached to speak. Sentences stopped midway when I entered the room. Three staff huddled together on the pathway, laughing. One looked at me, gave a meaningful glance to the other two. They turned and walked away. The science teacher changed his route across the school yard as I approached. The history teacher turned away slowly, deliberately, to give me a good view of his back. Astrid's sudden deafness meant I spoke to the air, again.

Four days after the riot I wrote home:

> Things go back to routine no matter how messed up they get. I've just spent four solid hours putting the house back together. I haven't picked anything up for days. As

I finished, I realized that the kids at school are doing the same. They have spread heaps of washing all over the grass around the dormitory. You can hardly walk from our house to the first dormitory for clothes spread out to dry. We talked to a few kids who ran when the riot started. Lots of kids are walking around with bandaids, proof that the police got hold of them during that night. But just to show that life goes on as usual, one girl came to Larry to get a pass to go to the hospital so she could get her arm bandaged. He asked if a policeman had hit her. No, she had a fight with her boyfriend. Now Michael is awake, his normal hungry self, so I'm going to feed him.

Put a group of people on a boat at sea or in a hotel during a blizzard, toss in a murder and a novel is born. Take a staff compound housing forty teachers, a hundred and twenty miles from the nearest city, spark a riot, and suspicion, fear, and the urge to shun and punish are ignited.

A few days later, I was in the garden, bent over beside the fence checking for ripe tomatoes. Graham was walking home on the path that led past our door. I straightened up and caught his eye by surprise.

"Hi, how're ya doing?"

He walked on, mumbled and examined his shoes.

"Have your classes settled down?"

He stopped, looked at me and blurted, "What the bloody hell is wrong with you? Don't you get it? Haven't you noticed, no one is talking to you?"

"Friends are still talking."

"I don't know who that could be."

He kicked at the gravel and hurried on.

It wasn't true no one was talking to us, but the group I called The Boys, the group that constellated around Winterstone, were definitely not speaking to us and were making sure we noticed. My tactic was to carry on as if nothing was happening—chirpily saying "Hi" to closed faces. I must have been both annoying and confusing to those who made a point of ignoring us.

We felt we were the loose ends, those suspected by the majority. More likely, we were part of the fractured majority targeted by the united minority. In the few weeks that remained of the school term, most of the teachers disappeared into the security of their homes.

Several days after the riot we invited Chris Zulu for a visit after school. We wanted to hear how the event played out with the Zambian staff. He was wearing a tie and sat on the edge of the couch, elbows on his knees, hands tightly clasped. We prodded him with questions. What did he know about Holsey? How had Holsey interacted with the students? Did Chris know who the student leaders were? Finally, in response to our insistence, Chris rose and told us calmly and firmly, "You cannot understand the situation because you are White."

Sound stopped. I felt hollowed out, my lungs cold. A roar of resentment raged inside my head. I thought, "You do not see me. You only see my skin. You do not know who I am." I said nothing and kept my face neutral as we said our goodbyes.

A few years later, we learned Chris had been appointed principal of the new secondary school in Chama, north of Lundazi. By that time, I was able to recognize what he had taught me. What it means to be the object of instant appraisal of your capacity, based on the colour of your skin. What it means to hear the soft, polite touch of condescension in the voices of many expatriates. What it means to be discounted by foreigners in your own home.

Escape

The interminable term ended in mid-December, a month after the riot. We still had another four months ahead of us, but for the moment, we escaped. Right after our last classes we went home to pack. I pulled together Michael's portable carry cot, a dozen diapers and three small shirts. We each jammed a few changes of clothing into our duffle bag, and we filled a cardboard box with groceries. Larry tied the canvas water-cooling bag to the front bumper of our Toyota and added three full plastic water bottles to the food box. Then we drove south on the familiar rust-red gravel of the Great East Road to spend a few days with Maggie, a Canadian CUSO volunteer who taught at the secondary school in Chipata.

She welcomed us warmly, "Come in. You poor things. You look done in. The baby looks great. Nothing's bothering him. Put your things in the spare room. That'll give you a quiet spot. I'll put the kettle on, then you can tell me what happened. We've been hearing so many rumours. Not just about Lundazi, other schools too."

Maggie listened patiently as, on that first night, we told and retold the riot story from all angles. We were trying to create a coherent tale that would help us grasp the abrupt changes at the school.

By the next evening, Maggie's house was jammed with more than a dozen people. Each term break, international volunteer teachers from all over Zambia took to the road and used each other's homes as drop-in hostels. Every corner of Maggie's house was stuffed with sleeping bags, duffle bags, and scuffed suitcases. At sunset, the school's generator roared to a start, but twenty minutes later it sputtered and died. Everyone knew that was the signal to dig out paraffin wax candles and jam them into empty beer bottles. We clustered around the light and the brown glass bottles reflected the flicker of candle flames and the red tips of cigarettes. The smoke drifted straight up then twisted into loose coils over our heads in the mildly muggy air. Our young, twenty-something bodies, dressed for the humid hot season, shone golden, sheened with sweat.

On the second night, we retold our story with more objectivity than the first night. Volunteers from the Copperbelt region added reports and rumours of riots in several secondary schools within weeks of Lundazi's night of smoke and tear gas. In all cases there were new Americans on staff. Our stories morphed into speculation these were CIA instigated disturbances. When our theories ran out, we talked of travel plans and snippets of Canadian news.

A man, older than most of us, maybe thirty, a Canadian by accent, moved into the clutch around the candles. He had a blonde brush cut and looked like he worked out in a gym, but there were no gyms in the country. He wore a white shirt and khaki trousers, not shorts. He listened intently, but without expression, to the conversations around him. (I would learn that intense was his only mode.) Then he turned to us and began asking questions about what we did at our school. When Larry told him about the school farm, the man introduced himself as Parker, formally shook hands, and quizzed us more thoroughly,

"What crops do you grow?"

"Maize and cotton, groundnuts and tobacco. Our students won the President's Medal for their high marks and good yields," Larry answered.

"And livestock?"

"Pigs and chickens. As a course requirement, our students learn about and care for the livestock."

I jumped in and chattered away, rambling on about the farm, our students and the dramas of the last few weeks. Parker seemed to be interested, even in the details of the riot. Eventually, I realized I was doing all the talking. I took a breath and asked, "And what about you? Where are you working?"

Parker described the company he administered. "It's a land settlement company, funded by several donors from Canada and Britain. The company subdivides farmland abandoned by White farmers at Independence. The Black farmers were kicked off that land onto reserves in the 1920s. Now Zambian farmers apply, and those that qualify bring their families and cattle and equipment to farm a block of land tailored to their resources." He explained more of the dry administrative details then talked about what a privilege he found it to work directly with Zambians far away from urban influences.

Parker looked at Larry. "There will be a position opening up with the company soon. You might be a good fit."

I was startled at the turn in the conversation, but at that moment Michael woke up, crying and calling from our room down the hall. I sensed that Larry hadn't warmed to Parker and wasn't interested in the hint of a job possibility. As I left to comfort Michael, I handed Parker a scrap of paper and asked him to write down his address. The next morning Parker was gone, but Larry had the scrap of paper in his shirt pocket.

We left Maggie's two days later and continued to travel throughout the Christmas break. We visited other volunteers who had once spread their sleeping bags on our living room floor, and they returned the favour. Finally, we went to a beach on Lake Malawi and introduced Michael to swimming. The holiday couldn't go on forever, but we stretched it to the end and returned to school the night before classes resumed in mid-January.

AFTERMATH

My story about how the world worked and how people behaved changed as we lived through the aftermath of that night. The staff fractured into small units. Nationality became important again. The Russians closed ranks; the East Indians became even more polite and more distant. Winterstone's acolytes pivoted tight around him. The rest of us broke into solitary singles and isolated married couples.

Each day, each and every teacher entered the staff room, picked up the day's notices, and left again to meet their students. Conversations were brief and stilted. When the January term opened, the new thirteen-year-old First Form students were innocent of the previous term's disruption. One hundred and ten of the suspected troublemakers were gone, expelled with no hope of return. New teachers, including several newly graduated Zambians, filled in the gaps left by the teachers who had managed rapid transfers or quit their contract after the riot. My old sense of a delicately balanced cohesion among our staff of many nations evaporated. Staff meetings shifted from argumentative to apathetic and back again. I smelled distrust and fear everywhere. I kept my head down and worked on our escape plan.

I said to Larry, not in jest, "It's getting so miserable around here I wouldn't be surprised if someone got killed."

One afternoon, he came home early from the farm.

"Pierre is dead. He hung himself in his clothes closet."

We were three, Larry, me and Michael. Pierre was one, isolated and mocked.

We all need to see the flash of an eye that acknowledges us; a voice that will chat, if only about the weather; a hand that will clasp a shoulder or feint a friendly punch. We need to eat and drink with another, at least once in a while.

There was no funeral, no announcement in the staff room. No

one ever referred to his death. Pierre, the solitary French volunteer, slipped away, poisoned by the invisible remnants of suspicion and fear that rose in our precariously balanced kingdom after the disappearance of Holsey and his flowing robes.

I thought about evil. When I was a child and I sat through my catechism classes at St. Mary's or listened during Sunday sermons, evil was named, but always with the assurance that good would prevail and ultimately triumph. Forgiveness, salvation and healing were always imminent, always available, just a breath or a prayer away.

Within our house, Dad could be in the blackest of moods, but we knew he would eventually get over it and return to his better self. "This too shall pass," was my mother's byword for problems, even when she was drowning in diapers and varicose veins. Dad told us satisfying tales about the comeuppance of his business competitors and his crooked landlord. He meant to assure us that, eventually, the scales of justice were balanced.

I was twelve and in Grade 6 when I overheard the boys whisper about places called Bergen Belsen and Auschwitz. At recess time they talked about Hitler's *Mein Kampf* and told each other stories of horrors beyond anything I ever imagined in my most heart-tightening nightmares.

In Grade 11, Mr. Andres, a Mennonite pacifist, taught us the history of WWII and the Holocaust. I rationalized that some madness had overtaken the people of Germany in a way never before experienced by humankind, and since I, a mere sixteen-year-old girl, grasped the depths of that evil, all the adults of the world would understand it too. I was certain that kind of insanity would never happen again.

In 1967 and 1968, during my first terms at Simon Fraser University, protests and demonstrations vied with class time for my attention. I enjoyed the soapboxing about academic freedom and freedom of speech. I thought I was original and radical, but maybe I had simply found a familiar but secular expression of the social-justice oriented Catholicism I had experienced in my teenaged years.

One evening at SFU, I squeezed into the circular meeting space of the rotunda. I listened to plans for a rally the following day. We sat or slumped over purple and red cushions, encircled by a tiled mural of cadmium orange and cobalt blue sunbursts. The warm air was humid with sweat and hormones as the speaker ramped up in intensity. Voices responded, "Right on." "Yeah, man." The blue-jeaned, tie-dyed bodies packed tighter and tighter as others joined the crowd in the round room. Bodies moved in an affirming rhythm of "Ye-e-e-s" and "No-o-o-o w-ay-ay." I breathed in the adrenalin and rode its waves, but then, as I felt myself being absorbed into a unified, throbbing animal that had surrendered its mind to the speaker, I dropped out of sync with the crowd. Fear expanded beneath my ribs. A voice in my head said, "This is how a mob begins." I unwrapped my legs from a yoga sit, stood up and carefully stepped between the legs, knees and hands of the listeners, momentarily touching their shoulders to keep my balance. They were oblivious of an individual choosing to walk away. I exited alone into the wide open mall where the concrete was slippery with rain.

When the surge of riot took control of many of our students at Lundazi, I could understand why some would pick up sticks and others would run the other way into the dark. When it was over, what I couldn't understand was why their teachers turned on each other.

It seems a long stretch from the Lundazi school riot to the evil of Nazi Germany, but for me that night and its aftermath cracked my naivety, my sunny assumption that adulthood was a thoughtful, reasonable stage in human development. As the eldest of six, then as a teacher, I was well schooled in the tantrums of four-year-olds, the exquisite agony of eight-year-olds who crumple under imagined slights, and the unthinking, gut-driven anger of adolescents. As a child, at every wedding and every year during the cycle of scripture readings, I heard St. Paul's words about love, ending with "Faith, hope and love abide. But the greatest of these is love." But before that familiar closing was the verse "When I was a child, I talked like a child; I thought like a child, I reasoned like a child. When I became a man, I put away childish things." These words were so embedded in me that I assumed at twenty-one, adults developed a rational, thoughtful filter between fear and their actions. Twenty-one was the age of majority, when a Canadian could drink legally, or marry, or both. Twenty-one was the star, the golden goal. I was a voracious reader, but I didn't connect the stories of the flawed adults I met in novels with the flesh and blood people who made up the community around me.

I came to realize that fear will drive a person to do almost anything to protect themselves. Fearful people cluster with the like-minded and rage at anyone who doesn't agree with them. At the school, some adults resorted to schoolyard tactics of isolation, shunning, name-calling and dirty tricks

I felt like we were the only ones under attack, and I carried a small worm of doubt—that I might be in the wrong or that I had a flawed character worthy of attack. But when Pierre died by his own hand and no one ever said a word about his death, I understood that he had been isolated in the poisoned climate to the point of despair.

I thought about my incomprehension of the 1930s Germany taught by Mr. Andres. I thought about the ordinary people of Germany at that time, and how they could have entered through the door of fear to find themselves in a new space, hating Jews. I had embraced the story of the 1960s, of peace, love and daisies sprouting from gun barrels. I believed we lived in a constantly evolving world that was becoming more peaceful, more tolerant, more unified, and ready to repair past errors. But a darker story had opened for me, a story of how, as individuals, we are fragile and contradictory, and how this instability in us reverberates throughout our world, a butterfly effect of trauma fanning more trauma in unexpected and seemingly disconnected places.

Doors of caution closed around my heart and my dream of a peaceful, multicoloured world faded.

January 1972

In January, the beginning of our last term and six weeks after the riot, new staff arrived to fill the places of those who had managed a fast transfer.

I have looked for and found an eight by eleven composite photograph taken in the first term of 1972, three months after the night of tear gas and fires. Thirty-six individual portraits of our co-workers are arranged around the school crest. The school motto "In God We Trust" is printed on a banner that waves over a line of three small crude drawings. The first drawing could be a pigeon or an eagle; next is a winged animal, possibly a lion, and the third is something that could be a lamp or a Molotov cocktail. Maybe it represents a candle stuck in a beer bottle, the only light most of our students had to study by when they were in grade school, before they enjoyed the electric light supplied by the secondary school's faulty generator. Under the drawings is an open book, the main icon of the crest.

The photo collage shows our new administration: Manyinda as headmaster and Landman as deputy headmaster. The balance of nationalities has shifted. There are eight Zambian staff, most of them newly graduated, eager to fill the empty positions created by the abrupt staff departures at the end of December. The twenty-six European staff represent England, Russia, Canada, Norway, the United States, India, Wales, Guyana, Northern Ireland, and Switzerland. From this collection I recognize Winterstone's group—The Boys— mostly British, mostly single.

As the term began, the dissonance increased. The new American couple held loud, profane public battles, waged in the street and the staff room, over whose turn it was to clean the toilet in their house. The battle implied they had chosen not to hire anyone to do their housekeeping. Chris Zulu nodded politely, always in a hurry, when we met. I never did ask his wife Amy how to cook wild mushrooms.

Manyinda accused Larry of stealing money from the school farm. An auditor was called in, who proved that Manyinda regularly bribed the farm workers to give him free eggs. The workers, trained by Larry in farm bookkeeping, had been methodically recording each of the free egg transactions but The Boys continued to stoke innuendo that Larry mismanaged the farm.

One morning Larry found all the pigs at the school farm on the loose. The hinges from the doors to their pens had been carefully removed with the correct tools for the job. The Boys sent a spokesperson to Larry to explain that the hinges didn't belong to the agriculture department, they belonged to the technical drawing department, and now they had been returned to the rightful owner.

We felt bereft of the once easy flow of staff life. We taught our classes and tended our backyard garden. We spent time with Jo and Ralph, the Welsh couple, also new parents; with Karoy from town; and with David and the new Canadians. A new, unsolicited relationship developed. Methuselah chose to live with us. He was a striped tabby cat with extremely long legs and reddish ears, the result of a cross between an amorous African wildcat and a domestic tabby. To get into our house he had to leap six feet straight up the stucco wall and crawl in through the bathroom window. One morning, when I woke to feed Michael just before dawn, I found the cat settled on our couch. We'd heard stories about a wild cat called Methuselah who would choose a home and assume his place in the household for an indeterminate stretch of time, and then, at the time of his choosing would disappear. We offered him pilchards in tomato sauce which were always available in 3-ounce tins in the Lundazi shops. He didn't turn his nose up at them. He was gentle with Michael, who explored the cat's fur and tail with the rough interest of a five-month-old. Methuselah provided a calm and regal presence in our home. He did not fawn, sympathize or distract while Larry and I talked and talked about our unhappiness at the school and what we might do next. The cat was simply there, providing a rumbling, meditative purr as the background for our discussions. Years later I read a saying of Julian of Norwich, "All shall be well, and all manner of things shall be well." In retrospect, that could have been the translation of Methuselah's purring.

The cat listened while we tossed around the idea of packing up and returning to Canada, but we adamantly agreed we didn't want to bail out, go home and move in with either of our families. The idea of being a "quitter" was repugnant to both of us. I kept thinking of the conversation that we'd had with Parker before Christmas. We decided to contact him and ask about the possibility of a job with the land settlement company. I wrote him a letter. By return mail we learned that he worked in Zambia under the auspices of the United Church of Canada and that his contract required he return to Canada for a one year sabbatical beginning in September, six months away. Over the next two months, our initial inquiry evolved into Larry applying for a contract, under the sponsorship of CUSO, to replace Parker as acting general manager for the company. By March we had an agreement in place for a one-year contract, along with a promise of housing. We agreed on six weeks for orientation, starting in May, followed by six weeks leave in Canada (our first time home in three years). Larry would take up full responsibility for the settlement in September. We had a way out.

The surprising piece of this puzzle coming together was Bedford. We asked, and he decided to join us. He was already three hundred kilometres from home, but he was willing to travel a further thousand kilometres from his family to an area with a different language and customs. I don't know why he made this choice, but it made our life much easier to have him with us. Maybe it was his turn to look for an adventure.

For us, our escape at the end of term could not come fast enough.

HISTORY

In our three years in Lundazi, after the sun set at six and the electricity came on, we would eat dinner, listen to the BBC World Service on shortwave, and finish up schoolwork. Sometimes we visited friends, but most weeknights we read in the quiet of our living room. Larry sat in the armchair and I tucked my feet up under me on the settee. The only sounds were the generator's hum and cicada songs.

We ordered books by slow surface mail from historic Blackwell's in Oxford, England and others from a bookshop in Toronto. When new books arrived, we slipped into their worlds for days on end and then traded them with other readers. Lawrence Durrell's four novels, *The Alexandria Quartet*, came into my hands on a trade. Durrell describes his characters from multiple points of view but in the same time frame, and then in the final book, the story is followed up several years later. From one book to the next it is impossible to be clear as to who is loved by whom or why. A man dies and the cause of his death shifts from illness to suicide to accident, depending on the volume. Durrell was playing with Einstein's theory of relativity and with Freud's insights, which I vaguely grasped, and I was captivated by the multiple points of view. I still have the paperback copies, which have been miraculously resistant to mildew.

As I looked back at the disintegration of our peaceable kingdom, I wondered if the story could ever be told from just one point of view. I wondered how others saw it and if there were larger influences at play. I started investigating how Lundazi's small police force could be so well equipped for a riot.

I began to search the internet, a tool none of us could have imagined at the time except in the world of science fiction. It brought me to Lundazi in 1964, seven years before the tear gas clouds drifted through our homes and classrooms. North of town there was an uprising, led by a woman called Alice Lenshina. Christopher, the policeman who rescued us on the road to Lundazi, had mentioned her. During our teaching years, we had heard scraps of disconnected stories of a religious madwoman, from north of town, whose followers had believed they could fly. Filled with fervour, they would jump out of trees to injury or death.

The historical record says Lenshina founded the Lumpa Church in 1953, a Christian-based sect focused on improving women's lives. She opposed polygamy, witchcraft, and the craftiness of politicians. Her 150,000 followers (a huge group for a rural area) melded their beliefs with the aspirations of the pre-Independence political movements led by Kenneth Kaunda and others (Kaunda became Zambia's first president). Both the British colonial government and the Independence leaders, while negotiating their way to self-rule, found Lenshina and her followers difficult and non-compliant. Both sides, the British and the pre-Independence forces, painted her sect as less than human—animals who covered themselves with their own feces in order to achieve Satanic powers. In 1964, a gun battle erupted north of Lundazi between Lenshina's followers, armed with machetes sticks and stones, and the Independence forces armed with NATO-supplied automatic rifles. A thousand Lumpa were tortured, killed, and buried in a mass grave about 100 miles north of Lundazi. Twenty thousand Lenshina disciples fled to the Congo. Because so many Lumpa church adherents remained in the Lundazi area, the district was stocked with riot gear and tear gas in anticipation of future clashes. When the school riot broke out, the Lundazi police had been prepared to use their arsenal for seven years.

In the years after we left the school, we kept in touch with Lundazi friends by handwritten notes and a printed Christmas letter. Of those who were present during the riot, Sonia and David responded every year, along with Grant, one of the geography teachers. I decided to email each of them to ask what they remembered of that night and the days that followed. Sonia said that Brian, as the headmaster, radioed Chipata when the riot began, and police reinforcements were sent up overnight. Those were the armed officers positioned around the classroom blocks while the teachers sat in the staff room and decided the fate of one hundred and ten students. Sonia also said that Brian fired Holsey because he was off topic in his curriculum and was teaching about Hitler. She said Holsey left town the day before the riot started.

In his email, Grant indicated he was as surprised as I was that Holsey was gone before the riot started. In reply to my question about who drove us through the tear gas to the police station, Grant was sure it was Dave. But Dave had left ten weeks before and at that time was driving across India on the overland route home to England. Grant claimed, "Holsey was immediately transferred to another school where he did the same thing—initiated another riot—but he was deported." Another teacher wrote that Holsey was spotted in Tanzania during the Christmas break, wearing a suit and tie, not West African garb.

We knew nothing of Holsey when he arrived and nothing of him when he left. He was like a character who stepped into the last act of a play with no introduction, no context, no foreshadowing, and then stepped out abruptly before the last scene, having altered the story and shattered the relationships of all the characters. Within a Google second, I found his obituary and a photograph of him wearing a West African robe with blue, white, gold and rust brown stripes, draped over a plaid shirt. The robe was embellished with an embroidered gold collar that expanded into designs of stars; amulets hung down his chest. It was a similar but more elaborate version of the gown he wore when he swept across the school grounds and exhorted our students and the Zambian staff to wear true African garb, not their Western-style clothing.

Leon Holsey died in July 2004, at the age of 83. That means he was born in 1921 and was fifty years old when he appeared on our staff in September of 1971. His obituary tells the story of a young man who was born, raised and educated in Baltimore and supported himself as a high school student by selling newspapers and scrubbing the marble steps of public buildings. A man who served in the merchant marine in WWII and after the war got a BA in Economics and Political Science, followed by an MA in Government and International Relations. He attended at least nine different universities and had a teaching career in several high schools, colleges and technical training schools, finishing up with thirty years teaching at Coppin State University. It is noted that he taught overseas in Zambia and Tanzania.

Twenty-three years after he had exploded his way through our school and returned to his position at Coppin State, his obituary described him as "very student oriented," among the vanguard of those promoting the "Afrikan-centred" approach to teaching, and one who "walked the walk...wore the garments and taught the courses." He founded the Society of Afrikan People of Ancient Antiquity Alkebulan Ancestry Inc. He was inducted into the Egungun Priesthood at the Oyotunji African centre in South Carolina and later initiated as an Adept of the Fon Spiritual System in Ghana.

The complaint in Lundazi was that Holsey didn't teach the required British history curriculum our students needed in order to pass the Fifth Form graduation exams that were set in England. He did not explain the finer points of British Constitutional History as mandated. Rather, he taught the history of the slave trade, the American Civil War, the cotton plantations, and the relationships between the White bosses and the Black women. I still wonder, did he teach to redress evil or did he have another purpose? Why did he visit the villages and give away watches and American dollar bills? Who funded him?

I emailed a friend, a historian, who taught in East Africa in the 1970s and asked what he thought of the story about Holsey. His response was immediate, "Holsey was an operative, a destabilizer. The US had them planted all over southern Africa at the time. They were there to discredit Black governments and to interfere with the movements opposed to apartheid. The US was heavily invested financially in the South African regime. Zambia resisted US influence and provided a base for the freedom fighter movement."

This seemed to fit with the rumours we had heard in Chipata of CIA involvement in riots in other Zambian secondary schools. Yet it seems incongruent to me that a Black American, who identified with his roots in West Africa, would knowingly take part in a plot to destabilize the Zambian government in order to strengthen the position of South African apartheid.

Holsey and Winterstone represented two strands of history. Winterstone arrived first at the school and had a year to establish himself as the grand old man. Holsey needed only ten weeks to create an impact. Holsey was Black, Winterstone White. Holsey was the American descendant of slaves, and Winterstone the inheritor of British colonial rule. Holsey's great-grandmother came from West Africa. Winterstone came to Lundazi from England via Tanganyika and a recent contract in The Gambia, a long, narrow, former British colony wrapped along the route of the river Gambia in West Africa. The river opens onto a harbour that, during the slave trade, enabled the filling of ships with human cargo.

Both men were middle-aged: Winterstone running from marriage and a disabled daughter; Holsey running towards the reclamation of his African roots. Winterstone drew around himself a group of young teachers, united in the camaraderie of sports and beer. Holsey's fiery explanations of colonial history fuelled some of the students who became his followers. Winterstone kept trying to speak Swahili to Zambians, and seemed to be unaware that Chitumbuka, the language of the Lundazi area, bore little resemblance to the language he had learned to speak years before in Tanganyika. Holsey seemed oblivious that the West African robes he wore were foreign to Zambians.

What was Winterstone's appeal? He portrayed himself as an "Old Africa Hand." The solitary individualist who could not tolerate the strictures of class and conformity in Britain. The man who had done his time in Africa. A man who had coped and survived "the heat, the flies, and the damn natives." A man who knew the "real Africa," now all but past, with plentiful wildlife, the adventure of safari, and the respect of the natives, who were skilled guides and trackers but always "knew their place." A man who played hard at sport and could hold his drink. A man who, just as the sun hinted its readiness to set, expected his servant to pour a good gin and tonic.

Winterstone had begun working in Africa long before the independence movements and he still cherished the lore of the Great White Hunter and the myth of The White Man's Burden described by Rudyard Kipling as Britain's moral obligation to civilize its brown subjects. I think that all the White teaching staff, Europeans, Canadians and Americans, no matter how sympathetic we were towards the aspirations of independent Zambia, were still infected with traces of those myths. We traded copies of Elspeth Huxley's *The Flame Trees of Thika,* in which she wrote of the trials and adventures of White settlers in Kenya between the World Wars. These tales were of life on an edge that could never be found at home, and the mystique of connection with the Africans who lived an intuitive life, close to the earth, raw and heroic, but of course unsuited to the higher complexities of self-rule. We lived only ninety miles from the Luangwa Valley, a rich and nearly untouched game reserve. Safari was a grand word to describe our weekend descent down into the heat of the valley where we slept in a grass thatched hut, under mosquito netting, weighted under heavy heat. In dawn's soft warmth we walked, alert for lions and leopards, with an armed "native guide" who still called his clients "Bwana."

In response to my email queries I was forwarded a copy of an account of the riot written by Duncan, one of Winterstone's group. I was curious, anxious and a bit afraid to read it. I didn't want to find our names in it, to be blamed again. At the beginning of his story Duncan noted that the date of the riot was 17/11/71, a symmetrical date. Fold it down the middle and the date becomes a mirror image of itself. After that date, I felt our community became a warped reflection of what it had been.

Duncan wrote that he was at home drinking with friends when he heard shouting. He looked out the window and saw students carrying burning torches marching towards his house. They rushed into his yard, tossed their torches onto the roof and ignited the grass fence protecting his vegetable garden. As soon as the students were out of sight and their cheering faded, everyone in the house moved across the street to Graham's house. Some huddled under Graham's kitchen table, while a mother and her baby hid in the wardrobe cupboard.

When the flames died down around the school, the group set out on foot through the bush. Duncan wrote, "We made our way to the police station, where other staff and school employees were gathered. The fear of the unknown and the isolation of the previous hour disappeared. The buzz of conversation and speculation was reassuring."

He found comradeship at the police station, whereas I sensed exclusion. By the time we arrived, the lines were already being drawn based on whether or not you left your house, or, if you left...when? Leaving the police station, some of us stayed in town overnight while others, in Duncan's words, "returned to Winterstone's to drink, analyze the causes, and define the perpetrators."

I didn't know there was a baby hiding with his mother in Graham's closet. It must have been the child of the British couple who were obsessed with germs. That night I didn't think of that baby or even of small Seka, Michael's morning walkabout companion. My memory and imagination hold only the feel of the blanket around my face as I tried to capture a bubble of clean air for Michael and get out of the house, through the tear gas and into the waiting car with our rescuer whose name and face I can't recall. Would I have been so firm in my "innocent until proven guilty" stance the next day if the students had thrown burning torches at our house?

Duncan again, "My house was a write-off, with the charred remains of grass fires, smashed windows, a hole in the roof and the general look of death hanging over it."

Our house was left untouched. We should have had a few broken windows or a charred grass fence to prove our solidarity with the staff the students had targeted.

The letter said that Brian, our headmaster, asked the staff to make up a list of possible perpetrators. Grant, in his email, bemoaned the fate of all those students who were expelled, their hopes lost, their lives turned upside down. I don't remember it that way. I recall that Grant agreed with the teacher who said it was a perfect opportunity to get rid of troublemakers. Duncan's letter confirmed my memory by describing how he led a group of armed policeman into his Fifth Form class "to select pupils who had shown themselves capable of leading a riot. I walked in behind the officer in charge who had drawn his weapon. I had no difficulty establishing order."

Larry insists that the fifth formers knew they would compromise the five years of work behind them and the futures before them, so they would have barricaded themselves in the classrooms and refused to join the riot.

Winterstone and his group were certain that the students rioted under the direction of Holsey, supported by a few sympathetic staff. But Grant says in his opinion the students may have been triggered by cutbacks in the dining hall that were instituted by Deputy Headmaster Manyinda.

Could it be the riot was about food, led by hungry students, rather than an anti-colonialist rising up, inspired by Holsey? They were teenagers and they were always hungry. I remembered my embarrassment in the first term English class when I used a British story about a man who needed to go on a diet. My students had been incredulous. "Madam, how could anyone ever have too much to eat?"

It is possible that our students marched on us in the dark because they were stressed by upcoming exams, frayed by November's heavy heat, and driven by adolescent hunger pangs. Maybe a few wanted to settle a grudge with Manyinda, who had trimmed the food ration. Maybe a few were angry with a teacher about a perceived injustice in the classroom. Maybe Holsey incited some to revolt against the remnants of colonial history represented by our white faces. Whatever the reason, the students who threw torches onto teachers' homes or burnt staff fences did not imagine that decades later, I would still struggle to understand their motives and the response of the adults in charge.

The Last Supper

The Kodachrome slides have developed an orange tint after almost fifty years. The slides, framed in stiff white paper, show us seated at small tables for two that have been pushed together to make one long dining room table for eight.

It is April 1972, and we have invited six friends to the Castle Hotel to say our goodbyes to Lundazi. On this night, Nadya and Volodya have joined us, one year since our trip to the Nyika Plateau. We have pulled close again. David has come, along with Karoy, who loaned Tobacco Board tractors to Larry for the school farm and housed us the night of the riot. The quiet Welsh couple, Ralph and Jo, were acquaintances before the riot, but we became friends as we found ourselves in the same boat, part of the disparate group censured by The Boys.

Each section of the table has a white cloth, not much larger than an oversized napkin, that barely reaches the edge of the table. Each table is set with salt and pepper, a bottle of HP sauce, a bottle of ketchup, one lidded glass butter dish full of soft margarine, a dinner bell, an ashtray, and a clutch of wildflowers—pink cosmos, orange and yellow zinnias, and purple asters—stuffed into a recycled pickle jar. The wall behind us is decorated with two identical Zambian tourist posters depicting spotted guinea hens with improbable purple wattles looking out from tall, overarching grass. The posters are stuck on the wall with long pieces of scotch tape that gleam in the camera flash. Karoy is wearing a T-shirt and khaki pants; Larry and Ralph wear white shirts and ties, and David and Volodya have gone one better, each in a dark sports jacket. Nadya is wearing a loose, knee-length maternity shift, and is about seven months pregnant. I have on a floor length white dress with short, embroidered sleeves I discovered hanging on a pole in the Mzuzu market. It still carries a whiff of wood-fire smoke. Jo took the pictures, so I don't see her in

Castle Hotel

the photos. Larry and David have raised their plastic wine glasses. Karoy and Ralph clutch a raffia-wrapped one-gallon wine jug and pretend to sing a maudlin song. Volodya looks at the camera with mock solemnity. He strongly resembles the man my youngest sister will marry twelve years from this time.

We eat the constant fare of the Castle Hotel.

Grilled fish.

"Look at this. It's full of bones." David holds up a thin piece of rib cage.

"But it's fresh," says Jo, a peacemaker, "I'm sure it was swimming in the dam with the hippos this morning."

Local greens.

"They must have learned how to cook vegetables from my British grandmother," says Larry. "Boil them till the colour drains out."

Rice.

Volodya picks out a small black stone he nearly swallowed along with his rice, "I will soon be needing a dentist if I eat too many of these."

Dessert.

Brilliant yellow Bird's Custard, made with boiled tinned evaporated milk. The dye crystals in the custard powder turn the milk marigold yellow when they meet moisture. The pudding, topped with a segment of mandarin orange from a tin, is served in scratched glass bowls.

"Pretty," I say.

After dessert, we leave the table and settle on small government-issue couches exactly like the ones in our homes.

Jo and I fuss a little because it is the first night we have left our babies at home in the care of a babysitter. Bedford stayed late to watch Michael, who always sleeps soundly. One of the Fifth Form girls is with Jo's son. David pours more wine and our broodiness fades. Nadya brushes her hand over her baby-round belly and declines.

A round of toasts.

"Proost!" from Karoy.

"Nazdorovje!" from Volodya.

"Iechyd da!" from Ralph.

For a moment, Karoy lays his head in my lap as he cradles the wine jug and croons to it. Ralph and Larry try to talk cars. Volodya starts to sing his favourite Tom Jones hit, "It's Not Unusual to be Loved by Anyone."

No one says anything serious or memorable. It's a night of silliness after six months of strain.

In the future, we will eat fine meals in other restaurants, some cooked by important chefs who would never allow a naked bottle of HP sauce on their table, but no meal will match our Last Supper in Lundazi.

Two years after our meal at the Castle Hotel, Larry and I passed through Lundazi. We were driving from our new home south of Lusaka, en route to the Nyika Plateau. We stopped at Mulla's for petrol. The pumps were the same. We could still watch the blue ball bounce inside the orange tinted glass window at the top of the pump, proof that the petrol was moving from the storage tank beneath the ground into the tank of the car.

We walked down the unchanged shopping street. Men rode by on bicycles, their parcels strapped onto the rear with bands cut from old inner tubes. Two oxen pulled a cart full of wood. The driver urged them on with a lazy flip of a whip. Primary school girls, in uniform, quick-stepped past us, arms linked, laughing. A pale-skinned man wearing a khaki safari shirt, the style beloved by expatriates, walked towards us. He had springy red hair jammed under a wide-brimmed hat, and as he passed, his grey-blue eyes looked right through us.

Who was he? What was he doing in our town? He could ask the same of us. I felt we were ghosts watching a movie of a place we had once been part of. Two years gone and there were no physical changes in the town, but we no longer had a place in it.

Sadness and loss washed over me. Our Lundazi life had ended. It was time to close the door and move on. I didn't realize the story was embedded in heart and muscle and bone and would flow through the remainder of our lives, elusive and magnetic with longing.

REUNION

For years, Larry and I daydreamed about winning the lottery, tracking down our friends from Lundazi and bringing everyone to the forest cabins of the Nyika Plateau. But we didn't buy any lottery tickets.

In the spring of 2003, thirty-one years after we said goodbye to Lundazi, we received a note from Sonia. Since her return to England she had nurtured links with ex-Lundazi staff, and she decided to organize a reunion. She hoped to gather a baker's dozen or so of the former staff for a good meal in a comfortable pub, to trade stories and renew friendships. Sonia started with the people we were keen to see: Dave, David, Ben, Don and Gay, Doreen, Joyce—and she was searching for the Russians. Using email and other tools of the new internet, her invitations moved farther and faster than stamps and envelopes would allow. She soon located Nick and Nina in Botswana, and Nadya and Volodya in Moscow. Her success inspired her to expand her search to those who taught at the school before we arrived and after we left. Even a few young adults, children of Lundazi teachers, were eager to come. Each connection led to another, and soon it was clear that no pub could hold the crowd.

Sonia kept us up to date on the expanding guest list and then told us of her search for Winterstone. His name revived the memory of our last six months in Lundazi. I remembered his hooded world-weary eyes. I still blamed him for poisoning my world, mocking my husband and sowing the seeds of dissension throughout the school. I still carried the worry that I, a young woman of twenty-three, should have been more cunning or wise, able to push back against a jaded man almost twice my age.

Larry was keen to go, but the thought of Winterstone had throttled my excitement and I delayed making a decision on tickets. Sonia's next email said that she had found Winterstone, who applauded the idea, but begged off because of ill health. Immediately, I booked two tickets to Manchester. More than sixty people had accepted, so she abandoned the idea of a pub lunch and booked a reception room at the Bromsgrove Golf Club, just outside Birmingham, for Saturday, July 5, 2003.

We stayed with Sonia the night before the reunion and helped her with the last-minute details. She had made a scrolled welcome banner and a collection of hand drawn and painted flags, "There's one for the country of each staff member, even those who can't come. Could you finish off the colours?" The collection included: England, Canada, Australia, India, Denmark, USSR, USA, Ireland, Wales, Indonesia, Guyana, Zambia, Botswana, Martinique, France and South Africa. I spread the banner across the living room floor and went to work. While Larry and Sonia went to pick up flowers, and a cake decorated with the Zambian flag, I stayed behind to manage the phone as people called to announce their arrivals and clarify directions. When the banner was done, I got dressed, then looked into the mirror. I noted my salt and pepper grey hair, took a breath, and slipped on my now contraband ivory bracelet and ivory earrings carved into miniature elephants.

Dave and David were at the reception room when we arrived, posting old photos on a display board. Edgy with anticipation, we arranged and rearranged items on a souvenir table: a bottle of Malawi gin, a wooden carving of a traditional farmer's hoe, a case of Castle Beer, old pamphlets from the Zambian Tourist Board. Everyone had been invited to bring memorabilia.

Dave said, "Do you think we'll recognize anyone? Do you suppose we'll have anything to say after the first ten minutes? Bloody hell, I sure hope this works. For Sonia's sake if nothing else."

At noon, Sonia posted me at the door with name tags. Nick and Nina walked through the entryway, and wrapped me in a great bear hug. Dozens of voices filled the entry hall and people flooded into the room. The women wore carefully chosen, form skimming dresses, suitable for middle-aged bodies; the men were in everything from their resurrected African print shirts to suits to motorcycle leathers. Ben arrived about ten minutes late. He told us later that he looked at the crowded room and wondered, "Who are all these old people?"

If we had been blindfolded, we would have known each other

instantly. Faces had crinkled and our bodies had slumped, but our voices and the individual notes of our laughter from our twenties were just the same as when we had said goodbye thirty years before.

I imagined if we were making a movie, I would direct a bird's-eye view shot taken from the ceiling of the reception room. It would show a swirling crowd of middle-aged men and women greeting, exclaiming, and embracing in delight and surprise. The camera would close in on two faces registering recognition, and then the scene would shift to a flashback, the same two, young again, in a moment under the warm Zambian sun. Off to the side, the camera would show a cluster of mystified young people watching. These were the children of the "old people," some the same age their parents had been when they were teachers in Lundazi.

Everyone exchanged stories, the condensed version of their lives. Hans and Lisbet, the parents of Michael's stroller companion Seka, explained that although they were divorced, they were great friends and ran a psychotherapy practice together. Erik, who photographed Michael soon after his birth, arrived with his wife and their three Viking-sized sons.

Doreen and Joyce, now each divorced from Ben and Dave, had shared a hotel room. I wished for fly-on-the-wall knowledge of their conversations the night before. Roy, the former Catholic White Father, who had married the Welsh midwife at Lumezi Mission and was now the father of six, travelled from Quebec.

The daughter of a former teacher said, "I am so glad I came. I have never been able to figure out my father, but this explains everything. Now I understand his stories."

I turned and saw Graham coming towards us. I froze. We had lost him as a friend when he became one of Winterstone's acolytes. He still looked like a young man, short and slight, with the same straight, limp hair. He reached out and shook Larry's hand firmly, "I want to apologize for treating you badly at the school. You did nothing to deserve it." The fist around my heart released. Larry and I stumbled over, "No problem, no problem. Good to see you. Tell us how you are and what you have been doing." Then we moved on to greet others. I felt the freedom that comes with vanquishing an oppressive ghost.

We sat down with Nick and Nina, the only Russians who made it to Birmingham. They had done contract work for their entire careers and had flown up from their current posting in Botswana. Both were tanned and carried extra weight. Nina's blouse buttons strained, and she was adorned in heavy gold jewellery. She was still full of compact feistiness. Nick, in white sports jacket and trousers, still wore his Lenin-style beard. As soon as we sat down, someone, I don't remember who, asked the terrible question, "Who do you think turned Nadya and Volodya in to the Russian Embassy after they travelled with you to the Nyika Plateau?" My breath stuttered. Nick jumped in emphatically, "It was Olga. She was always a miserable person. She really disliked Volodya. We always thought she was assigned to watch and report on us." My breath returned, fear evaporated, and relief settled in. After thirty years of wondering whether or not Nadya and Volodya carried the suspicion that we had betrayed them, it had never occurred to us that there had been an informer within the Russian ranks.

Nick said, "We were a family in Lundazi. We have never found such a quality, such a community again. Our life in Botswana is close but not the same." Nick promised to carry our greetings to Nadya and Volodya, who had wanted to come but had been blocked by Moscow bureaucracy. Their absence was my only sadness that day.

The serving staff announced a generous buffet lunch, but the talk went on and on and no one moved until the servers began to walk around the room with samples of the food and pointed us toward the feast. After lunch, David showed a film stitched together from cine film shot by staff members on November 4, 1969, the official opening of the school. With the magic of old film, a lens and light, we sat and watched our younger selves gather in front of the school as we waited for President Kaunda to arrive.

On that day, the camera recorded images of thousands of people: our students, the staff, Lundazi townspeople, administrators and politicians. In the film, our students wear their best pressed uniforms: the girls in white blouses and green dirndl skirts hiked to mid-knee, the boys in white shirts and slim-legged black trousers, a nod to the Beatles. The teaching staff are dressed in the best they own. Canadian Barb wears a proper lady's straw hat, white gloves, clip-on earrings, and she is chewing gum. Veronica, the deputy headmaster's wife, is all in white, with a tall head wrap and a ruffled, knee-length Western-style dress. Manyinda, her husband, gesticulates importantly, jabbing his finger at the camera, giving orders. A petite, feisty nun with a short, practical veil and a modest calf-length skirt tips her face to speak to a tall, blue-turbanned shopkeeper. The Boy Scouts march past in their khaki uniforms. Drummers beat time on bush-crafted drums decorated with leopard skins. Some of the Scouts wear green tams; others have tall, feathered headgear.

The camera shifts to a Zambian Air Force plane—a Canadian built Buffalo—as it lands on the dirt runway of the seldom used landing strip a short walk from the school. President Kaunda appears at the exit door in his standard grey safari suit, waving his signature white handkerchief. He is followed by four sunglassed unarmed security guards. In the next frame, Kaunda gets out of a Mercedes and walks through the throngs of townspeople. Every Lundazi home must have been empty and every shop shuttered that day.

The president visits classrooms: the sewing room where the girls run new treadle machines; the business room where they type on new typewriters; and the home economics class where the girls cook on new, woodburning cookstoves that look like my grandmother's stove. The boys sit at desks, writing notes in an economics class. The camera moves to the spartan school dining hall, which has been transformed into a banquet hall for hundreds. There are table settings for everyone—napkins pleated and arranged in water glasses, and centrepieces created from local, soon-to-fade flowers. We eat curried elephant and cornmeal porridge and toast the president with Coca-Cola.

Early in the film, the camera catches my sulky face in the crowd. I remembered feeling hot and overwhelmed. I took for granted the president's arrival—after all, he had personally welcomed our cuso group into the country just two months before. I didn't yet understand the importance of the school for the thousands milling around, who had never had a chance at education before Independence.

When the screen went dark, Sonia introduced two young volunteers, a man and a woman, who were current teachers at Lundazi Secondary. Before coming to Birmingham, many of us had cobbled together random bits of news from Zambia and concluded that the school was gone—the staff houses taken over by the town administration, the classrooms open to the sky and populated by weeds. This was before Google Earth, before the time when we could look down on satellite photos of the school compound in the present and trace the path to the staff room or follow the road into the now crowded town of Lundazi. The woman shared her photos of the school farm, the library, and the classrooms—still serviceable, but with peeling paint and the glass gone from the window frames. Ebony-skinned students wearing clean, tidy uniforms filled every desk and grinned for the camera.

The young man explained how he would like to help revive the library. Larry and Dave looked at each other and simultaneously decided to auction some of the memorabilia. The bottle of Malawi gin got the bidders going and we cleared most of the souvenir table, raising four hundred dollars to translate into new library books.

Brian arrived late in the afternoon with his new girlfriend. He made a good, short speech and then we all sang a heartfelt, raucous, sentimental version of the Zambian national anthem. A baffled server standing close by whispered to me, "Who are you people?" Near six o'clock, the servers began to stack chairs. We had run overtime. We moved outside for a group photo, followed by reluctant goodbyes and long embraces as the tyranny of train schedules pulled us apart, possibly forever.

As I collected my camera and shawl, I stopped and thought of those who were not present. None of the African teachers and only one of the East Indian staff was there. Everyone who attended was an expatriate who had taught in Zambia at the new government's invitation to fill a gap and do ourselves out of a job. There had been eight Africans on staff when Larry and I arrived. Manyinda had died, Evaristo and the two South Africans would be over seventy if they were still alive, and Chris Zulu, our age and hopefully still a principal, would not have access to the internet and was out of reach.

Finally, I thought of Bedford, the Zambian who had kept our daily life running smoothly with home-baked bread, fires started on time, and laundry ironed free of skin-burrowing larvae. He should be fifty-five, as I was, but as a man who had three wives by the age of twenty-six, I wondered if he had escaped the scourge of AIDS. I could only hope he was healthy and had realized his plan to become a professional driver.

For those Sonia had gathered in Birmingham, Zambia had provided a landscape where we tested ourselves and met challenges we would never have had at home. Throughout the afternoon, each of us had said, in different ways, "We got more than we gave." Most of us carried the question of whether our time had contributed to the lives of our students or infected them with the shortcomings of Western culture.

We were able to revisit this question ten years after the Birmingham reunion when Larry and I reconnected with Peggy. We had shared the adventure of buying a drum on a Malawi beach with her and her now deceased husband Nigel. Peggy spent her whole career working with small Canadian projects overseas. She was confident that low key projects, the ones that brought people face to face in classrooms, in technical schools, in forests and small farms, had long-term positive impacts. Her response gave us some peace with the questions that had run as an undercurrent through our day in Birmingham.

When everyone was gone and the doors of the reception room were closed, Dave, David, Larry, Ben and I drove to a nearby restaurant, The Old Penny. We found a table by a window, where we sustained the crucible of the reunion, floating in a bubble out of ordinary time. Then, in the warm, summer evening, we drove along winding hedgerowed roads to Herefordshire, the land of Elgar, to spend the night in the family cottage Dave had restored over many years. It was almost eleven when we arrived and the air was chilly inside the small stone house. We didn't want to bother lighting the fire, so we stood and chatted amongst the lovingly collected mismatched furniture. At midnight we were still talking. We struggled to define the magnetic pull that brought us back to each other like homing pigeons. Could the magic be found in shared shopping lists, the men repairing cars together, the borrowing of cake pans and ingredients, the isolation, and the smell of longed-for rain pattering November's dry dust? Without a definitive answer, we finally gave in and went to bed.

Hours later, in a perfect English summer morning—slightly chilly, slightly overcast—we straggled together again as the sun teased its way through the milky haze. We brought kitchen chairs and a small table onto the enclosed lawn. We had run out of words. We sat together in comfortable, companionable silence over coffee, scrambled eggs and cool toast. Eventually, Larry, Ben, David and Dave got up to wander around the stone cottage that Dave and his brothers had reconstructed over many years of weekends and summer vacations. David examined the pump for the water system and began to describe how to dismantle the whole thing to improve its efficiency. Years dropped away. The men slipped back to the way they had been with each other half our lives ago. They bantered and challenged each other with rapid wit, outrageous puns, and a touch of Monty Python. I watched and listened and remembered. I realized I loved the four of them when they were together. I also knew that part of their performance was for me.

Dave had invited anyone remaining in Birmingham to drive out and join us at his cottage for afternoon tea. After lunch was done, we brought the rest of the chairs and tables onto the lawn and set out teapots, cups with saucers, cream and sugar, and cakes iced in pink and lemon yellow. When everything was ready, we stopped to listen for cars approaching. Soon we heard the crunch of tires on the gravel at the edge of the road and the sound of engines stopping. There were twenty of us. We picked up the threads of yesterday's conversations, less intense than the day before, more reflective. We knew that the enchantment was soon to end. The sun moved lower in the sky, the air began to chill. A few of the women pulled light summer sweaters or shawls out of large handbags. Conversation continued, even though the schedules of impending planes and trains began to impose their demands for departures.

Hans, still slim, still blonde with short cropped hair, consulted some notes then returned them to his pocket and stood up to speak. On common impulse we all stood with him in a circle. His hands moved together as if he were going to pray, then he steepled his fingers and began in his careful, Danish-accented English,

"I have been thinking all through the night about the power of our time together in Lundazi. That time shaped much of what we became afterwards."

He stopped, looked up to the treetops then back to our faces.

"I have noticed that most of us continue to work as teachers, social workers, or in some form of community development. No one has pursued wealth."

His fingers interlaced then returned to their steeple shape.

"We are still searching. And sometimes we find small communities of like-minded people who want to work together. We still have this hope, in spite of our age and experiences, to 'change the world' for the better. We know this moment together will not happen again, but we will not forget it and we will not forget each other."

He stopped speaking and briefly bowed his head. We stood silent. The trees had turned to silhouettes around us. The pearly grey light of dusk erased the evidence of age and the voices from our youth called out our final, reluctant goodbyes.

When we returned to Canada, I wrote to our sons, "Trust your life. There is an invisible thread running through it."

Acknowledgements

I wish to express gratitude to my village:

Betty Taylor, my writing partner and first reader,

Yvonne Blomer, the midwife of the tale,

Rhonda Ganz, for her creative input,

the Thursday Writers for their inspiration and support,

those who read drafts and offered responses toward clarity: Magdalene and Conrad Vanderkamp, David Mason, Nadya Ignatova, Ed Hamel, Jennifer Friesen, and Linda Picciotto,

those who offered alternate viewpoints: Stuart Cox, Ben Goodman and Natasha Gludovacz-Samoilova,

Eric Bach, Carol Sherwood, Wayne Thom, and Josephine Fletcher for photographs and drawings,

the staff of Lundazi Secondary School who shared our adventure,

Bedford Silungwe who chose Kondwani for our son Michael's middle name,

and Sonia Williams who kept us together.

About the Author

PHOTO: CAROL SHERWOOD

Mary Bomford started life in Station Master's houses along the CPR prairie line. Her family settled in Chilliwack, BC, but at eighteen she was off again to the Faculty of Education on the brand new campus of Simon Fraser University, then on to Zambia, England, Winnipeg, the Peace River country, and Vancouver Island.

She arrived in Zambia as a Canadian CUSO volunteer, filled with earnest confidence in the transforming power of Western education and technology. Experiences both dramatic and subtle turned most of her convictions inside out: the pragmatic warmth of her Zambian midwife, her uncle's doppelganger recognized in a Zambian colleague, live caterpillar barrettes adorning her students' hair, and a student uprising.

The microcosm of the Zambian secondary school opened her to new ways of seeing the world. She realized she had learned more from the new country and its people than she had taught and the gift of that time continues to offer new perspectives each time she revisits it.

As a writer, Mary has attended the Banff School of Fine Arts and has taken workshops in short story and memoir in Fort St. John and Victoria. During her teaching career Mary taught students from Grade 1 to Grade 11 in Canada and Zambia. She maintained her link with international issues as a workshop leader with Amnesty International, coordinated fundraising with African AIDS Angels, and worked with women in Malawi and Chile.

She and her partner Larry have been married for fifty-three years and have two sons and four grandchildren. She lives in Saanich, BC.